D1154780

# THE MIND IN ACTION

BY

**ERIC BERNE, M.D.**

SIMON AND SCHUSTER
NEW YORK
1947

MANUFACTURED IN THE UNITED STATES OF AMERICA
AMERICAN BOOK–STRATFORD PRESS, INC., NEW YORK

To my mother
Sara Gordon Berne

# *ACKNOWLEDGMENTS*

———————————

THANKS ARE DUE to the various audiences of soldiers and civilians in California, Utah, and Washington who helped me clarify my formulations by their questions, comments, and objections. I especially appreciate the personal assistance given to me by the following individuals:

The publisher's staff, and especially Henry Simon, were of major assistance in preparing the manuscript and offering constructive suggestions. Dr. Paul Federn gave me much advice which he left it my option to follow or disregard. He has no other responsibility for the contents. Robert Peel, of Denton, Texas, and Frances Ordway, of Carmel, California, gave me invaluable time-saving assistance with the typing. Major, now Dr. Samuel Cohen, of Philadelphia, and Major, now Dr. Paul Kramer, of Chicago, helped me by their consideration while it was necessary to work on the manuscript under the difficult conditions of army life. Colonel and Kippy Stuart, Doris Drake, Louise Masters, and Captain, now Dr. George Ambrose were also of help during this period. To those who read the manuscript, or who listened while I read it at the Short home in order that they might make suggestions, I offer a toast of Carmel wine in memory of much help and many pleasant evenings. These include Marie Short, Jake Kenny, Mr. and Mrs. John Geisen, Muriel Rukeyser, Dr. and Mrs. Russell Williams, Mr. and Mrs. Frank Lloyd, Sam Colburn, Gretchen Gray, Katie Martin, and a score of other Carmelites.

E. B.

Carmel, California
January, 1947

# PREFACE BY DR. A. A. BRILL

THIS BOOK *is unique in more than one way. The author is a well-trained psychoanalytic psychiatrist, an avowed Freudian, and yet it took a number of chapters before I was actually convinced of it. For unlike those who espouse certain theories and plunge right into the midst of them, Dr. Berne maintains such an objective and un-biased attitude that he at first gives the impression of a keen prober rather than an ardent adherent of Freud.* The Mind in Action *starts with a sort of biological survey of the general aspect of mental development. It is a lucid exposition unencumbered by technical expressions which explains the normal functions of the brain, in terms of feeling and action; the most powerful urges and their control in childhood and adult life and the reaction of the whole organism to the environment. Dr. Berne has the happy faculty of documenting and presenting abstruse mental processes in such a simple and alluring way that he can hold the interest of even a jaded psychoanalytic reader. But following him for a few chapters one realizes that Dr. Berne endeavors to embody Freud into everything that touches on and appertains to the functions of the mind.*

*In my efforts to explain the author's mode of operation it occurred to me that psychoanalytically Dr. Berne is just about 40 years younger than the present writer. In other words he belongs to the* post bellum *period of psychoanalytic recognition, and hence can evaluate Freud's contribution as part and parcel of the whole progressive development of psychiatry. In other words Dr. Berne is a young Freudian who like the new generation of Egyptians "did not know Joseph" and hence could follow a new path and expound the new psychology without the affectivity of the older Freudians. The psychoanalytic theories were well established when Dr. Berne mastered them; that is why he could complacently survey the whole field of psychoanalysis, the* fons et origo *as well as all the deviations from it, and then easily separate the kernel from* the sheaf. *Having read everything written on Freud and psycho-analysis since I first introduced him here I feel that Dr. Berne has succeeded in presenting "the mind in action" in a manner that will interest and instruct not only the intelligent layman but also the psychoanalyst and physician.*

# CONTENTS

---

# CONTENTS

## THE GROWTH OF THE INDIVIDUAL

### CHAPTER FOUR

## DREAMS AND THE UNCONSCIOUS

## PART 2:  Abnormal Development

### CHAPTER FIVE

## NEUROSES

CONTENTS

CONTENTS

CHAPTER NINE

# PSYCHOANALYTIC TREATMENT

# Appendices

APPENDIX A

# BEYOND SCIENCE

APPENDIX B

# MAN AS A POLITICAL ANIMAL

# AUTHOR'S FOREWORD

---

THE OBJECT of this book is to make the dynamics of the human mind intelligible to those who are more interested in understanding nature than in using big words or memorizing definitions. I have attempted to put ideas on a practical level which will give as clear and simple a picture as possible of complicated happenings. Long words have been avoided wherever this could be done without sounding clumsy. The object is to give the reader a better understanding of himself and others, and not to make a tea-room psychiatrist out of him. For those who want more details, the bibliographies should be an ample guide, and for those who want a technical vocabulary, a short glossary is appended.

Every psychiatrist has his own way of looking at people, derived from his own clinical experience. The ideas set down here are based on what I learned from my teachers, principally Dr. Eugen Kahn, Professor of Psychiatry at the Yale School of Medicine, and Dr. Paul Federn, of the New York Psychoanalytic Institute, modified by my own thoughts, observations, and interpretations of the psychiatric and psychoanalytic literature. My teachers did the best they could for me while I was in their hands, but otherwise they are in no way responsible for what I say. It is taken for granted that most of the ideas, like the ideas of every dynamic psychiatrist, are based on the work of Sigmund Freud, but the emphases and the manner of formulation are my sole responsibility, and no group of psychiatrists or psychoanalysts has authorized me to be their spokesman.

In order to help in preventing misunderstanding on the part of professional readers of what I am trying to say, notes are added at the end of each chapter, in which qualifications and reservations are made, and the more technical aspects of the matters dealt with are discussed. Any of the books referred to in these notes may be obtained from Robert Brunner, the psychiatric bookseller, 1212

Sixth Avenue, New York 19, New York, or from J. W. Stacey, Inc., 551 Market Street, San Francisco 5, California.

For the sake of clearer understanding, a short semantic glossary is desirable in addition to the technical glossary at the end of the book:

*He* refers to human beings in general of either sex. Where *she* is used, according to the context it may imply that a phenomenon occurs more frequently among women than among men. *We* in an appropriate context refers to "the majority of those psychiatrists for whom I have the most respect." *Is* in a sentence referring to technical matters means "seems to be, in the opinion of most thoughtful psychiatrists and from my own experience with the problem." *Seems to be* means "appears to me, from many observations, but not enough to make me certain in my mind, though corroborated by the opinion of one or more psychiatrists for whom I have a high respect." *Philosopher* is used to mean anyone who likes to think about what he reads. Tensions are spoken of as being *relieved, satisfied,* and *gratified.* The latter two are incorrectly used in this connection but their use prevents repetition and serves to emphasize the idea that "tension" and "wish" are almost synonymous.

The pseudonyms of the patients described in the case histories are not arbitrarily chosen, but are nearly all derived and "Americanized" from historical and mythological sources related to the case in question. This may intrigue some readers, but it need not complicate matters for those who are not interested in names. The case histories represent types and not individuals, and any resemblance to any living individual in external circumstances or characteristics is accidental and unintentional.

While many of the case histories exemplify commonplace occurrences, some of them are meant to illustrate clear-cut types of mental illnesses and emotional abnormalities; that is, they describe pathological personality types. In such instances the situations and reactions dealt with may occasionally strike the reader as unusual. This is more a matter of degree than of quality. If the reader will consider carefully, he will find that while the intensity of the reactions of our subjects may sometimes be startling, their modes of reaction are far from unique. The histories serve to emphasize by exaggeration things which everyone may find to some extent within himself and those around him. If this is not apparent at first thought, it may become clearer with the lapse of time. This means that the mentally ill do not have different instincts, but only express differently those which are universal among human beings.

# INTRODUCTION

A PSYCHIATRIST *is a doctor who specializes in helping, advising, and treating people who suffer from emotional difficulties, poor judgment, and, in severe cases, abnormal feelings, beliefs, and sensations. The objects of his study are the motives of human beings, and the question he asks is: "Why does this individual have a need to feel, think, or act the way he does?" Since the workings of the body affect the emotions and the emotions express themselves through the body, the psychiatrist, like other doctors, must start with a sound knowledge of anatomy and physiology; he must know what the stomach, the blood vessels, the glands, and the brain look like and how they work. He must also know how certain chemicals such as alcohol affect the mind, and how the mind can affect certain chemicals of the body, especially those which are manufactured by the sex glands, the adrenal glands, and the thyroid gland.*

*While he is building up his knowledge of the way the human body works, the student psychiatrist must also be observing how human beings from various kinds of homes behave in different situations in the country where they are living. In listening to orphan immigrants and Boston aristocrats talking about their children's report cards, he notices the differences and similarities in the bodies and minds of the parents, and wonders how these things affect their children's progress in school.*

*After he has become familiar with the different ways in which healthy people react in mind and body, the student begins to observe sick people. He studies individuals with stomach ulcers, for example, and tries to see what they have in common in their stomachs and their feelings, and whether there is any connection between their emotions and what the X-rays show. He talks to people with abnormal fears and observes the reactions of both their minds and their bodies to see if he can find in what way each has gone wrong.*

INTRODUCTION

*Besides doing the preventive work of mental hygiene, such as giving advice to young couples who are about to be married, and to mothers who are having problems with their children; and taking care of people who are abnormally sad or excited, or who have abnormal feelings and impulses, it is the psychiatrist's province to deal with certain conditions which involve special organs of the body as well as the emotions, or which result from taking excessive quantities of certain drugs. For this reason, if for no other, he has to have a sound knowledge of the working of the body. Among these latter conditions are syphilis of the brain and spinal cord, epilepsy, delirium tremens (which may seriously damage the heart and brain), and alcoholism and drug addiction, both of which cause physical symptoms. In giving the various forms of shock treatment in serious mental cases, he must understand the effects of certain powerful drugs, insulin, and electricity on the human body.*

*In addition, the psychiatrist is often called upon to decide the part played by the emotions in cases of stomach ulcer, high blood pressure, thyroid disease, heart disease, backache, paralysis, asthma, skin diseases, and other conditions which are often difficult to treat by ordinary medical methods. In such cases, he must have a sound knowledge of the workings of the affected organs.*

*Before trying to help his patient, the psychiatrist likes to know what kind of an egg he came from; that is, what his forefathers were like in body and mind, and under what influences the egg developed into the adult human being. After he has found out these things, the psychiatrist can judge better what the individual started with and what he went through which brought him to his present condition. He tries to discover what assets and liabilities his subject came into the world with, and then how he has been handling life with whatever he has.*

*Many features of the personality are based to a large degree on inheritance. Heredity determines the upper limits of abilities and when they are normally going to increase or decrease. For example, it determines whether a man could possibly be a great musician or mathematician (and chess playing should be included here as well), and at what age he will be able to have complete sexual relations. Environment, however, determines what he actually does. In other* words, heredity determines possibilities, and environment determines how closely these are approached. But to spend too much time asking which is more important in real life is as impractical as asking: "Which is more important for strawberries and cream, the strawberries or the cream? Do the berries float in the cream, or does the cream surround the berries? Which is more important in measles, the measles or the child?"

There is no proof that environment cannot change some of the so-called inherited qualities of the mind. Nearly every human ability can be improved by proper training, and the opinion that a disability is "inherited" does not mean that the sufferer should give up. The study of the glands in years to come is going to be very important for changing those things we now regard as inherited, just as psychiatry is now becoming more and more important for changing those qualities we regard as being due to environment. Therefore, instead of asking what is due to heredity and what is due to environment, we should ask rather, "Which qualities can be changed with our present knowledge, and which cannot?"

This book is about the human mind as the psychiatrist sees it. We shall therefore begin by studying what different people have to work with and what they are trying to do with what they have, and then go on to see how they grow and develop, what can go wrong in the course of development, and what can be done about it if things turn out unhappily. After that we shall discuss some of the mysterious happenings in the mind which baffle us in our present state of knowledge, and finally we shall attempt to show that psychiatry can be of practical use in dealing with groups of individuals, such as political parties and nations.

# PART

# 1

---

# Normal Development

---

### CHAPTER ONE

# WHAT PEOPLE HAVE
# TO WORK WITH

---

## I

## Can people be judged by their appearance?

EVERYONE KNOWS that a human being, like a chicken, comes from an egg. At a very early stage, the human embryo forms a three-layered tube, the inside layer of which grows into the stomach and lungs, the middle layer into bones, muscles, joints, and blood vessels, and the outside layer into the skin and nervous system.

Usually these three grow about equally, so that the average human being is a fair mixture of brains, muscles, and inward organs. In some eggs, however, one layer grows more than the others, and when the angels have finished putting the child together, he may have more gut than brain, or more brain than muscle. When this happens, the individual's activities will often be mostly concerned with the overgrown layer.

We can thus say that while the average human being is a mixture, some people are mainly "digestion-minded," some "muscle-minded," and some "brain-minded," and correspondingly digestion-bodied, muscle-bodied, or brain-bodied. The digestion-bodied people look thick; the muscle-bodied people look wide; and the brain-bodied people look long. This does not mean that the taller a man is the brainier he will be. It means that if a man, even a short man, looks long rather than wide or thick, he will often be more concerned about what goes on in his mind than about what he does or what he eats; but the key factor is slenderness and not height. On the other hand, a man who gives the impression of being thick rather than long or wide will usually be more interested in a good steak than in a good idea or a good long walk.

Medical men use Greek words to describe these types of body-build. For the man whose body shape mostly depends on the inside layer of the egg, they use the word *endomorph*. If it depends mostly upon the middle layer, they call him a *mesomorph*. If it depends upon the outside layer, they call him an *ectomorph*. We can see the same roots in our English words "enter," "medium," and "exit," which might just as easily have been spelled "ender," "mesium," and "ectit."

Since the inside skin of the human egg, or endoderm, forms the inner organs of the belly, the viscera, the endomorph is usually belly-minded; since the middle skin forms the body tissues, or soma, the mesomorph is usually muscle-minded; and since the outside skin forms the brain, or cerebrum, the ectomorph is usually brain-minded. Translating this into Greek, we have the viscerotonic endomorph, the somatotonic mesomorph, and the cerebrotonic ectomorph.

Words are beautiful things to a cerebrotonic, but a viscerotonic knows you cannot eat a menu no matter what language it is printed in, and a somatotonic knows you cannot increase your chest expansion by reading a dictionary. So it is advisable to leave these words and see what kinds of people they actually apply to, remembering again that most individuals are fairly equal mixtures and that what we have to say concerns only the extremes. Up to the present, these types have been thoroughly studied only in the male sex.

*Viscerotonic endomorph.* If a man is definitely a thick type rather than a broad or long type, he is likely to be round and soft, with a big chest but a bigger belly. He would rather eat than breathe comfortably. He is likely to have a wide face, short, thick neck, big thighs and upper arms, and small hands and feet. He has overdeveloped breasts and looks as though he were blown up a little like a balloon. His skin is soft and smooth, and when he gets bald, as he does usually quite early, he loses the hair in the middle of his head first.

The short, jolly, thickset, red-faced politician with a cigar in his mouth, who always looks as though he were about to have a stroke, is the best example of this type. The reason he often makes a good politician is that he likes people, banquets, baths, and sleep; he is easygoing, soothing, and his feelings are easy to understand.

His abdomen is big because he has lots of intestines. He likes to take in things. He likes to take in food, and affection and approval as well. Going to a banquet with people who like him is his idea of a fine time. It is important for a psychiatrist to understand the natures of such men when they come to him for advice.

*Somatotonic mesomorph.* If a man is definitely a broad type rather than a thick or long type, he is likely to be rugged and have lots of muscle. He is apt to have big forearms and legs, and his chest and belly are well formed and firm, with the chest bigger than the belly. He would rather breathe than eat. He has a bony head, big shoulders, and a square jaw. His skin is thick, coarse, and elastic, and tans easily. If he gets bald, it usually starts on the front of the head.

Dick Tracy, Li'l Abner, and other men of action belong to this type. Such people make good lifeguards and construction workers. They like to put out energy. They have lots of muscles and they like to use them. They go in for adventure, exercise, fighting, and getting the upper hand. They are bold and unrestrained, and love to master the people and things around them. If the psychiatrist knows the things which give such people satisfaction, he is able to understand why they may be unhappy in certain situations.

*Cerebrotonic ectomorph.* The man who is definitely a long type is likely to have thin bones and muscles. His shoulders are apt to sag and he has a flat belly with a dropped stomach, and long, weak legs. His neck and fingers are long, and his face is shaped like a long egg. His skin is thin, dry, and pale, and he rarely gets bald. He looks like an absent-minded professor and often is one.

Though such people are jumpy, they like to keep their energy and don't fancy moving around much. They would rather sit quietly by themselves and keep out of difficulties. Trouble upsets them, and they run away from it. Their friends don't understand them very well. They move jerkily and feel jerkily. The psychiatrist who understands how easily they become anxious is often able to help them get along better in the sociable and aggressive world of endomorphs and mesomorphs.

In the special cases where people definitely belong to one type or another, then, one can tell a good deal about their personalities from their appearance. When the human mind is engaged in one of its struggles with itself or with the world outside, the individual's way of handling the struggle will be partly determined by his type. If he is a viscerotonic he will often want to go to a party where he can eat and drink and be in good company at a time when he might be better off attending to business; the somatotonic will want to go out and do something about it, master the situation, even if what he does is foolish and not properly figured out, while the cerebrotonic will go off by himself and think it over, when perhaps he would be better off doing something about it or seeking good company to try to forget it.

Since these personality characteristics depend on the growth of the layers of the little egg from which the person developed, they are very difficult to change. Nevertheless, it is important for the individual to know about these types, so that he can have at least an inkling of what to expect from those around him, and can make allowances for the different kinds of human nature, and so that he can become aware of and learn to control his own natural tendencies, which may sometimes guide him into making the same mistakes over and over again in handling his difficulties.

## 2

## Where does human energy come from?

In order to understand anything in this world, we have to ask first, what parts does it consist of and how are they put together, and secondly, where does its energy come from and how is it conducted into the proper channels. To understand an automobile, we must first describe the various parts and where they are, and then see how the energy of the gasoline is changed into rolling motion through the workings of the mechanism. To understand a frozen water pump, a moaning radio, an inspiring comet, a fair waterfall, a growing tree, or an angry man, we must follow the same course. The construction is called *structure* and the working is called *function.* To understand the universe we study its structure and function. To understand an atom we study its structure and function. Then we can navigate a ship, and make an atom explode.

We have seen that in structure the human being consists of three kinds of tissue and that the way these are put together will partly determine how he acts and reacts. If we now study the glands and the brain, we shall have the beginnings of an idea as to how the energy of a human being is controlled as he functions.

The energy of man comes from food and oxygen, as far as we know. The amount of food he eats, together with the amount he has stored in his body, determine the amount of energy he can release by means of oxygen. The result of digestion is to change the food into fairly simple substances which can be stored and used as required, to release energy by changing chemically. Vinegar and baking soda fizzing in a glass produce heat, which is energy. In a more complicated way, body chemicals and oxygen fizzing in the body produce heat, so that a certain amount of food produces a certain number of calories of energy for the body to use. How this heat is changed into the kind of energy needed by the body is not yet clearly explained.

We can recognize human energy in two forms: bodily energy and mental energy—just as we can recognize that the energy used in going for an automobile ride comes partly from the car and partly from the driver.

The glands have much influence in determining how fast bodily energy is used and for what general purpose it is employed. The thyroid gland acts like an accelerator and keeps the individual running at high speed or low speed. It may keep him running faster than his food provides for so that he uses up all kinds of reserve chemicals, such as fat, to supply the energy needed, and thus a person whose thyroid is overactive tends to lose weight. On the other hand it may slow him down so much that he takes in more food than he can use, and the excess is stored as fat and other substances, so that the person whose thyroid is underactive may put on weight.

If we compare the thyroid to an engine accelerator, we may say that the adrenal glands, which are found attached to the kidneys, are like rocket fuses. When we need an extra push, the adrenals release a sudden huge supply of energy. This happens usually when we have to fight or run; the adrenals are the glands which gird us for action when we are angry or afraid. Sometimes we are angry or afraid without being able to do anything about it, so that we are unable to use up the extra energy. Something has to happen to this energy and since the normal path of expression is blocked, it may exert itself on the muscles of the heart or other inner organs, causing pounding and other disagreeable sensations. In any case, the extra energy does not simply vanish; if it is not used up at the time by fighting or running away, or by palpitations of the heart or contractions of the other internal organs, it is stored up until it finds a chance to express itself directly or indirectly, as we shall see farther on.

Both the thyroid and the adrenals are set differently in different people. Because of their thyroids, some people are always on the go and some are always sluggish. There are other reasons for such differences in energy output besides the thyroid, but one always has to think of this gland in trying to account for restlessness or sluggishness. In the same way we have to think of the adrenals when the question of differences in excitability arises. Some people's adrenals are set on a hair trigger, so that their bodies are frequently in a state of turmoil, while others never feel the surge of strength that comes with profound anger.

The thyroid affects the total amount of the individual's activity, regardless of what he uses the energy for. The adrenals release additional energy to aid the individual in separating himself from things which threaten him or stand in his way, whether he accomplishes the separation by running, or by destroying the threatening force, or by causing it to leave in a hurry.

The sex glands also affect the output of energy, and like the adrenals the energy they release has the quality of supplying vigor for certain special purposes. We may say that the adrenals assist the instinct of self-preservation by releasing added strength for separation or destruction. The testicles and ovaries assist the sexual instinct by giving added interest to certain constructive activities. Their earthy purpose is concerned with sexual union, but part of the energy they release can be usefully applied in any romantic or sublime activity which has the feeling of approach, affection, or creating.

In thinking about these glands, it should be understood that we have no right to say that they are the source of the energy and desire for creating and destroying; but they do serve in some way to give added zest to such desires, and to release *extra* energy to accomplish them. Older people whose glands are wearing out can still create and destroy, but they usually do not have the same passionate excitement and concentrated energy that younger people do.

Furthermore, the glands have nothing to do with the special way the released energy is applied. For instance, the adrenals make the muscles of the arms and legs stronger and quicker, but they do not determine whether the limbs will be used for fighting or for running away. The sex glands make the individual feel strong and restless and increase the attractiveness of outside objects, especially other human beings, usually of the opposite sex, but they do not determine how he goes about getting closer to people, nor whom he chooses. With glands alone and no brain, a human being would show little more initiative than a bottle of fermenting wine. This can be shown by removing the outside parts of the brain from a cat. Under the influence of the adrenals, the cat will then go into rages with almost no provocation at all, and be prepared for violent action, but he neither knows the true object of his rage nor can he deal effectively with anything that really threatens him. He becomes steamed up but does not know how or against whom to act. The brain is necessary for effective action in accomplishing a definite purpose.

The energy of thinking and feeling is harder to understand than the energy of moving, and little is known about its origin. It is known that energy is used whenever the mind is active, and it can be shown that the brain gives off electric waves and uses up oxygen. This may mean that the energy used by the mind is not completely different in kind from the energy used by the body; it may well be the same energy used in a different way. It can be shown experimentally that there is a difference in electrical pressure between the brain and the body, and between the different parts of the brain, and that these differences change when the mind is active. This shows that mental activity is accompanied by electrical changes.

A good deal of mind energy is used in doing nothing, or rather in keeping from doing things. One of the main functions of the brain is to keep the individual's activities toned down, and prevent the rest of the nervous system from running wild, as it does in the cat without a brain. Keeping a firm grip on the lower nervous system requires energy, just as keeping in hand a team of restless horses does.

Mental energy is also required to keep certain ideas and feelings apart in order for the mind to remain tidy. If all sorts of ideas and impressions were allowed to run together without hindrance, the human mind would be as disorderly as a haystack. If ordinarily separated ideas or feelings are allowed to come together, as in jokes or embarrassing situations, the energy formerly used to keep them apart is released, and can then be used for other purposes; for example, it may play a part in starting an explosion of laughter, tears, or blushing.

In situations involving social prestige, for example, the feeling of respect which "inferiors" may have is usually kept separate, by the use of mental energy, from the feeling of resentment which such situations arouse. When the pent-up resentment is allowed to express itself openly, the energy which was formerly used to keep it in check is released, and this in addition to the energy of the freed resentment may be enough to awaken a smile or a laugh on the part of the listeners.

This is illustrated by the case of the woman who got on a trolley car and refused to pay her fare. When the conductor insisted that she would have to pay or leave the car, the woman said haughtily:

"You can't force *me* to pay. I'm one of the directors' wives."

The conductor was not impressed.

"I don't care if you're the director's *only* wife, you'll still have to pay," he replied, amid the smiles of the other passengers.

In this case the listeners sympathetically went through in their minds the same process of defiance and freeing of resentment as the conductor did in actuality. He used the energy thus freed for talking; they used theirs for smiling. Added to this in both cases was the energy released by bringing openly together the ideas of "wealth" and "polygamy." The laying open of these and other hidden connections freed blocks of energy which were used by the various parties concerned for laughing, smiling, talking, or expressing irritation.

We see, then, that our energy comes from the food we eat and the air we breathe, and that the glands play an important part in determining the vigor with which it is released and the direction which it takes, while the mind, in the end, determines the exact purpose for which it is used. If it is desired to change the amount or direction of a person's energy output, therefore, there are three points of attack. Changing the production of energy from food and air belongs to the field of internal medicine, and is a problem which arises in cases of heart, lung, and thyroid diseases, anemia, and so on. Changing the release of energy by glands is something we know little about at present, but which both the internist and the psychiatrist take a great interest in. The control of energy output by the mind is the problem of psychiatry and that is what we shall deal with in the rest of this book.

3

## What is the brain for?

The brain is often not too accurately compared to a telephone exchange, because it is concerned in making connections between ideas, and between things that happen and what we do about them. Even in this respect, the brain is more complicated than anything man could manufacture. There are more possible connections in one brain than there would be in a world switchboard if every living human being had a telephone. In addition, one part of the brain seems to be able to substitute for another in an emergency with more ease than would be possible with any man-made switchboard.

The brain is enclosed in the top part of the skull. It is split part way down the middle and is about the size of a large coconut. The spinal cord is shaped like a thin cane with a knob on top of it. The brain surrounds this knob and is connected with it by a million little nerve cords.

People often wonder how much of the brain is really used, and how much of it one could do without. Sometimes the brain is injured before, during or after birth, and then we can answer these questions, for the injured part may liquefy after a while so that the brain substance disappears and a collection of watery fluid replaces it. It is amazing in such cases to see how much of the brain can be destroyed without the individual or his friends knowing that there is anything wrong. One man had several of these large pools of fluid inside his brain, so that from birth only about half of the tissue was left, yet he apparently went through high school normally, and was doing a good job as an auto mechanic at the time he came to see the doctor. The only reason he wanted medical attention was that he suddenly began to have epileptic convulsions. Until these began, neither he nor his family had suspected that there was anything wrong with him. It was only when he went to see a specialist that anything extraordinary was noticed. Because of certain small irregularities in his vision and muscle development, which had never interfered with his work enough for him to notice them, the neurologist took special X-rays, which showed up the holes in his brain.

Some parts of the brain have special uses, but other parts are capable of gradually replacing each other. If one of the special parts liquefies, the individual will not be able to carry on whatever function that part of the brain is concerned with. If one half of the rear end disappears, the individual will be unable to see one half of what is in front of him, and will be blind on one side (not in the right eye, for example, but in the right half of each eye). If both sides of the rear end liquefy, he will be almost completely blind. In some cases, the duties of even these special parts can be taken over by other sections of the brain. An apoplectic stroke, or shock, as it is sometimes called, is due to destruction of a part of the brain which controls certain muscles. When this portion is destroyed, the muscles stiffen and the individual is unable to control them normally. With long practice, however, other parts of the brain can often be taught to take over, so that some apoplectics regain control of themselves after a stroke. In the case of the mechanic mentioned above, it happened that most of the destroyed brain tissue did not have any special function, so he was able to carry on normally.

The reason so much brain tissue can be dispensed with is that the brain usually acts as a whole. In this, as in many other ways, it works differently from a telephone exchange. If some of the telephone exchanges in France were destroyed, there would be less telephone service in that country. But if a man learns the French language, that knowledge cannot be partly destroyed by destroying any special part of the brain, because he knows French with his whole brain and not with any part of it. There is no "bump of languages." * One might almost say that the absence of some parts of the brain no more interferes with knowledge, thinking, and other aspects of the mind than the absence of one leg does. Indeed, in real life, the latter often causes more mental symptoms than the former.

The brain should be regarded as part of the energy system which is a human being. If we look at it in this way, we may allow ourselves to suppose that the brain has another function just as important as being a sort of telephone exchange, and that is, to store energy. There is some evidence that this is actually what the brain does. We may remember in the case of the cat with the top removed from its brain, that the animal seemed to be unable to store any of its feelings, and gave way immediately to rage on the slightest provocation. Similarly, the animal was unable to store any memories of what had happened, and was unable to store the impulse to move its limbs when they were stimulated. In the case of human beings who have whole brains, the ability to store mental energy is highly developed. Normal adult people can store their feelings until it is more convenient to express them at some later time, instead of flying into frequent rages without restraint; they can store memories, and recall them later; they can store the desire to move their limbs in response to stimuli, as they must do in the dentist's chair. In rare cases it is necessary to cut off the front part of the brain in human beings for certain types of illness, and then we see things which lead us to believe that the individual is unable

---

* There is an apparent exception to these statements in the complicated condition called "aphasia," which we need not go into here.

to store his feelings and impulses as well as he could when the brain was all there. After such an operation, the person will act more impulsively and show many of his feelings more quickly than he did before.

Many otherwise mysterious things can be explained if we suppose that it is a function of the brain to store energy. From this point of view, the brain is the organ of waiting.

One of the most important things in family and social behavior, and the relationships between human beings, is the ability to store energy without distress when the individual's judgment tells him that it is advisable to wait before acting. If our supposition is correct, it is the brain which stores the energy released by the glands and other sources until the proper moment arrives, and in this way the storage capacity of the brain would play a part in preventing people from doing foolish things just because their tensions encouraged them to. We may even imagine the brain in everyday life being charged and discharged like a living storage battery, as illustrated in The Case of the Ten Dollar Slap.

Midas King, the owner of the Olympic Cannery, was a plump, fidgety, somewhat irritable viscerotonic. Things did not go smoothly in the cannery during the war. Everyone was working at top speed, the staff was continually changing, and mistakes, sometimes serious ones, were frequently made. The days were a continual series of annoyances to Mr. King, but he always tried to control himself at the office. He came to Dr. Treece for psychiatric treatment for high blood pressure.

Mrs. King, who accompanied him, told the doctor of an incident of the previous evening. Upon coming home from the office, Mr. King had seemed peaceful enough until their little three-year-old boy had done something bad; whereupon Mr. King had suddenly given him a terrible slap on the head. Mr. King had felt that he was justified, but his wife had told him he had gone too far, and had taken the boy in her arms and soothed him. The cause of Mr. King's burst of anger was that the child had torn a dollar bill into pieces. Mr. King now felt sorry for what he had done.

"I think I see the situation," said Dr. Treece. "The boy tore up a dollar bill, but instead of slapping him one dollar's worth, you slapped him ten dollars' worth, isn't that it?"

Mr. King and his wife agreed that that was a good description of what had happened.

"The problem is," said the doctor, "where did the other nine dollars' worth of annoyance come from?"

"Of course he brought it home from the office, poor dear," replied Mrs. King.

"His feelings got charged up at the office and discharged at home," said the doctor. "And now, after some years of this kind of thing his blood pressure doesn't come down after a restful week-end as easily as it used to. So we have to find out how he can keep from becoming so easily irritated during the day, isn't that it?"

We might remark here in passing that the child, like the criminal, learns what punishment to expect for any given misdeed. This amount of punishment he is often prepared to accept without holding a grudge. But if he is punished ten dollars' worth for a one-dollar crime, he feels nine dollars' worth of resentment, since, inexperienced though he is, he nevertheless realizes somehow that he is being made a scapegoat for someone else's sins and resents this unfairness.

This little example shows how the storage of energy and its manner of release are all-important in keeping the body running smoothly, and in relationships with other people both at work and in the home. Besides feelings, knowledge and experience are also stored, in the form of memories. In mentally defective individuals there is not much ability for this latter kind of storage, so that morons and imbeciles do not learn easily, and having profited little from their previous experiences, their judgment is poor. The two kinds of storage are distinct. A man's ability to store knowledge has nothing to do directly with his ability to store feelings. That is why so many "intelligent" people make such fools of themselves in their relationships with others, and is also partly the reason that being slow of understanding does not prevent a person from getting along with others. We admire people for their intelligence, but we like them for the way they handle their feelings. Those who wish to develop their personalities, therefore, must decide whether they want to develop one side or the other, or both. If they develop only their storage of memory images, they may be admired, but not necessarily liked. If they want affection as well as admiration, it might be of help to develop their ability to store their feelings and express them in an acceptable way.

While these are both things of the mind, the brain is probably the organ of the body most directly concerned. It is the organ of learning and waiting, which, we suppose, stores memory images and feelings; it is as well the central organ which deals with the connections between ideas, and with what goes on outside ourselves and what we do about it.

# 4

## Why people act and feel the way they do

A person acts and feels, not according to what things are really like, but according to his mental image of what they are like. Everyone has images of himself, the world, and those around him, and behaves as though those images, rather than the objects they represent, were the "truth."

Some images have the same pattern in almost every normal individual. The Mother is virtuous and kind, the Father stern but just, the body strong and whole. If there is reason to think anything to the contrary, deep down in their minds people hate to believe it. They like to continue to feel according to these universal images, regardless of whether they correspond to what is really there. If they are forced to change them, they become sad and anxious, and even mentally ill.

People's images of their own bodies, for example, are very difficult to change. A man who has lost a leg finds it hard to settle down until he has gone through a period of sadness or "mourning" during which he succeeds in changing his body image to correspond to his new situation. Even then, deep down in his mind, he keeps his old image of himself. For years after he has lost his leg, he may see himself as a whole man in some of his dreams, and sometimes he stumbles because for a moment he forgets. These things show that his mourning has not been completely successful.

People's images of their parents are also difficult to change. In some dreams, the weak father may be strong, the drunken mother pure, and the dead still living. It is hard work to change an image when it has to be done, which is one reason that people hate to do it. If a loved one dies, the effort of changing one's mental image of the world to correspond to the new situation, which we call "mourning," is quite exhausting, and leads to tiredness and loss of weight. Oftentimes mourners, when they get up in the morning, are more tired than when they went to bed and feel as though they had done a hard night's work. The reason is that they *have* done a hard night's work, altering their mental images.

There are other images which belong only to certain individuals because of special circumstances, and these also are hard to change. "The phantom in the bedroom," the mental image of a man's first wife, may spoil his relationship with his second wife; "the mother with her hand on the doorknob" is a mental image which may keep a woman from growing up emotionally even when she is far away from home; she always feels as though everything she did were being criticized by her absent or dead mother as if the latter were listening outside the room.

The story of Nana Curtsan illustrates another type of individual image which may persist and influence conduct after the reality has changed. Up to the time of her father's tragic death, Nana had been quite plump. Because she had no mother, and her father was a drunkard, she was starved for affection, and was willing to do anything to get it. As a result she got a very bad reputation, which distressed her; but she felt quite helpless to control her craving for male company, and because of her poor figure she had to go to extremes to obtain it.

After her father died, she lost a good deal of weight and her true figure emerged from its cushion of fat like a slender, graceful sculpture from a block of stone. Two of her old friends, Ralph Metis, the banker's son, and Josiah Tally, the cashier at the bank, were so dazzled by her new-found beauty that they began to think of marrying her, in spite of her reputation.

Unfortunately Nana was unable to change her image of herself. In spite of what her mirror and her comrades told her, she continued to think of herself as a physically unattractive girl who had to go to extremes in order to gather affectionate garlands. She persisted in her previous conduct and the result was that with the assistance of the horrified parents of Ralph and Josiah, she lost her chance for a good marriage.

The story of Nana, who did not give up thinking of herself as "the homely Dryad," is just the reverse of that of many a middle-aged or elderly woman, who continues to believe that she is "the enchanting Sylph" of her youth, and acts accordingly, sometimes with pathetic results, and sometimes, by good fortune, with charming success.

Such mental images, which guide our behavior, are charged with feeling. When we say that we love someone, we mean that the image of that person in our minds is highly charged with constructive, affectionate, and generous feelings. When we say that we hate someone, we mean that that person's image is charged with destructive, angry, and hostile feelings. What the person is actually like, or how he appears to other people and how they feel about him, does not come into the picture except indirectly. We don't fall out of love with Pangyne and in love with Galatea, but out of love with our image of Pangyne and in love with our image of Galatea. All that Galatea does is make it easy for us to form a lovable image of her. If we are particularly anxious at the moment to fall in love, we help her along by picking out the lovable things to emphasize in our image, denying or neglecting the undesirable qualities. Thus it is easier for a person to fall in love "on the rebound" than it was in the first place, because when the image of his first love breaks down, it leaves an empty space in his mind with a large charge of feeling which is urgently looking for a replacement. Driven by the anxiety of the vacuum, he romanticizes the image of the next woman who comes along so that she can fill the niche quickly.

Though we like to cling to our images and are loath to alter them, over a period of time we do have a tendency to make them more romantic than a vanished reality. Old people think of the dubious past as "the good old days," and some long for home when they are away from it and are often disappointed in it when they return. Most people are glad to see old friends and old enemies after a forgotten interval, since they have softened the bad and emphasized the good in their images of them during their absence.

Hector Meads and his family were good examples of how

people tend to make their images of absent things and people more romantic as time passes. Hector was the only child of Archie Meads, who owned the Olympia Garage. Through no desire of his own, Hector became an employee of the U. S. Government and was sent to a small island in the South Pacific. When he returned after twenty-nine months, he was restless, fidgety, irritable, and dissatisfied at home. He grumbled so much and seemed so strange that his mother, a nervous woman at best, became quite agitated from worrying about how to please him.

After six weeks of restless roaming around the house, listening to the radio, and drinking wine, he went to work for his father. He quit that because he was unable to get along with the customers and with Philly Porenza, the mechanic with holes in his brain. He and Philly had been good friends before Hector went away, but now Hector complained that Philly was a loafer and didn't understand what life was really about. Hector also quarreled with his former girl friend, Ann Kayo, the police chief's daughter, and took to dropping over to Foamborne Street to see Nana Curtsan occasionally. He tried working at the Hotel Olympia, McTavish's Dry Goods, and the Depot Meat Market, but it was six months before he finally settled down to a job, in King's Lumber Yard. He was always finding fault with his boss or with working conditions. He was certainly not the easygoing boy who had left Olympia more than two years before.

What had happened was this: when Hector and his family had said good-by on his departure, they had each kept an image of what the other looked like. While he was away from home and lonely, Hector had often thought about his family, Ann, Philly, the garage, and various places around Olympia. He thought about the good things and the bad things too. As conditions grew worse and he became more lonely and uncomfortable on his little island, Olympia and its people had come to seem increasingly desirable to him. There were so many worse things on the island, that he had gradually forgotten all the bad things about Olympia. Home as he now remembered it seemed more and more romantic to him. He expressed these feelings in his letters.

The people at home went through the same sort of change. They all missed Hector and would often think how amusing and cheerful he was. They gradually forgot all the bad things about him, his thoughtlessness, untidiness, and carelessness about his work. They were touched by his letters, and their feelings became more and more romantic as the months slipped by.

By the time he was due to come home, Hector had a very exaggerated idea of how wonderful Olympia was, and Olympia had an exaggerated image of how wonderful Hector was. In both cases, the images were based on the way things were the day Hector left, with a lot of romance added.

In the meantime, of course, both the real Hector and the real Olympia were changing. Hector saw a lot of trouble over there on his little island, and he was no longer just a trying but lovable boy who liked women to fuss over him. He was thoughtful and self-reliant, and a man among men. Olympia had seen trouble too, and was no longer just a sleepy little village, but a town among towns. Ann was grown up and sophisticated, though still kind and beautiful; his parents were a little older and a little more set in their ways. Philly Porenza had turned a little sour on the world after he had started having convulsions.

When Hector returned, both he and the townspeople were shocked. Both thought they were prepared for changes, but their images of each other hadn't changed the way the realities had; in fact they had changed in the opposite direction, if anything. Their new images were so far from the new realities that even with the best will in the world they couldn't get used to each other at all for about six weeks.

In many people it seems to take about six weeks for a mental image to change to correspond to a new reality. People don't really feel at home in a new house until they have been there about six weeks. By that time their image of "home" has had a chance to change to resemble the reality of the new house. After six months or so, the altered image has become solid enough so that the individual can settle down permanently without further anxiety from that source.

Though the individual himself may change his images gradually as time passes, he does not like to have others try to change them for him before he is ready. That is why people shout and become anxious during an argument. The better the logic of the opponents, the more anxious they make the individual for the safety of his cherished images, and the louder he shouts to defend them; and the more anxious his opponents make him, the more he dislikes them. We have an understandable but unreasonable tendency to dislike people who "beat us" in an argument, who tell us that our loved ones are not all that they are cracked up to be, or who try to make us like people of whom we have a hateful image. In the old days, would-be conquerors often executed messengers who brought them bad news. It was not the messengers' fault that they had to disturb the emperor's image of himself as a world conqueror, but unfortunately they did, and they suffered the consequences of the anxiety they aroused. It is still worth a man's neck to disturb an emperor's image. Nowadays the ax falls more subtly and the execution may be postponed, but sooner or later it comes. It is always wise to be tactful in undertaking the pleasant or unpleasant task of bringing a superior, a friend, a husband, or a wife face to face with the fact that their images and reality do not correspond, or in other words, that they have made a mistake in judgment.

What is called "adjustment" depends on the ability to change one's images to correspond to a new reality. Most people can change some images but not others. A religious person may be willing and able to adjust to any change but a change in religious outlook. A good business executive may be able to change his image of a business situation in a few minutes on the basis of new information brought from the market, but be unable to change his image of how children should be raised on the basis of information brought from the nursery school. A poor businessman may not be able to change his image of a business situation as rapidly as the market changes, but be able to change his image of his wife from time to time as she changes in reality, so that his marriage is a continued happy success. (It may be judged from this that flexibility is often more important than intelligence for success in any field).

Images are made of stuffs of different flexibility. Some people have brittle images, which stand up against the assaults of reality with no change up to a certain point, and then suddenly crack wide open, causing great anxiety to the individual. These are the rigid personalities. Others have waxy images, which melt before the eloquent words of a salesman or critic. These are the suggestible personalities.

It is most clearly in matters of love that people show the quality of their mental images and how they handle the problem of trying to make reality and images correspond. Some men, for example, have such rigid images of the ideal woman that they must marry that they will have no compromise. They never meet anyone who fits perfectly into the pattern they have in mind, so either they never marry or else they marry again and again, hoping that eventually they will find a woman of low melting point who will pour herself into the long prepared mould. (Incidentally, this is an excellent example of how the same basic psychological characteristic can lead two people by different routes into exactly opposite courses of conduct, which is one claim of psychiatrists that outsiders have difficulty in understanding).

The successful man is the one whose images correspond most closely to reality, because then his actions will lead to the results which he imagines. A man's failures depend upon the fact that his images do not correspond to reality, whether he is dealing with marriage, politics, business, or the horse races. A few lucky ones can make their successes by simply describing their mental images, which may correspond to what a lot of people would *like* theirs to be. These are the poets, artists, and writers, whose images, therefore, need not match reality in order for them to get along. A surgeon, on the other hand, must have images in absolute accordance with reality. A surgeon whose mental image of the appendix was different from the reality in any respect would not be a good surgeon. The whole training of surgeons and engineers is a meticulous attempt to make their images correspond with reality. A scientist is a professional image-sharpener. A man who buys a lottery ticket is an example of how anxious people are to make the world match their images with as little effort as possible.

This idea of images is useful in thinking about mental illnesses as well as in studying character. A man with the condition known as hysterical paralysis, for example, may be thought of as a man with an altered image of his own body. He is paralyzed because he has a highly charged image of himself as paralyzed. He is paralyzed "in his mind," and because his mind has control of his body, it makes the real body correspond to the mind image as much as possible. In order to cure the hysterical paralysis, the psychiatrist has to offer some other image for the patient to charge with feeling. If the patient removes the charge of feelings from the false body image to a new image formed with the assistance of the psychiatrist, the paralysis will vanish. Since none of this process is under the conscious control of the patient, it cannot be brought about by ordinary methods.

The case of Horace Volk, which we shall hear more about in a later chapter, illustrates this. Fear of his father and other strong emotions altered Horace's image of himself so that in his mind his voice was paralyzed, and hence in reality he could not talk above a whisper. Dr. Treece, the psychiatrist, with careful handling, succeeded in diminishing the intensity of Horace's warping emotional tensions by making the boy weep; and then by suggestion he helped him to form again a normal body image. During this process, Horace formed a strongly charged image of the doctor, which absorbed some of his abnormally strong tensions and helped to relieve the pressure which was distorting his image of himself. When the pressure was thus relieved, Horace's body image returned by "natural elasticity," as it were, to its normal state, and he was then able to talk as usual. None of this could have been done by conscious willing on Horace's part. Even the simpler part of the procedure, the weeping, was beyond his conscious control. It is very difficult for even a talented actress to make herself shed real tears by willing them.

A great man is one who either helps to find out what the world is really like, or else tries to change the world to match his image. In both cases he is trying to bring images and reality closer together by changing one or the other. Einstein's work caused nearly all physicists and mathematicians to change their world images to correspond with the "reality" he had discovered. Shakespeare helps people to have clearer images of what the world is like. The Messiahs of various religions were good men who would have liked the world to correspond to their images of what it should be like.

Some evil men try to change the world by force to match their images of what they want it to be. Hitler had an image of the world as a place where he had supreme power, and used force to try to make the world correspond to his image.

In the mental illness called "schizophrenia," the patient imagines that the world does correspond to his image of it, and does not bother to check. He differs from the aggressive reformer or conqueror in that he is unable or unwilling to do the work of changing "I want" into "is." Sometimes he starts out as a reformer, and finding that this change is too difficult to bring about in reality, he changes it in his own mind and rests content with that.

One of the most important things in life is to understand reality and to keep changing our images to correspond to it, for it is our images which determine our actions and feelings, and the more accurate they are the easier it will be for us to attain happiness and stay happy in an ever-changing world.

# 5

## How emotions change experience

The mental images we have been talking about cannot be thrown upon a screen, nor even clearly explained to ourselves, but this does not mean that we must doubt their existence. No one has ever seen an atom or electricity, but we must not for this reason doubt the existence of the forces of nature or we shall be quite unable to understand the physical world. Nature proceeds *as if* what we speak of as atoms and electricity existed, and so we suppose that they do exist. Similarly, human beings proceed *as if* the kind of mental images we have been talking about existed, and so we suppose that they too exist. We shall speak from now on as though dynamic mental images were as real as electrons and gravity.

These dynamic mental images consist of two things: a representation, and a charge of feeling. The charge may be "positive" or "negative," love or hate, and often is both. The representation gives the image a shape, and the charge gives it energy.

It must be clearly understood what is meant when we talk about a representation, shape, or idea. Shape, as far as a dynamic mental image is concerned, includes function as well as structure, and so shape in our minds means more than physical shape. Everyone knows the physical shape of an airplane. The mental shape, representation, or idea of an airplane includes not only its appearance, but also some idea of what it does and how it works. It is easy to see, therefore, that one must have intelligence as well as eyes to form good representations, and that other things being equal, the more intelligent a person is, the more complicated and accurate his representations of the things around him will be. Furthermore, the accuracy of his representations has nothing to do with how he *feels* about airplanes. Some people who understand airplanes very well dislike and fear them, and some who have no idea how they manage to fly love them. Thus the representation of an airplane may be a "positively" charged image or a "negatively" charged image, regardless of whether the shape of the image is simple or complicated, accurate or inaccurate.

The distinction between feeling and representation is frequently seen in social relationships. People can often remember exactly how they feel about an individual without being able to remember his name, or they may remember a name without being able to recall what its bearer means to them. Mr. and Mrs. King were once planning a party, and Mrs. King asked, "Shall we invite Mr. Castor, that interesting horseman from Hawaii?"

"I remember the name well," replied Mr. King. "He is a tall fellow with hearts and flowers tattooed on his arms, but I can't remember how I feel about him, nor whether I like him or not."

In this case it is apparent that Mr. King had a good representation of Mr. Castor, and remembered his shape well. His image was clearly formed, but he could not bring up the attached emotional charge, so he did not remember just how he felt about him. Mrs. King then suggested: "Shall we invite that marvelous fellow What's-his-name, that that hateful Mrs. Metis hates?" It was plain that she didn't remember much about the shape of Mr. What's-his-name, not even his name, but she did remember the strong and pleasant feeling charge of his image; she didn't recall who he was exactly, but did feel that she liked him, mainly because her enemy Mrs. Metis hated him.

What this means is that an image can be broken up, and the feeling and representation separated from each other, so that the

feeling remains conscious and the representation becomes unconscious, or vice versa. In such cases, the feeling separated from its
representation "floats" in consciousness, and may "support itself"
by becoming attached to another representation which has something in common with its own. This helps to account for slips of
the tongue and other mistakes which are made in everyday life. If
it is the representation which floats, it supports itself on another
image.

Different people have different abilities to store charges and
representations. A mind which cannot store ideas with clear-cut
shapes cannot learn properly. Individuals who have this difficulty
are called mental defectives. Only after repeated and prolonged
attempts to form well-shaped representations do they understand
the things around them. At the same time, they have to express
their feelings like anyone else, but not having clear-cut images,
they make mistakes and get into trouble.

Sometimes the problem is different. A mind which was once
able to understand things and form good representations becomes
twisted so that distorted feelings and distorted representations result. An aeronautical expert, for example, may come to feel that
airplanes have a personal enmity toward him and follow him
around in an attempt to injure him. The result of this distorted
mental image of airplanes is that he cannot be understood by those
around him and is unable to get along normally in the world. Many
such abnormalities are found among the schizophrenics we have
already spoken about, and since they act in accordance with their
distorted and abnormally charged images instead of in accordance
with normal ones, their behavior is difficult for healthy people to
understand.

This should help to make it clear why a "nervous breakdown"
has little to do directly with intelligence, and why people with
"nervous breakdowns" may be able to remember and to think
about certain problems as well as or better than the average person. A "nervous breakdown" of any kind is a disturbance in the
way feeling charges are distributed on the individual's images of
his own body, his own thoughts, the things and people around him,
and so forth, so that some of the images are distorted; while mental
deficiency is a subnormal ability to construct and store shapes or

representations. Mental illnesses have to do with emotions; mental deficiency has to do with understanding. Sometimes, it is true, people suffer from "nervous breakdown" and mental deficiency at the same time, but this is just an extra misfortune, because the two conditions are separate.

Human beings would be much simpler if they just learned automatically from experience and formed images to match what actually happened to them. In this case they would resemble adding machines, which form absolutely correct and rigid conclusions from the keys which are punched by the outside world; or pieces of clay, which bear a true and unvarying imprint of everything which touches them. The reason we are not like these dull objects is that our inner spirits give new and individual meaning to everything which happens to us, so that the same event is experienced differently by every person, and each one forms his view of what happened to suit his own emotional make-up. If an adding machine does not like the look of a 9 in a column of figures, it cannot change it to a 6 for the sake of beauty, but a human being can. If clay feels that an imprint is too sharp, it cannot round the corners, but a human being can round the corners of his experiences to suit himself.

The forces within the individual which change his way of experiencing are the forces of love and hate, in various forms which we shall hear more about. All his images are molded out of their true form by these two feelings, and since he acts in accordance with his images and not in accordance with reality, every one of his acts is or can be influenced by love and hate. The individual's images are also molded by three ideas or wishes which are fixed deep in the unconscious mind of every human being and which he can never completely get rid of. These three beliefs are: the immortality of his being, the irresistibility of his charms, and the omnipotence of his thoughts and feelings.

No matter how much an individual protests that he at least has shaken himself free from one or all of these, they remain hidden in the depths of his being and are most likely to influence his behavior whenever he feels anxious or insecure. The most easily observed of the three is the "omnipotence of thought," since many superstitions are based on the idea that thoughts and feelings are all-powerful. This concealed belief becomes especially active in certain emotional disturbances.

Wendell Meleager dreamed frequently that he killed his mother's brother. After he heard that his uncle was killed in an automobile accident, Mr. Meleager began to suffer from palpitation and insomnia. He took to reading books on superstition so that he could avoid doing anything which they said might bring him harm. Whenever he saw a policeman, he became shaky and felt faint. In short, he behaved exactly as though he himself had murdered his uncle; he finally had to give up his law practice temporarily because of his anxieties.

Although actually he had no connection with his uncle's death, and consciously his feeling was one of affection for him, his unconscious image of his uncle was charged with murderous thoughts. He certainly unconsciously overestimated the power of these thoughts, since when the event took place he behaved as though he had been the direct and malicious cause of his relative's death. His way of experiencing the announcement was warped because he had a warped image of his uncle in his unconscious mind, and unconsciously believed in the omnipotence of his destructive thoughts.

The individual's belief in the irresistibility of his charms shows itself most clearly in dreams, where the dreamer may experience without surprise the joys of winning effortlessly the affection of the most desirable men and women. A reflection of this is seen in some elderly people who are unwilling to admit that they have lost the sexual attractiveness of their earlier days.

The belief in immortality is recognized by most religions, and in spite of all conscious attempts at resistance it also persists in the minds of even the most atheistical heretics. No one can really imagine his own death. If he tries, he will find himself surviving as a spectator at the funeral. If he tries to eliminate the funeral by picturing a bomb explosion, he may see himself being blown to bits, but he cannot imagine himself absent when the smoke clears away. Furthermore, this web of infinity extends to the past as well as to the future. No one can honestly imagine himself coming into being from nothingness. This is expressed by the frank or disguised ideas of reincarnation which are found in some religious systems.

It is the forces of love and hate, and of these three wishes or be-liefs, which lend color and individuality to human life, and keep people from becoming machines or clods. It is these same forces which make trouble when they get out of control. It is noble for them to shade our images under the eyes of our intelligence; but when they color them completely and take over control from the rational mind, steps must be taken to restore the balance.

We should try to become aware of how much our feelings affect our behavior, our experiences, and our ideas of the people and things around us, so that we can try to avoid unreasonable actions, excessive worry, and mistakes in judgment. From psychiatric experience the suggestion comes that when in doubt, for the sake of one's own happiness, it is wiser to act, feel, and think from love than from hate.

# 6

## How people differ from one another

We are now able to understand some of the differences between human beings.

As we have seen, their bodies are often unequally developed in various directions; in some people the digestive organs, in others the muscles and bones, and in still others the skin and brain predominate. When one system is out of proportion to the others, more thought, feeling, and action often seem to be devoted to that system. So we have viscerotonic, somatotonic, and cerebrotonic minds, each with its own way of reacting, which we may summarize as soothing the environment, mastering the environment, and getting away from the environment, respectively. Thus constitution determines in the beginning something of how a man handles his surroundings.

His glands influence greatly the strength of his urges and the amount of energy he can put into satisfying them, as well as the speed at which he uses his energy. There is another important factor which the glands undoubtedly influence but which we know little about, and that is mood. Some lucky people are always gay, and some unlucky ones are always sad. Most people swing between mild sadness and mild happiness. Of course people's moods are affected by what happens to them and how well things go, but there is more to it than that. It is sometimes surprising to see how much misfortune a person in a good mood can suffer without getting downhearted, and it is equally surprising to observe how many "nice things" can happen to one in a sad mood without cheering him up. People differ in the speed with which they change from happiness to sadness, and vice versa.

The efficiency of the brain, we may suppose, affects the ability of the individual to store his feelings and postpone satisfactions until the best possible moment. Some people are prudent and some are impulsive. Some can stand waiting and some cannot. While it is not always wise to wait, it is always desirable to have the ability to wait if it should become advisable. This is something people can usually improve.

There are different kinds of impulsiveness. Some people have a quick, impulsive, and proper reaction to each situation; others go along showing very little reaction to a number of situations, and then suddenly and impulsively release a burst of stored-up energy. The first kind is understandable and others sympathize with it; they know why the man got angry and he doesn't have to explain it to them. The second kind is difficult to understand and makes others feel uneasy; they feel that maybe the man had a right to get angry, but he shouldn't have got *that* angry. This latter type of reaction occurs unexpectedly, and since it uses energy released not only by the situation of the moment, but also that pent-up from other situations, the reaction seems to go too far, and the onlooker questions it in his mind.

Another useful feature to think about is the relationship between imagination and action. Some people are too much given to day-dreaming. Since they cannot by any means carry out all the dreamy desires they become conscious of, they may go through life feeling perpetually disappointed. Cerebrotonics in particular are apt to daydream, mull things over, and carry out few of their plans. Other people have few conscious desires which cannot be handled in a practical way, so that they do not indulge much in fantasies they cannot carry into action.

The first group may in this connection be regarded as having a weak "barrier" between the unconscious and conscious parts of the mind, and a brittle "barrier" between the conscious mind and deliberate action; they daydream freely but do little about it. The other group have a strong "barrier" between the unconscious and conscious minds, and a flexible "barrier" between the conscious mind and action; they daydream little, but act freely. The "inhibiting" first group usually go no farther than thinking about their images; the "repressing" second group try to make the outside world correspond to them.

In this section we might also consider what is generally called "intelligence," as measured by "intelligence tests." The possible intelligence of an individual depends on the constitutional ability of his mind to form and retain accurate representations and relate them to each other. The amount of intelligence that he actually shows and uses depends on this ability minus the effect his emotions have in blinding him to facts and distorting his images. This means that by straightening out a person's emotional life, we may be able to increase his usable intelligence to its highest possible level. In one experiment, some mentally defective children from an institution were paired off with foster mothers chosen from a nearby home for delinquent girls. Each child then received motherly love and attention which had previously been lacking in its life. Under this emotional influence, there was an increase in the intelligence which the children showed. Furthermore, the intelligence which the "mothers" showed also increased, since they too had filled a gap in their emotional lives: each one of them now had a child to love. Loving and being loved increased well-being and intelligence in both parties.

It is said that there are three kinds of "intelligence": intelligence with abstract ideas, mechanical intelligence, and intelligence in getting along with people. It would not be surprising to find that cerebrotonics had the highest average abstract intelligence; that somatotonics had the best mechanical intelligence; and that viscerotonics had the highest average social intelligence. Since there are so many mixed types, however, it is difficult to study this matter properly.

The differences between people and their ways of handling their inner energy depend upon many things. So far we have discussed mainly factors which are already influenced at birth, that is, "constitutional" factors: physical build and the corresponding mixtures of reaction patterns; the activities of various glands; the ability to store energy and the manner in which it is released; and, also, the plasticity of images and the ability to form and retain clear-cut representations and keep them from being too much distorted by emotions. These are among the basic things that people have to work with in forming their personalities as they grow and develop in their surroundings.

## Footnotes for Philosophers, Chapter One

1. *Physique*

The ideas used in this section are modified from Sheldon:

*The Varieties of Human Physique*, by W. H. Sheldon et al. Harper Brothers: New York, 1940.

*The Varieties of Temperament*, by W. H. Sheldon & S. S. Stevens. Idem, 1944.

While these ideas seem to be useful in dealing with normal people, their superiority over Kretschmer's classification remains to be demonstrated in regard to psychotics.

2. *Endocrines*

In the text we have not distinguished between the adrenal cortex and the adrenal medulla. The discussion refers to the medulla. Other generalizations and omissions have been made for the sake of clarity and simplicity. One of the most interesting books containing scientific information about the endocrine glands is:

*The Nature of the Beast*, by Ruth Crosby Noble. Doubleday, Doran & Company: New York, 1945.

Further information about psychic energy can be obtained from Schilder, who gives references to the literature on the subject:

*Mind*, by Paul Schilder. Columbia University Press: New York, 1942. Chapter XXI.

3. *Brain*

The concept of the brain as the organ of waiting is a useful one for didactic purposes. The mode of "storage" of "energy" is a legitimate subject of inquiry. For a discussion of the function of the brain consult:

*Man on His Nature*, by Sir Charles Sherrington. The Macmillan Company: New York, 1940.

4. *Images*

The idea of images presented here is modified from Freud, Jung, Schilder, and Burrow. Compare:

*Psychological Types*, by C. G. Jung. Harcourt, Brace & Company: New York, 1933.

5. *Presentations*

This discussion of images, charges, and representations has as its foundation the Freudian concepts of presentation and cathexis. Freud's ideas about these subjects are scattered through his collected papers, but there is some popularly available discussion, with some remarks about the omnipotence of thought, in "Totem and Taboo," which can be found in:

*The Basic Writings of Sigmund Freud*, edited by A. A. Brill. The Modern Library: New York, 1938. Pp. 873 to 877.

It appears as though a development of these concepts might eventually lead to a graphic method of representing metapsychological ideas, similar to the method of analytic geometry. An image might be represented by the curve of the intensity of the cathexes at its various points, rather than in its objective form.

Hans Vaihinger is the expounder of the "Philosophy of As-If."

6. *Individual Differences*

The hypothesis that mood is partly dependent upon endocrine influences, reasonable though it sounds, is still in the speculative stage. The idea of strongly "inhibiting" types versus strongly "repressing" types is a clinically and didactically useful restatement of the concepts of introversion and extroversion (in the Freudian rather than the Jungian sense). The subdivision of intelligence into three spheres can be found in Thorndike. For a general discussion of intelligence, see:

*The Measurement of Adult Intelligence*, by David Wechsler.

The Williams & Wilkins Company: Baltimore, 1944.

The factors mentioned in this section can be tabulated into a useful structural classification of personality. Kahn's classification, upon which this one is partly based, is discussed in:

*The Anatomy of Personality*, by H. W. Haggard & C. C. Fry. Harper & Brothers: New York, 1936.

*Psychopathic Personalities*, by Eugen Kahn. Yale University Press: New Haven, 1931. (Out of print.)

Perhaps it is not quite correct to say that the viscerotonic "soothes" his environment, but this statement avoids, at this stage of the game, the issue of incorporation.

### CHAPTER TWO

# WHAT PEOPLE ARE TRYING TO DO

—————————

## I

## What is a human being?

A HUMAN BEING is a colorful energy system, full of dynamic strivings. Like any energy system, he is continually trying to reach a state of tranquillity. He "has to." That's what energy "is for"; its mysterious function is to restore its own balance.

When the forceful mixture of air and gasoline is exploded in the cylinder of an automobile by the spark, it "has to" expand in order to regain its equilibrium, which is upset by compression and by the electric flash. When it expands, it pushes powerfully against the piston, which "has to" move, just as a man has to move if his equilibrium is upset by a heavy thrust. When the piston shoots downward, it upsets the equilibrium of the whole engine, which "has to" turn in order to regain its balance. If everything is in order and the car is in gear when the engine turns, the car "has to" move. That's the way it was made.

Men are also made so that when certain things happen inside or outside, certain other things have to happen sooner or later in an attempt to restore the balance.

In a human being, energy off balance, or tension, shows itself physically and mentally. Mentally it shows itself in the form of a feeling of restlessness and anxiety. This feeling arises from an urge to seek something which is able to restore the balance and relieve the tension. Such urges are called wishes. Only living things can wish, and living things live by wishing. Sexual desire, ambition, and the desire for approval are some of the more complicated human wishes to which we have given names. There are many others, conscious and unconscious, some of which we have given names to and some of which we have not. One of the most interesting jobs of psychology today is to recognize wishes and study their connections with each other.

The tensions in a good automobile do not have any trouble finding relief, because the insides are arranged on purpose so that the tensions can act in only one direction at a time. But the human being has different wishes pushing him in different directions at the same time, and this may make him quite uncomfortable. A simple example of this is a young lady with the hives at her first college dance. She has a wish to scratch and a wish not to scratch; and even a very well brought up young lady will feel fidgety while she is waltzing because of such a conflict between her wish to keep her good manners and her desire to scratch herself.

The problem with human beings is that it is necessary to postpone the relief of some tensions in order to avoid setting up new and even more painful tensions, such as embarrassment. This has a lot to do with why some people get splitting headaches and burning pains in the stomach, while some do not. We shall see later that the necessity for the human energy system to postpone the relief of tension is the cause of many interesting things.

A human being is a living energy system whose tensions give rise to wishes which it is his task to gratify without getting into trouble with himself, other people, or the world around him.

2

## What human beings are looking for

Human beings, if nothing interfered, would tend to act in such a way at every moment as to try to relieve their strongest tension by gratifying their dearest wish. Every wish that is gratified brings them closer to their goal, which is a feeling of peace and security, or freedom from anxiety. Anxiety is a sign of tension, and is reduced as the energy balance is restored. No one ever quite attains the goal, because new wishes are springing up all the time, and there are too many wishes trying for satisfaction at once, so that the mere possibility of gratifying one often increases the tension of the others. Even in sleep there is no peace, and the clattering snorer stirs uneasily sooner or later.

Life is full of irritations like sour cigars and bitter women who left the tickets in their other purse, as well as less humorous inner and outer frustrations which threaten to keep people from being able to gratify their wishes, and thereby increase their tensions and anxiety. It is not events themselves which are important, but their effect on the possible fulfillment of desires. The same thing can happen to two people at the same time and make one of them anxious and not bother the other, depending on their wishes concerning the future. The anxiety may seem to be due to the event itself, but it really arises only because the event affects the possibilities for gratifying wishes. Two automobiles might get flat tires at the same moment on the same stretch of road, but the amount of anxiety which this accident would arouse in each driver would depend entirely upon his wishes concerning the immediate and distant future; how much of a hurry he was in, his financial state, who was with him, and so on; and perhaps in some cases, to take a forceful example, upon the state of his bladder. Some playful high school boys, far from feeling any anxiety, might regard the event as a lark. Anxiety about losing a job may seem to be caused by the employment situation itself, but it only arises because of the threat to the individual's wishes to be able to fill his stomach, impress his neighbors, and make his children happy. A man who has no family cares and no wish to eat regularly nor impress his neighbors with his stainless steel possessions may never be subject to this type of anxiety, and may be perfectly content to be a hobo or a philosopher living in a barrel. What makes anxiety possible is the wishes inside and not what goes on outside. No wishes, no anxiety. A corpse never gets stage fright, so matter how large his audience.

People think they are looking for security, but what they are really looking for is a feeling of security, for actual security, of course, does not exist. The feeling of security is increased by having means available for the relief of tensions and anxieties, and the gratification of wishes; this helps to secure balance in the energy system which is a human being. When we see how conflicting our chief wish tensions are, we shall understand why "seeking freedom from anxiety" does not always correspond to what we commonly think of as "seeking a safe situation."

Lavinia Eris offers an example of how feelings of security and insecurity depend more upon what goes on in the mind than upon what goes on outside. During her college days, Lavinia's hobby was collecting specimens of insects and snakes, some of them poisonous, for the zoology museum. At first she was terrified when she had to approach a rattlesnake, but after the novelty wore off and she learned how to handle the beasts, she felt competent and secure. A few years later, however, she began to have frequent nightmares about rattlesnakes, and in this case the novelty never did wear off; each night was as terrifying as the last. The nightmares, which were caused by powerful conflicting tensions, remained fearsome to her, and she could never feel secure during these dreams even in the absence of outside danger. With the real snakes, however, she had soon begun to feel secure even though the outside danger remained the same. The anxiety caused by the conflicting wishes which were at the bottom of her nightmares was greater and more enduring than the fear caused by actually handling the dangerous reptiles.

Human beings seek to attain their goal of a feeling of security by striving to obtain means for gratifying their wishes, but unfortunately other wishes and outside forces interfere. While the fear of outside forces will wear off if it becomes clear that they can be managed or that they are no threat to the attainment of desires, the anxiety linked with wishes does not vanish until means for the relief of tensions become available.

3

## Which urges are the most powerful?

The two most powerful urges of human beings are the creative urge and the destructive urge. The creative urge gives rise to generous love and giving, ardent procreation, and joyful building up. The tension which drives man toward these constructive goals may be called *libido*, and its most important function for the human race is to ensure that procreation will continue. It therefore finds its most concentrated expression in sexual desire. The destructive urge activates hostility and hate, blind anger, and the uncanny pleasures of cruelty and decay. The tension which lends force to such feelings may be called *mortido*. It finds its most concentrated expression while fighting for survival, so that when properly applied, it aids in saving the individual from inside and outside dangers. In familiar language, libido is the energy of the life-wish which preserves the race, and mortido is the energy of a death-wish which, when turned against a real antagonist, helps to preserve the individual.

Naturally these two drives, which may urge the individual to opposite courses of conduct toward the people and things around him, often come into conflict with each other. Such disagreeable conflicts can be handled in several ways. Usually they are dealt with by pushing one of the wishes out of consciousness and pretending that it does not exist. In peacetime people have a tendency to pretend that mortido does not exist, and in wartime they try to pretend that libido does not exist toward the enemy. Always, however, the wish they are trying to ignore interferes with their conduct in spite of themselves so that neither loving nor hateful behavior is ever pure, and people never act completely constructively nor completely destructively. They are only too apt, without consciously willing it, to bite the kind hand that feeds them and feed the hateful mouth that bites them.

Another way of handling the conflict is to allow one feeling to hold sway one moment and the other feeling to govern the next. The man who alternately loves and hates is often as puzzling to the onlooker as a man who alternately takes bites of ice cream and cheese; the onlooker may not stop to think how significant it is that both foods could come from the same udder.

Creative and destructive drives, which find their culmination in sexual relations and killing, are the raw material which man and civilization have to work with. In order to preserve himself, society, and the human race, man must apply destructively directed energy to useful purposes, such as destroying greed, selfishness, and disease, and constructively directed energy toward spiritual as well as material progress. The mental development of the individual depends upon his struggle to apply these forces within him to the most productive ends.

There is a difference between wishing and trying to gratify wishes, between feeling love and hate and expressing them. The strength with which the individual expresses his love and hatred for others and for himself, and tries to gratify his libido and mortido, may be called aggressiveness. A man with strong feelings may fool himself and others by expressing them weakly, and a man with weak feelings may do likewise by expressing them freely.

Besides aggressiveness of expression, we should consider the direction of love and hate. Some people direct their love mostly toward others and others direct it mainly toward themselves. The direction of various quantities may change from time to time. Similarly, one can be very hateful toward others, the most aggressive act in this case being murder; or one can be very hateful toward oneself, the most aggressive act then being suicide. Both murder and suicide are expressions of aggressiveness; the only difference as far as mental energy is concerned is in its direction.

In most people's lives, such extremes are not found. Libido and mortido are well controlled and hidden by each other and possibly by other forces, so that many people go through life without realizing how powerful these two urges are and how much they influence motives and conduct. In fact, we are now ready to say that human behavior is largely determined by the tensions of libido and mortido, which upset the mental equilibrium of the human being and drive him to act in such a way as to make it possible to restore his energy balance. By obtaining possibilities for gratifying his creative and destructive urges he can diminish his feelings of anxiety and approach the feeling of security which is his goal. As we go along, we shall see how complicated it is for him to express these urges, how many things can go wrong while he is making the necessary adjustments and compromises, and what happens if he fails to handle his wishes and tensions in a practical way.

The chemicals in the blood must play a considerable part in determining the strengths of libido and mortido. Though one might suggest that the sexual chemicals from the ovaries or testicles influence libido, and that the "fear and anger" chemical from the adrenal glands influences mortido, it is not proven that injecting any of the chemicals we know about so far will make people more loving or more hateful. The results with animals are far more striking than with human beings. Rats which are injected with the "maternal" hormone of the pituitary gland, for example, will show a definite increase in loving motherly behavior. But in spite of the fact that nothing is proven in regard to human beings, we must nevertheless keep the various glands in mind when we discuss these powerful urges.

Many people question the origin of destructive urges, but few deny their existence. Because they do not show themselves plainly at all times does not mean that they are not present. The desire to procreate does not show itself plainly at all times either, but no one denies its existence. Anyone who has children in the house will have to admit that they are destructive and hostile at times, and there is no evidence that they grow out of these tendencies and much evidence to show that they simply express them more cautiously and subtly in later years, as is the case with their affectionate urges. Destructive urges are also manifested in dreams. A person's dreams are his own productions and he can form them into any shape he pleases. That people so often dream about destruction must mean that it pleases some part of them. The chief argument among psychiatrists is whether destructive urges are inborn or whether they develop as a result of thwarting the creative urge. We need not enter into this argument for our purposes, since people behave as though they had always had destructive tendencies and whether they develop during the first few months of life or are present at birth, does not alter what we have to say about their later development.

A human being is one who causes things to happen, and what he causes to happen, and how, and when, depends a great deal upon his two most powerful urges, the aggressiveness with which he expresses them, and the way he solves the conflict between them.

## 4

## The problem of a human being

The problem of a human being is the same as the problem of any energy system, namely, to "find" the path of least resistance for the discharge of tension. An electric battery, which also is an energy system, finds the path of least resistance in a circuit instantly, in a small fraction of a second. A flooding river or a tornado, which are other energy systems, finds the path of least resistance in a matter of hours. The human energy system may take years to find such a path, and can delay indefinitely because it is able to store energy.

The psychic tensions within a human being manifest themselves mainly, if not entirely, as libido and mortido, and these two forces strive for immediate expression. This means that man has a tendency to try to take what he wants when he wants it, and to destroy immediately anything that gets in his way, annoys him, or crosses him up. We can see this direct action often enough in a young infant who has not yet learned from sad experience to restrain himself. Unfortunately, if an adult attempts to do such things, there is interference from two sources: other human beings who also want what they want when they want it and wish to eliminate whoever or whatever gets in their way; and nature, which won't always supply what he wants when he wants it, and won't change in order to make his life easier.

Not only do nature and other people cross him up and keep him from carrying out his wishes on the spot, but they are also continually threatening to destroy him. Every energy system around him, including foaming oceans, roaring columns of air which we call winds, thunderous and earthshaking volcanoes, snarling wily animals, and other struggling human beings, is also striving for possibilities to reduce its tensions directly as they arise. Not only may he be upset because these other dynamic things interfere with him, but also he has to watch out that he does not interfere too much or in the wrong way with them. His problem is therefore to find out the best way to handle other energy systems in order to gratify his wishes speedily with the least danger.

In some parts of the world, magic is used for this purpose. For a small fee, such as three toads' hearts or a hot record for his sidewinder gramophone, the Akan-Ashanti witch doctor will put a hex on his customer's love rival by sticking pins into a wax image of him. Natives who live where there are hurricanes may believe that the wind likes raw steak, and sacrifice cows to the wind god to protect themselves from future frustrations. In some parts of the world, people like to pretend that death is a waiter who likes big tips, so they feel good about giving a lot of money to charity. In our country, of course, people don't believe in any of these things, and feel that the best method is to try to find out how people and nature are likely to act under various conditions, and how to get what is wanted from both of them with a reasonable hope of success. It appears that the more accurately we judge our surroundings, the more likely we are to get what we want.

We can see that in order to gratify their wishes without getting into trouble people have to learn to control their libido and mortido; that is, they have to learn to wait. They also have to learn how to handle and judge their surroundings so as to reduce the danger of being thwarted or destroyed when they finally do act.

This is a problem of control. Man has to learn to control three groups of forces: himself, other people, and nature. This is called the Reality Principle, for the more realistic he is, that is, the more accurate he is in his observations of these three things, the more rapidly and fully will he be able to satisfy his libido and mortido in safety. The Reality Principle requires him to form clear-cut images.

Most people have pretty good images of some of their surroundings. A good farmer understands the workings of nature. A successful businessman understands what people are apt to do under certain conditions. But only a rare individual has an accurate idea of what his own libido and mortido can make him do without even being recognized. It is in this last respect that the greatest and most frequent errors are made.

Fortunately we have within us a way of handling this threefold reality that has to be kept in such nice balance. This system is called the Ego, and is supposed to work in accordance with the

Reality Principle. It is supposed to make accurate observations and judgments of the individual's inner tensions and of the tensions of the energy systems around him, and is then supposed to guide his behavior accordingly, to his best advantage. It has to help him postpone his satisfaction when advisable, and to try to arrange the world around him so that he can eventually attain them.

To do these things, it has to have some kind of mastery of his psychic energy, and some kind of mastery of people and things. Thus the Ego is the "organ of mastery." The energy for this function is obtained from part of the libido and mortido energy which is gradually split off in infancy, and becomes separated from, and actually in many ways an opponent of, the rest of the libido and mortido energy. The Ego energy is used in controlling the remainder in accordance with the Reality Principle as the person learns about reality. People get great pleasure from mastering their own bodies in swimming and diving, from mastering a little rubber ball that flies around a golf course, from mastering little paper dolls that are called playing cards, and from mastering the mechanics of an airplane engine. There is a double satisfaction in all these things; they satisfy not only the primitive libido and mortido, but also those portions of libido and mortido which are split off and obtain their satisfaction by mastering things through the Ego.

Psychiatrists, for good psychological reasons, have come to think of the enormous amount of primitive libido and mortido, left after splitting off the relatively small portions required to form the Ego, as "those things," or simply "It." The libido and mortido of the Ego, and the libido and mortido left in "It" are often opposed to each other rather than working together, because one of the tasks of the Ego is to master and control "It," which always fights back. "It" wants immediate expression and satisfaction, and the Ego often wants "It" to wait.

Because psychiatrists in different countries speak different languages, they have found it convenient, like other scientists, to use for scientific terms Greek and Latin words which have been known throughout the world since ancient times. They therefore usually speak of "It" in the old Roman tongue, as "Id," or "the Id." The libido and mortido left in the Id are then spoken of as the "Id instincts."

We should make sure that we understand at this point that just as what pushes the piston of an automobile is a force, and not a little man, so the Ego energies and the Id instincts are forces, and not little men sitting in the mind with their hands on their holsters, ready to fight each other at the drop of a temptation.

The reason life is so difficult is that the Ego is in such a complicated situation. It has three forces to contend with, control, and finally find expression through to the satisfaction and safety of the individual: the Id instincts, the forces of nature, and other people. Most individuals are aware of the reality of nature and other people, but they do not realize clearly that the Id is also a reality, and an important and troublesome one to be reckoned with. One reason for this lack of appreciation is that the Id is in concealment and finds all sorts of ways of fooling the Ego.

No matter how clever a man is with other people and with the things around him, he will not be very happy unless he is clever with his own Id as well. In the end it is not the ability to charm women or to make money that leads to happiness, but the ability to make peace in one's own mind. The problem of the human Ego in a difficult world is to find the path of least resistance for the safe satisfaction of the creative and destructive urges.

# 5

# How do human beings express their urges?

As long as the individual postpones relief of any Id tension, the energy which is tied up in the "repressed" wish is wasted. In addition, it is hard work for the Ego to keep the lid on the Id, and a good deal of energy is wasted in just keeping that part of the Id hidden. It is much like having a secret police force to keep part of a nation from freedom of speech. The nation is weakened not only because a lot of its citizens are discontented and are not allowed to help in the national tasks, but also because many of them have to spend their time watching the discontented ones. If the latter could be satisfied, not only would they work for the nation instead of against it, but the secret policeman would be unnecessary and they too could be put to some useful task. Anyone who has seen healthy soldiers guarding military prisoners, while their comrades were out fighting the enemy, will understand this metaphor.

If the Id can be safely satisfied, the Ego can relax, and both Ego and Id can then devote additional energy to doing something useful for the individual and for society.

Nature has provided methods for partly getting around this double waste of energy, so that Id wishes which are not allowed to express themselves directly and completely can express themselves indirectly. This means that some, at least, of their energy may go to useful purposes, and it also means that the Ego can at least partly relax as the Id tension is reduced.

For a short time it may do no harm simply to press the Id wishes out of the conscious mind and assume that they don't exist. We should never forget, however, that to assume they don't exist does not abolish them. Eventually they will find their way out somehow in spite of all we can do. If an individual doesn't understand this, and fools himself by thinking that while everybody else may have unconscious creative and destructive urges, he doesn't, he is liable to get himself into trouble. We have already got ourselves into the trouble of a second world war by this kind of thinking. The more we know about our Id wishes and how to recognize and control them, the better off we shall be, and the sooner they will stop driving people into sad sexual situations and "justified" spitefulness.

One indirect way that the Id wishes express themselves after a while, when they have been kept pressed out of consciousness, or "repressed," by the Ego, is to wait until the Ego is asleep at night, and then show themselves in disguised form in dreams.

This does not afford a great deal of relief, however, and if the tensions are powerful and there is no other way out, the repressed Id energy may affect the individual's body and behavior to such an extent that the Ego loses control of a part of the body or a part of the mind. This loss of control expresses itself as a neurosis. A neurosis, or psychoneurosis, which for our purpose is the same thing, is therefore a disguised expression of an Id wish. We shall hear more about this later.

We are mostly interested at the moment in how the Id affects our normal everyday behavior, and how people manage to let off steam without their adult lives becoming a series of violent adventures. This is mostly done by substituting some other object or some other activity for the original goals of their wishes, something close enough to the real gratification to calm the Id down temporarily and distant enough not to give rise to threatening consequences.

The primitive need of the libido is to approach another human being as closely as possible, most of the time one of the opposite sex. Obviously the actual method of satisfaction will depend partly upon age. The closest an infant can get to another person is to suck at his mother's breast, and this is the beneficial goal of the libido in young infants of both sexes. If the child is bottle-fed, he will need extra cuddling to make up for the nursing pleasure he is deprived of. After puberty, the closest approach that can be made is the sexual embrace. In old age, holding hands and talking may be the only possible method of satisfaction of this primitive need.

While sexual contact provides the most direct satisfaction of libido, anything which gives the feeling of "approach," whether it be physical, mental, or emotional approach, may help to relieve libido tension. Thus moving closer, talking more intimately about common interests, or feeling an emotion together are of value in this respect. Even doing the same things at the same time, though far apart, may help. Many couples who are separated make an agreement to think of each other every day at supper, write letters to each other at the same hour every day, and do other things which "draw them together though they are apart." In some situations, however, such "fore-pleasures," instead of relieving libido tension, build it up further or mobilize it in larger quantities. In such cases it is true within certain limits that the more of these mental and emotional fore-pleasures that precede the sexual act, if one is to take place, the more pleasurable and complete will be the final satisfaction. Women seem to realize more clearly and at an earlier age than men that the more love between a normal couple and the more things they have in common, the more satisfaction they will get from the sexual relationship.

If sexual relationship with the opposite sex is delayed too long because of outside circumstances or the threats of conscience, there are other possibilities. First, some satisfaction can be obtained from courtship and social meetings. Secondly, some people can obtain almost complete satisfaction without any partner or with a partner of the same sex: that is, by masturbation or homosexuality. In the first case they have the proper sexual object, a person of the opposite sex, but don't accomplish the sexual aim, which is intercourse. In the second case, they don't have the proper object, but do accomplish the sexual goal of orgasm. In both cases something is out of place, so we speak of libido displaced from its proper aim, and libido displaced from its proper object.

Some of the most interesting and socially useful displacements of libido occur when both the aim and the object are partial substitutes for the real aim and object. This occurs in what is called sublimation, that is, an activity which helps bring other people as well as its creator closer to the sublime or "higher" things of life. Many mental functions are organized to bring such refined forms of pleasure to people. A good example is painting. Here the artist substitutes as object the model for a love partner (and this model need not be a person, but may be some inanimate object, such as a landscape or a bowl of fruit), and as aim the thrill of artistic creation for the thrill of love-making. The life of Andrea del Sarto is a good example of how an artist expresses himself through his painting when the direct expression of love meets with opposition.

Similarly the poet substitutes imaginary, or at least imagined, people and things for the real woman he cannot find or have, and again the ardor of creation for the passion of love. Dante exemplified all these things in the relationship between his poetry and his Beatrice. Sublimations can also occur in less talented people, who get some creative thrill from carpentry, and even from adding to their collections of sea shells or postage stamps, or getting a new station on the radios they have so lovingly built.

It must be understood that there are other satisfactions in sublimation besides the ones we have mentioned. We are only trying to point out in part how the pent-up libido uses these activities as an indirect way of relieving the mental tensions that result from ungratified primitive wishes.

The energy of mortido finds similar indirect methods of expression. One primitive need of mortido is to eliminate another human being, usually one of the same sex. Even among birds, fishes, and non-human mammals, this sexual distinction between the objects of libido and mortido can be seen. Flickers, jewel fish, elephants, and dogs, are usually loving and "approaching" with members of the opposite sex, while they readily become enraged and try to "eliminate" members of the same sex. Among human beings, when the restraining veneer of politeness wears off, the same is usually observed, as anyone can verify by visiting a saloon.

Since in our country in peacetime mortido can usually satisfy itself completely only once, whether by murder or suicide, it is much more mysterious to us than libido. In wartime psychiatrists learn more about it, since they are given the task of studying its effects in the raw. The Orientals, from Morocco to Yokohama, know far more about it than we do. In our democracy, where kindness is supposed to be rampant, mortido is even more severely repressed than libido, and so takes us by surprise in even more explosive ways. In everyday life libido gets a chance to drain off in various activities, but mortido has fewer such opportunities. Rages are less frequent than orgasms in the life of the well-adjusted individual.

We had better not neglect mortido too much in thinking about how to prevent war. Much of the peacemakers' attention seems to be directed to the problem of "exports," as though in hope of preventing war by regulating these. This seems very much like trying to eliminate babies by regulating women's clothes. Changing the conditions of the external objects will do little to change the strength of the primitive drives, which in the end will have their way.

Just as anything which gives the feeling of "approach" will help to satisfy libido, so anything which gives the feeling of "separation" will help in the case of mortido. Leaving town, quarreling, sarcasm, and doing everything differently "just to be stubborn," are indirect ways of gratifying mortido. Strangely enough, we know from experience that constipation belongs here also, though on first thought it may appear to be the reverse of "elimination."

In their direct satisfaction, both mortido and libido show two faces. Just as libido can be satisfied to different degrees in different people by either approaching or being approached, so mortido can be gratified by either running away or being run away from. The passive man's libido wants the woman to come to him, while the active man goes after the woman. In the same way, the passive man's mortido urge is to run away, while the active man wants to chase the other fellow away by fighting. Thus when mortido is awakened by danger, some people run away and some fight it out. This force has two emotions to deal with, fear and anger, and whichever one is stronger in any situation will determine the individual's behavior. In either case, the task of separating the individual from the outside threatening energy system is accomplished. (Those who object to the above formulation of "active" and "passive" are referred to the note at the end of the chapter.)

Mortido has the same possibilities for indirect expression as libido. Instead of eliminating a person of the same sex, it can attack him without eliminating him, as in making sarcastic remarks, business competition, or athletic competition. Or, it can eliminate an individual of the opposite sex, as in the case of a man who murders his wife from jealousy, where the real object is a person of the same sex; or it can eliminate the individual himself, as in suicide; or it can eliminate an animal instead of a person, as in hunting. In the first case, we have the proper object but the final aim is not accomplished, and we see mortido displaced from its aim; in the other cases we have a different object, but the aim of elimination is accomplished, and we see mortido displaced from its object. Mortido can also be sublimated, as in stonecutting, carpentry, and mining, which create beautiful or useful things by attacking inanimate objects. Surgery involves one of the most useful sublimations of mortido.

The reader is now acquainted with several psychological pairs of great importance in understanding people, which may be listed as follows:

    i.  Creative urges and destructive urges
   ii.  Libido and mortido
  iii.  Inwardly directed energy and outwardly directed energy

iv. Approach and separation
v. Aim displacement and object displacement
vi. Active and passive

Let us now go back to the orphan girl Nana, and see some of these pairs in action. We shall also see how unreasonable and undiscriminating the Id is, and how libido tension and mortido tension both try to find expression at the same time whenever possible.

We already know some of the reasons for Nana's early promiscuity. Her mother's early death, her father's dissolute habits, and the complete lack of family life left a deep hunger for affection or anything that looked like affection. When she was nineteen, her father was killed in a daylight attempt to hold up an armored car in front of the First National Bank of Olympia. From the reckless way in which this attempt was made, it was obvious that he had little wish to live and therefore little fear of the threat of death. As he often said, "A fellow that don't care to gamble any more don't care which way the dice fall." The ensuing scandal made it difficult for Nana to earn an honest living, and after a while she was forced, in spite of her repugnance for such sordid relationships, to take money from her numerous boy friends. It became the custom among various men of the town to go down to Foamborne Street and visit Nana when they were drunk. The fact that Mrs. Fayton, the town prostitute, screamed jealous vituperation at her on the street added to Nana's distaste for her profession.

In order to better her circumstances in the only way she could, she consented to live with Mr. Krone, a tall, ugly, thin old miser who fell in love with her. She thought she hated Mr. Krone, who often beat her viciously just as her father had done, but much to her own surprise, when he died a short time later she mourned him bitterly, in spite of the fact that he willed his hoard of money to the Anti-Vivisection Society after he had promised it to her. She was thus forced to return to her old way of life.

It was only a matter of time before Nana caught a venereal infection, which she contracted from Mr. Meleager, a dignified-looking corporation lawyer who frequently went to Chicago on business. She was shocked and incredulous when Dr. Pell told her what the condition was, but she improved rapidly under regular treatment. When it seemed to her that she was cured, she neglected the doctor's warnings and secretly saw two of her favorite visitors again. The result was that Ralph Metis and Josiah Tally both caught the disease from her.

The chief emotional tensions in Nana were first, a hunger for the affection she had never received in childhood; secondly, a hunger for beautiful things, exaggerated by the drab surroundings she had lived in all her life: what money she earned beyond her living expenses she spent on reproductions of beautiful pictures and books on art, which she kept secretly hidden in her closet and never mentioned to any of her male friends; thirdly, resentment against her father for never having given her the kind and amount of affection she desired; fourthly, resentment against society in general, which she blamed for killing him and for having made her life miserable.

The springs of her conduct were her unsatisfied Id tensions, mostly dating from early childhood. Their expression was now made easy by her "independence" and increased loneliness since her father's death.

It was unreasonable, of course, for her to place the blame for her father's death on the bank which hired the armored car, but that is just what happened. This is typical of the way the Id works.

Her way of living enabled her to gratify her starved outwardly directed libido in more ways than one. It did not supply a normal emotional "approach" to another human being, but it did give her a poor substitute. It also supplied her with money to gratify her sublimated creative urge, which showed itself in the secret interest in art which she was ashamed to acknowledge because of a conflict between her inner delicacy and her self-repugnance. By enabling her to dress expensively, it also gratified her inwardly directed libido, or vanity.

It relieved her inwardly directed mortido because to a woman of her sensitiveness such a life brought much suffering. Mr. Krone gave this aspect a more direct relief by beating her. It gratified her outwardly directed mortido to take some of his precious money from the old miser, and to give her disease to her two friends, resulting in a permanent "separation" from them which satisfied her destructive urge.

If we disregard her explanations of why things happened and

look only at what did happen (a procedure which psychiatrists commonly employ), we can see at least two examples of object displacement. Mr. Krone took the place of her father in many ways, and the similarity added to her unconscious pleasure in punishing him financially as well as in being nice to him. That she wasn't completely aware of this displacement of mixed feelings from her father to Mr. Krone was shown by the fact that she herself was surprised when she wept at the old man's death. Ralph and Josiah, the two men connected with the bank, to whom she gave her disease, were scapegoats for "the bank," which she unreasonably wanted to punish for her father's death.

Both activity and passivity played a part in her punishment of the three men. Mr. Krone she actively punished, going out of her way to spend money extravagantly and to make him jealous. The other two men she punished by her passivity. She did not go out of her way to infect them, she simply yielded passively to their persuasions and omitted to tell them of her condition, all in good faith, since at the moment she thought of herself as cured.

One of the most important things to notice is that in nearly everything she did, she gratified both libido and mortido at the same time. This was most clearly shown on the night of the catastrophe, when she obtained sexual pleasure from the two men and at the same time gave them the disease. It also showed in her mixed feelings towards Mr. Krone. In fact, without being clearly aware of it, she had the same sort of ambidexterous, double-edged attitude towards all concerned, including herself. Such double-valued attitudes, involving love and hate at the same time, are called "ambivalent," and both feelings strive to obtain gratification simultaneously in everything the individual does.

Some people might object that since she "didn't know" that she still had the disease, it isn't fair to talk this way about what happened. It is true that her Ego may not have known that she had it, but the uncertainty was there in her Id, as she found out later when she came to the psychiatrist for treatment. By "forgetting" and by the sins of omission, ye shall know the Id.

# 6

# How do people handle their surroundings?

People usually handle their surroundings in such a way that either libido or mortido, or preferably both, obtain some satisfaction from almost everything they do. These satisfactions are gained through the feeling of "approach" or creation, and "separation" or destruction. The Id, however, has little if any ability to learn, or to put things in what we usually think of as their proper order.

The Ego, which normally controls the faculties by which people handle things, such as their limbs and their thinking, is different. The Id can only wish, while the Ego can learn and arrange. The Id is like a petulant Roman Emperor, and the Ego is like a faithful servant trying to carry out his unreasonable demands. The Emperor says: "I wish to have hummingbirds' tongues for dinner!" The servant has learned where and how to get what the Emperor wants, and how to arrange for his food to be cooked to his taste. The Emperor could never catch a single hummingbird by himself. When he wants anything, he has to get it through a servant, who is his means of communication with the world outside the palace. In the same way, the Id says: "I want to have a wife and some children!" The Ego then has to arrange the individual's life for the next few years so that the wish of the Id will be gratified. The Ego handles the environment in two ways: by arranging and by learning. Just as the work of the Id can be picked out in everything the individual does by noting which wishes are *actually* gratified by the end result (without consideration of how they are gratified or what protests the individual makes); so the work of the Ego is demonstrated by the amount of arranging of ideas and actions which has taken place, and what the individual *thinks* he has done. In dreams, the work of the Id can be detected in the wishes which are gratified by the dream; and the work of the Ego is harder to see unless much arranging has taken place. That is why a dream frequently seems strange or silly to the Ego when it awakens in the morning. In studying mathematics, the work of the Ego is easy to see in all the arranging and learning that has to take place, while the work of the Id is hidden and it is difficult to see what unconscious wishes are gratified by noticing that two plus two equals four.

In a way, the Id is more "natural" than the Ego, just as a cow is more "natural" than a steak. A steak is a cow which has been arranged by a human Ego. Nothing in nature is arranged. Trees grow naturally in forests. Only when the human Ego enters the picture do they grow in regularly arranged patterns in orchards. Weeds grow where they find the best nourishment, or where the wind drops their seeds. Only the Ego can make flowers grow in neat rows. It is the Ego which cages animals, cuts canals in straight lines, sees patterns in the stars in the sky, and makes "opposites which exclude each other." In nature and in the Id, there are no "opposites which exclude each other." Everyone is now familiar with electrons and atoms. Is an atom hard or soft, dark or light, good or bad? We cannot even say whether it is matter or energy, time or space. It is both and neither. Along with the idea of "opposites which exclude each other" in physics and psychiatry, we have to drop the idea of "cause and effect" as we are commonly accustomed to think of it. In nature, things are not "caused," or "explained." They simply occur at "different" times. Our Egos invented the ideas of "cause" and "explanation." They are not a part of nature. Such ideas are just another evidence that our Egos like to put things in order. Things don't happen "because." They happen "when," or "as if," and we shall have to be content with that.

In the Id, then, love does not exclude hate. Love and hate may exist side by side at the same time towards the same person and may be interwoven in all our feelings towards that person. But people tend to think of them as opposites which exclude each other, and so the Ego may experience "surprise" on finding that in some cases the extremes of affection and destruction are expressed almost simultaneously. Extreme affection is often closely linked with total destruction. That's why a violent man frequently murders a woman with whom he is passionately in love. The police, who have to deal with realities and not with arranged ideas, realize this, and in such cases the first person they question (and not the last person, as our "logical" Egos might want us to think) is the lover. This idea is so familiar that it sounds "logical," but it is also "illogical," and comes from practical experience and knowledge of the way the Id instincts fly in the face of logic.

The second important faculty of the Ego is learning. People learn about reality by keeping in mind things that will enable them to make general statements, which are a kind of prophecy. A man who does not pay attention to his surroundings may get caught in the rain again and again. But if he lives in one place long enough he comes to learn that a certain kind of cloud brings rain. He generalizes, that is, prophesies, that low black clouds bring rain. From many observations of the sky his Ego extracts or abstracts the ideas of lowness and blackness, in order to make this generalization. The Id is unreliable in this respect because it makes too many unrealistic generalizations which do not work. The child's Ego may learn, if he sees the sight every year, that the visit of the doctor with his black bag means a new baby. The Id makes false generalizations because it does not abstract the proper meanings from all that happens: in dreams, which are the best material for studying the Id, a doctor may mean a baby no matter what he is carrying, or a black bag may mean a baby even if it is not carried by a doctor. If the Ego figured things out that way, it would get nowhere. The problem of correct learning has also been studied from the point of view of conditioned reflexes.

The Id is more like nature in the raw than the Ego, but it is not competent to handle reality because it does not arrange things or generalize in a practical way. People can best handle their surroundings efficiently by observing, learning, generalizing, and arranging, with the aid of the Reality Principle, and by controlling their Id instincts accordingly. Strangely enough, however, in spite of all this, the Id often shows more wisdom than the Ego, an apparent contradiction which we shall hear more about in the section on Intuition.

## 7

## How does a human being grow and change?

It is easy to understand that one "purpose" of libido is to keep the adult human being forever wishing to reproduce. If the libido expresses itself in undisguised form, as it may in many young people, we have an individual who is "continually chasing after the promise of an orgasm," as St. Cyr has aptly said. It is evident also that mortido helps the individual to survive, by giving him the wish to eliminate anything which threatens him. When the individual is living among civilized people, however, he has to disguise these primitive urges. Because life is so complicated, and Id drives are filtered through the Ego, only on special occasions do we see either libido or mortido in the raw.

The Id can only wish. It cannot learn or think or grow or change much, if at all (except perhaps that its strength changes at special periods of life, as during puberty). It is governed by tensions striving for release. There are only two things which can happen to the Id wishes: they can be gratified partly or completely, or they can be thwarted. When they are gratified, there is a relief of tension, as can be seen in anyone who has just had normal sexual satisfaction, or who has just injured himself in an unsuccessful attempt at suicide. When they are thwarted, tension piles up, and further attempts to relieve it result.

Since the primitive creative and destructive urges themselves cannot be basically changed, growth or change in the human personality takes place by changing the manner in which these tensions are relieved.

The Id can only express itself in ways which the body and the surroundings make available. In the newborn infant, many things are undeveloped. The Id of a nursing child cannot express itself in any way which requires walking, because the nerves and organs of walking are not yet fully developed. Many pleasures are denied to the infant because his control of his own body has to await the ripening of the nerves to the various organs and muscles. He makes the best of what he can use. At birth, the most important movements he has at his command are sucking and making sounds. Any gratification of libido or mortido has to be gained through these and other largely undeveloped mechanisms. Since the Id instincts usually gain more satisfaction when another person is involved, it can be observed that the infant's greatest contentment comes from sucking at the breast.

As the child grows, his nervous system acquires control of more and more actions—allowing new ways of gratifying his Id—until the age of strength and puberty when adult sexual activity and aggression, the final goals, become possible. His possibilities for getting satisfaction increase, and so does the variety of his activities, since human beings like to branch out when they can. After the period of sucking pleasure, he learns to control his bowels and bladder, and then he is able to get more pleasure from them. As he learns to use his hands and legs, he has even more ways of getting satisfaction. Later in life when his sexual organs mature, he uses them to relieve mental tension. As each new stage is reached he more or less outgrows the pleasures he obtained at the last stage, and uses in a more matter-of-fact way the organs which have been abandoned as pleasure givers. He thus goes through stages of mouth pleasure, bowel and bladder pleasure, body pleasure, and sexual organ pleasure.

Many times, however, the human being will hang on to an old way of getting satisfaction if he is not very successful with a new way, or if circumstances make it difficult for him to experiment with it, as in the case of an orphan child who is deprived of many opportunities for development and therefore continues to suck his thumb after infancy, remaining fixed at one of the early stages. Or, he may develop normally but return to an earlier stage in times of stress, giving up on occasion some of his most recently acquired methods of releasing tension, like an older child who sucks his thumb when his mother is away on her vacation and stops when she returns.

Besides going through the various organ stages in a natural way by keeping pace with the growth of his nervous system, his body, and his glands, the normal human being may change the speed, the manner, the frequency, or the object of his gratifications as he grows up. These changes are greatly influenced by the Ego, usually in accordance with the Reality Principle. He learns that certain ways of getting satisfaction often lead to greater dissatisfaction in the long run, so he tries to be more sensible about it. He profits from experience. The Id seems to be "lazy" and set in its habits, and tries again and again to obtain gratification in the same old un-profitable ways unless the Ego takes a very firm hand. If the Ego doesn't have a watchful eye, the Id compels the individual to repeat the same simple, childish mistakes over and over.

Not only does the Id have a tendency never to learn, using again and again the same childish and unsatisfactory methods in attempting to obtain gratification, but it may even content itself at times with false realities, such as imagination, dreaming, and even convincing the Ego that its imaginations are real, which is what we call "hallucinating." Thus in an alcoholic delirium released mortido may seek satisfaction through visions of sinister snakes and monsters, instead of by actual killing or suicide. These visual hallucinations seem real to the individual, because of crippling of the Ego's "reality test." Many a young man seeks to satisfy his libido by imagining that some beautiful woman is in love with him, when actually she may not even know that he exists. If he really comes to believe his fabrications, these false convictions are called "delusions."

As people grow up, they tend to become more dignified in their behavior, and more careful to restrain themselves from doing anything which might lose them the good opinion of themselves and their neighbors, so that mortido tensions tend to turn more and more frequently back on the individual himself. A child may vent his mortido in a temper outburst without being too embarrassed, but a grown man who is angered and irritated by his fellow workers usually tries to control himself, with the result that the mortido may take it out on his own body.

Two of the commonest ways it does this are by elevating the blood pressure and by changing the caliber of the blood vessels of the stomach. If such a conversion of a feeling into a bodily reaction takes place too frequently, more or less permanent changes may result. The blood pressure may stay up instead of coming down after a restful weekend, as we saw in the case of Mr. King; or the continual disturbance in the circulation of the stomach may eventually result in a small area being digested away from the wall of that organ, causing a "gastric ulcer." The prevention does not lie in slapping one's stenographer or kicking the foreman in the fundament, but in learning to keep from being irritated by little things, including financial losses. After all, you can take your stomach with you, but not your money. Too often, a man prefers to keep his mahogany desk and let the surgeons have his stomach.

As the individual grows, the Ego becomes more efficient in accomplishing its three tasks: relieving libido, relieving mortido, and reducing the threat of the outside world. Farming is a good example of this, where mortido gives the energy to attack the earth, and libido gives the energy to nurse the growing crop; while the sale of the crop reduces the threat of starvation and at the same time increases the chance of getting further libido and mortido satisfaction, by making it easier to find a wife.

The personality of the normal human being grows and changes as he learns new methods of gratifying libido and mortido, using new organs and faculties as control of them is learned, and abandoning previous infantile ways. The Reality Principle assists in this growth by helping to fight the compulsion to repeat over and over the old and now less efficient and even dangerous methods of attempting to gain satisfaction.

## 8

## Why do human beings control themselves?

A playful little child makes no effort to control himself until he learns that direct expression of libido and mortido does not pay. When a lusty infant wants to break something, he smashes it. When he wants to put his arms around somebody, he hugs her. As he grows up, he learns that similar conduct may in the end lead to more pain than pleasure, that immediate relief of one tension may lead to damming up of a greater tension. It is then up to the Ego to judge, if it is capable, which line of conduct will give the greatest relief of tension in the long run.

If the infant breaks his father's musical saw, he gets spanked or scolded. This is painful and leads to great mental tension. Next time he feels destructive, he may stop to think as follows: "Will smashing this fifteenth-century Ming vase relieve more tension than the resulting spanking will create?" If his father has a firm and callused hand, the answer will be: "No!" So the vase remains on its pedestal behind the rubber plant.

Later on in life, the same person may have to answer the question: "Will stealing the policeman's girl relieve more tension than having my skull beaten in with a shillelagh will create?" Again the answer is: "No!" so the policeman's girl remains on her pedestal down by the rubber plant.

Punishment results in increased tension in several ways. Let us consider here only the increased libido tension due to loss of opportunity to love and the increased mortido tension due to the inability to retaliate. The spanked child is forbidden to hug his father for a while, nor can he gratify his resentment by taking him out to the woodshed. Even if he is only scolded rather than spanked, the result is the same.

In some cases, when mortido is directed inward, so that the person craves suffering, punishment may relieve more mortido tension than it creates, and being spanked may be a pleasure. Many adults as well as children get mortido satisfaction from being punished. That is one reason why certain people are always getting into scrapes. For them, suffering, rather than acting as a preventative, is one of the attractions of a dangerous life.

Most people, however, like to avoid what is commonly thought of as "punishment," and find ways of handling their Id instincts so that satisfaction may be postponed if there is any danger of suffering. In this way they hope finally to obtain complete or partial gratification without tears.

Since actual physical pain is rarely used as a form of punishment for adults in this country, people control themselves mainly to avoid the mental pain which results from increased tensions. They refrain from crime, for example, in part because libido and mortido frustration would make it disagreeable for most people to be sent to the penitentiary; they would lose their self-regard and the regard and company of their friends, and they would be helpless against the many people they would hate, including themselves. The types of sexual activity and outbursts of violence which occur in prisons demonstrate the increase of Id tensions in those who are cut off from decent society and shut up by themselves.

It will be noted that we have made no direct mention here of conscience, which after all is what we generally think of as keeping most people well behaved. We have, however, already hinted at its existence when we used such terms as "loss of love," "loss of opportunity to love," and when we spoke of loss of self-regard, and self-hate. In the next section we shall see how these things are related to conscience, and whence the latter develops. People are not born "good" or "bad," but they learn their standards of conduct at a very early age from those around them. When the child is "bad," the parents should always stop to ask themselves: "How much are *we* at fault? Have we given the child a good example to imitate?"

## 9

## How does a human being make a decision?

People have two ways of making a decision. The first is by thinking. We consider the possibilities on both sides, weigh them, and decide more or less in accordance with the Reality Principle. The second is without conscious thinking. We should be in a continual turmoil of indecision if we had to think about every little thing we did during the day. If we had to decide, each time we buttoned a button, which finger went over the button and which finger went under it, we should take as long as little children to get dressed. So the mind has ways of making decisions for us without conscious thought on our part.

One of the ways in which we make decisions without being aware of it is the automatic thought-saving way called habit, which saves us effort in handling simple everyday situations which do not involve any strain on the Id. There are people who do have to think and elaborate about every unimportant thing which would be done from habit by most; these people then have so much to worry about, as we shall see later in the case of Ann Kayo, that they use up time and concentrate energy on worrying so that they have little time left to carry on their normal occupations effectively. Investigation shows that ordinary actions such as buttoning a button or washing the hands, which have little emotional meaning to the average person, have taken on a special significance for such people. Their libido and mortido are too heavily displaced onto trivial objects, and have made too many images uncertain. Since habit can only be used in handling lightly charged situations involving clear-cut images, such "obsessed" individuals have trouble doing things from habit. Parts of the world around them have become too "libidinized" and "mortidinized."

The Id itself supplies an unconscious force for making decisions in more emotional situations. This force is based on emotional attitudes which we gather in early childhood from our parents and others whose love we value and are at pains not to lose. After early childhood, people are able to make certain decisions without conscious thought in accordance with what they imagine the desires of these loved ones would be. They behave as if they said to themselves, for example:

"That is the way I have to do because that is the way my father would have had me do if he were here by my side. If I didn't do it that way I might lose his love, as I learned when I was an infant."

The important thing to notice is that they do *not* have to say this to themselves, but the result is the same *as if* they did say it. In this way time and energy are saved in making decisions.

Naturally, children whose fathers were not there to bring them up, or whose parents played their roles badly, will have a disturbance in this aspect of their development, which may cause them increasing grief and trouble as they go on in life.

This unconscious mechanism, then, incorporates the lessons learned in childhood about how to avoid losing people's love. The individual learns in infancy how he "ought" to behave, because his parents become angry when he does not behave as they think he "ought" to, and this feeling of "oughtness" gets so deeply ingrained that it becomes a part of his unconscious self. There is also some "oughtness" acquired later in life, that is, after the age of five or six, which remains conscious in the form of what is called "conscience," and this also plays a part in helping to make decisions. The "unconscious conscience," however, is a more important problem than the "conscious conscience" because it is formed earlier, is more deeply rooted, more powerful, harder to change and control, and affects people's conduct without their clearly realizing it and often in spite of themselves.

When the individual grows up, of course, his parents are not standing beside him to punish him if he does not do as they think he ought, but their powerful and heavily charged images are there in his unconscious mind, which is just as good, since, we remember, he will act in accordance with his images anyway rather than according to what is really there. The fact that the images of "ought-ness" may be twenty or forty years old may make no difference, since they are unconscious, and we know that the unconscious does not age and that its images are imbued with a feeling of immortality which keeps them fresh and young. As for inflicting the punishment if he does transgress, his parents do not have to be there for that either. His own Id takes care of it.

Just as a part of his libido is normally turned inward upon himself, so that he respects and admires and protects himself, so a part of his mortido is turned inward to help supply the energy for punishing himself. When he does something he learned as an infant he ought not to do, this part of the mortido kindles the images of his absent parents in chastising him. The feeling we get when we do something we feel we ought not to do is called "guilt." Even if the individual is not aware of feeling guilty, the unsatisfied tension of inwardly directed mortido resulting from "wickedness" shows itself as a "need for punishment." Guilt and the need for punishment mean that the individual's unconscious and conscious parent-images, and their successors, have become active and are threatening to punish him much as his real parents used to do. Until this need for punishment is satisfied, it will continue to exist, and quantities of this tension may pile up for years, eventually driving the individual into scrape after scrape in an effort to obtain relief. For this reason, inwardly directed destructive energy must be controlled since, like the rest of the Id energies, it may go too far if the Ego does not realize in time what is going on and put a stop to it. The need for punishment may get the individual into a serious accident through "forgetfulness" or "carelessness."

We can see now that the Id tensions are a little more complicated than we hinted at first. There are tensions of outwardly directed libido and tensions of inwardly directed libido; and tensions of outwardly directed mortido and tensions of inwardly directed mortido. All four groups are clamoring for satisfaction, and it is up to the Ego to keep them all under control. One of the most important and difficult tasks for the Ego to carry out is to see that in gratifying any of the other three tensions it does not unduly increase the tension of the inwardly directed mortido. In other words, "guilt" may cause more tension than is relieved by doing what we do, and some people who cannot control this may punish themselves to a disastrous extent for some trivial trespass.

The unconscious images of the parents and their successors, incorporating the lessons learned in early life, are charged with mortido and some libido split off from the rest of the Id. This system, which helps decide the individual's behavior, is called the Superego. The question of guilt and the need for punishment is complicated, because they are connected with many elements, all of which help in making decisions. The first is the Superego proper just described. Another one is the Ego Ideal, which consists of the individual's conscious and unconscious images of what he would like to be, patterned after certain people whom he admires, identifies himself with, would like to imitate, and who possess certain qualities which he regards as ideal. Another is his conscious image of what is right and wrong, which he gets mainly from his religious preceptors, school teachers, and other authorities: these form what is commonly known as "conscience."

These three elements are the most important. For simplicity, we shall loosely include them all under the name of Superego.

Since "doing his duty" by moving his bowels properly is one of the child's first lessons in "oughtness," the period of bowel training is an important one in the formation of the Superego. This is a good example of the well-established but rather complex connection between mortido and the bowels, which we shall meet again.

It should be understood that the mortido involved in the Superego is a quantity split off from the rest of the Id energy, so that the Supergo is free to work more or less as an opponent of the Id. Thus finally the Ego has at least three energy systems whose needs must be considered before acting: the Id wishes, the outside world of reality, and the Superego.

The decisions of a human being may therefore be made consciously or unconsciously. Conscious decisions are regulated, we like to think, by the Reality Principle and the conscious conscience. Unconscious decisions may be simplified and energy saved by means of habit in the case of actions which have little emotional significance. In most emotional situations, decisions depend on the result of the conflict between the unconscious forces of the Superego and the Id. Once the decision has been made without the individual being aware of the real forces behind it, he takes upon himself the task of finding justifications for it and convincing himself and others that it has been made in accordance with the realities of the situation. This is called "rationalization."

10

# To whom the good of all this?

Who is "I"? We have described the Id wishes as giving pleasure to "the individual" when gratified. We have told how the Superego guides the Ego, and punishes "the individual" for his sins. We have studied the manner in which the Ego, between these two forces, has to guide "us" through the dangers of the environment. For whose benefit are all these forces working? Is my Ego I? Or is my Id I? Or is my Superego the real I?

A woman described her Self as being something that controlled the rest of her being; she thought of herself as someone driving a donkey cart. The donkey was the thing in her which thought, controlled her bodily movements, remembered things for her, and did her work of writing stories for her. When she couldn't remember something, her Self blamed the "donkey," whose job it was to remember and to compose sentences. What was the Self she was talking about?

As far as we have gone, we should have to say it was either the Superego, or an observing part of the Ego. In the latter case, we should have to suppose that the Ego is a system which in some mysterious way can look at itself, much as the parts of the body can feel one another. This is one way of accounting for the feeling people can have that they can watch their own minds at work as though they were someone else, just as they can grasp their own legs as easily as though they were someone else's.

Another way of explaining this is to suppose that there is a fourth part to the personality, for whose good the other three exist. If there is such a fourth part, psychiatrists and psychologists know little or nothing about it. Religious people might say it was the soul. Scientists have no answer at present. We have avoided the question so far by describing the human being simply as an energy system, a system of forces continually trying to regain or maintain its equilibrium, and not trying to "please" anybody or anything or any part of itself, any more than the earth is trying to "please" anybody when it goes around the sun.

Although the "driver" for the donkey cart of the human mind could logically be either the Superego or a part of the Ego itself, we may, if we like, regard the feeling of people that they can watch their own minds as a manifestation of a fourth system of tensions in the mental apparatus. This would be the same system of tensions which normally pushes living things continually in the direction of "progress." We may suppose the existence of such a system in order to explain why people grow and why the human race tries to get "better," and why animals gradually become more efficient through evolution, and why a creative love of beauty is added to the mind as that energy system becomes more complicated from the jellyfish up through the frogs and monkeys to man. We can forget the question of whose "benefit" this is for and still suppose that there is a force within us which keeps us striving to go "onwards and upwards."

As we shall see later, a neurosis has many advantages for the individual. If he is better off in many respects with his neurosis, what is the force which makes him "want" to get better? What is the curative force of nature which makes sick bodies and sick minds strive to become healthy again so that they can continue to grow? What makes an embryo grow? Why doesn't it just stay an embryo? Growing is hard work and uses up a lot of energy. What made some jellyfish evolve into men? Why didn't they just stay jellyfish forever? Evolving is also hard work.

For an answer we can go back more than two thousand years to a great Semite named Zeno. Zeno wandered and wondered for many years. His wandering came to an end in Athens, in ancient Greece, but his wondering did not. Zeno talked a great deal about "Physis," the force of Nature, which eternally strives to make things grow and to make growing things more perfect. The idea of Physis was not originated by Zeno, but he did much of the thinking about it in connection with the growth and development of living things. Many philosophers since have talked about the creative force of Nature which makes all things grow in an orderly and "progressive" way.

If such a growth drive exists in the minds as well as the bodies of human beings, how can we fit it into our energy scheme, and what is its connection with the other tensions of the mind? We may remember that we have talked about inwardly and outwardly directed mortido, and outwardly directed libido, but so far we have said little about inwardly directed libido. It may be that growth energy comes from the tension of inwardly directed libido. This explanation seems too simple, however; for example, just the reverse might be true, and libido might be only one aspect of growth energy. Perhaps Physis does not exist at all, but in spite of our inability to be definite about this subject, there are so many things which happen *as if* there were such a force, that it is easier to understand human beings if we suppose that it does exist.

We shall henceforth take the liberty of supposing that Physis is a force to be reckoned with in studying the human mind, and avoid the question of whether it is a force separate from inwardly directed libido. We have not solved the problem of who is the "driver" for whose benefit the Id, Ego, and Superego maintain their nice balance of tensions, but we have learned that there are other possibilities in the human mind which we must not neglect to think about.

## Footnotes for Philosophers, Chapter Two

In this chapter, we have ventured onto the very battleground of modern psychiatry. The subjects dealt with are difficult, but some orientation is absolutely necessary if the reader is to understand what follows. Our didactic purpose precludes an adequate presentation of dissenting opinions. The viewpoints chosen are those which the author has found most productive in clinical work.

1. *Tensions*

It seems legitimate and profitable to think about the dynamics of the mind in terms of various formulations of the second law of thermodynamics, thus attempting to bring psychological phenomena into relationship with the general laws of energy, in order to unify our concepts with those of other branches of science. Some of the formulations which seem potentially useful are as follows: *

"All systems tend to approach a state of equilibrium."

"The entropy change of a system depends only on the initial and final states of the system, independently of the previous history of the system, and when a system changes from one given state to some other definite state, no matter by what irreversible or reversible process, the entropy change is the same."

And the entropy equation: "$dS = dq(rev)/T$."

Le Chatelier's principle is equally worth considering.

2. *Anxiety*

Cf. *The Problem of Anxiety*, by Sigmund Freud. W. W. Norton & Company: New York, 1936.

Or, for easier reading:

*New Introductory Lectures on Psychoanalysis*, by Sigmund Freud. Idem, 1933. Chapter 4, "Anxiety and Instinctual Life."

3. *Instincts*

The question of whether the destructive urge is primary, or is secondary to libido frustration, leaves practical psychiatry in much the same position as the parent problem of heredity *vs.* environment. As a test of objectivity, one may start off with the assumption that libido only arises as a result of mortido frustration, that sucking, for example, is the result of a frustrated desire to bite, and that later when he has his teeth, the infant proceeds to carry out his "real" aim; or that in puberty, genital sexual desire arises as a substitute for the desire to kill,

* Abstracted from Frederick Hutton Getman and Farrington Daniels, *Outlines of Physical Chemistry*. New York: J. Wiley & Sons, 1943, 7th ed.

and so on. If this train of thought is followed through carefully, it emphasizes the difficulty of solving the problem of the death instinct. At any rate, the pertinent question for psychotherapy is not how much the child is born with, but how much can be modified.

The most easily accessible references concerning the death instinct are:

*Beyond the Pleasure Principle*, by Sigmund Freud. The International Psycho-analytical Press: London, 1922.

*Man Against Himself*, by Karl A. Menninger. Harcourt, Brace & Company: New York, 1938.

For a critical discussion:

*New Ways in Psychoanalysis*, by Karen Horney. W. W. Norton & Company: New York, 1939. Chapter VII.

The term "mortido" is taken from Paul Federn in preference to the term "destrudo" suggested by Edoardo Weiss.

5. *Mental Mechanisms*

Cf. *General Introduction to Psychoanalysis*, by Sigmund Freud. Garden City Publishing Company: New York, 1938. Chapter 23.

The etymology of the term "sublimation" implied in this section is dubious but mnemonic. For the sake of simplicity, and at the expense of accuracy, I have taken liberties with the terms "active" and "passive." In the case of mortido, for example, there are at least four possible "voices" or courses of action:

"I hurt him"; "I am hurt by him"; "I hurt myself"; "I avoid being hurt by him."

6. *The Ego*

For a pertinent discussion of some of the problems mentioned here, see:

*Language in Action*, by S. I. Hayakawa. Harcourt, Brace & Company: New York, 1941.

*Science and Sanity*, by Alfred Korzybski. Science Press Printing Company: Lancaster, Pa., 1941.

7. *Psychic Growth*

Cf. "Three Contributions to the Theory of Sex," in *The Basic Writings of Sigmund Freud*, op. cit.

9. *Superego*

Cf. *New Introductory Lectures on Psychoanalysis*, op. cit., Chapter 3.

10. *Physis*

The idea that the personality can watch itself by one part of the Ego boundary "looking at" or "touching" another was suggested by Paul Federn. Freud felt that the Superego was the "watcher." Our patient's "donkey cart" is similar to the "horse and rider" cited by him.

The conception of Physis used here is Gilbert Murray's, and is most simply described in one of the Haldeman-Julius Little Blue Books, "The Stoic Philosophy," by Gilbert Murray, Appeal Pocket Series No. 210, Appeal Publishing Company, Girard, Kansas. Bergson is the best known author on the subject of creative growth, and his book is now easily available:

*Creative Evolution*, by Henri Bergson. The Modern Library: New York, 1944.

Schopenhauer is among the others who have something to say on this subject. Freud, in *Beyond the Pleasure Principle*, has expressed his disbelief in the existence of such a general creative force, terming it a "pleasing illusion." He himself was none too sure at one time, however, that something like Physis did not assist Ananke as the motive force in evolution. "This view of the struggle for existence," he says, "need not detract from the significance of 'inner evolutionary tendencies,' if such are found to exist." (*General Introduction to Psychoanalysis*, op. cit., p. 310.)

### CHAPTER THREE

# THE GROWTH OF THE INDIVIDUAL

---

I

## What is the difference between an adult and a child?

ADULTS ARE MUCH more like children than children are like adults. To many children a truck is a Big Car. It takes them a long time to understand that a truck is made to haul goods and a car is made to haul people. Similarly, to many adults a child is a Small Adult. They do not understand that (roughly speaking) it is a child's job to learn to handle himself, while an adult's job is to learn to handle his environment. Though an adult is often a Big Child, a child is never a Small Adult. The idea that a child is a miniature adult we may call the Homunculus idea about children. (Homunculus, meaning a cute little hombre, is a nice word for a mother to have in her vocabulary, even if it is misleading.)

How does a child differ from an adult? A child is helpless. As he grows older, his helplessness grows less, but he still depends upon his parents to show him the proper way to do things. As they show him how to do some things, he has ever new things to learn but as we have said, he cannot learn to do anything his nervous system is not ready for. The time when the various nerves, such as those to his legs and bowels, ripen depends upon the quality of the nervous system he inherits from his parents. Sometimes not even the nerves of breathing and sucking are ripe at birth.

The child's images are vague. It is all he can do to tell the outside world from himself. His images grow sharper as he learns to pick things out. After all, adults have had a good many years of experience in picking out the important things to make their images sharp, and even then they are not so good at it. The child has had no such experience and accordingly we must be patient.

Minerva Seifuss, for example, was always an extraordinarily clever child for her age. When she was a little toddler, she occasionally upset things, as all toddlers do. One time she upset an ashtray and was told in no uncertain terms that she must not do it again. Her mother, of course, understood that the important thing about an ashtray is that it contains ashes; but at Minerva's age, clever as she was, her attention was attracted by more primitive things. The child was only too eager to please, but she picked out the wrong thing to be impressed with. The ashtray in question was colored a bright blue, and Minerva said to herself: "I must please mother and never upset one of those bright blue things again." The following day she thought nothing of going ahead and playing with a bright green ashtray, and as a result she was thoroughly scolded by her mother, who cried: "I told you never to play with an ashtray again!" Minerva was mystified. She had carefully avoided all blue dishes, in accordance with the way she had interpreted her mother's desire, and here she was getting scolded for playing with a green one! When her mother found out what was wrong, she explained: "See, these are ashes. That is what we are interested in about these dishes. An ashtray is something that holds these gray grains. Don't upset anything that has this stuff in it!" Then for the first time Minerva understood that an "ashtray" was not a blue dish, but something that contained gray dust. After that, everything was all right.

If mother does not appreciate the child's difficulties, and explain things carefully to him in a way that makes it clear exactly what she means, punishments may become quite senseless to him; and if this happens time after time, he may finally give up trying to be good and do as he pleases, since he feels that he will never understand what she wants anyway. He may come to regard punishments as unpredictable "Acts of God," which happen periodically no matter how he tries to behave. Nevertheless he resents them and may go out of his way to revenge himself on his mother. All this might in many cases be avoided by following the example of Mrs. Seifuss and pointing out to him clearly and unmistakably what it is that one wants him to watch out for.

An infant is mostly occupied with the basic things of life, breathing and eating, and these are his concerns before everything else.

An adult knows with some degree of certainty that if conditions are right he will eat when the time comes. The child may feel insecure because he doesn't know what the required conditions are, except that it all depends on mother. He soon gets the idea that the first guarantee for security from fright and hunger is that his mother should love him, and he begins to make efforts toward winning her love. If he should feel that he is not sure of it, he becomes anxious and afraid. If his mother does things he cannot understand at his particular age, it can upset him no matter how clearly she may understand them herself. If she has to interrupt his feeding without a caress to take care of his sick father, it might make him just as afraid as if she interrupted it because she didn't care. A frightened child is an unhappy one and a difficult one. If he sees an opportunity to revenge himself for some such scare he may do so. He cannot think clearly enough to realize that such conduct may do him more harm than good.

A child's life is full of shocks and amazing things which we cannot fully appreciate after we grow up. Imagine what a shock it must be to a child to be born! And how surprised he must feel when he first looks at writing! His mother says these black marks are "cat." Well, but he knows that a cat is a furry animal. How can black marks mean the same thing as a furry animal? What an amazing thing that is! He would like to learn more about it.

## 2

### What does a newborn baby think about?

This is really an illogical question because a newborn baby probably doesn't think at all. His mental life as far as we know consists only of feeling and yearning, and must resemble pure poetry.

The newborn baby has just come through one of the most trying journeys of his life, namely, the trip through the birth canal and his emergence into the outside world, where he is completely dependent on others for his safety and comfort and has no idea how to make his needs known before he discovers that crying in a certain way will bring help. His heart has to push the blood around his body in an entirely new way because some of the blood vessels used after birth are different from the ones used before, and his circulation is none too efficient at first. Furthermore, he has more need for the nourishing blood, especially in his head, for his brain at this period requires extra blood food for growth. His lungs too may take time to become fully accustomed to their new job, so that breathing also may be a problem.

He must now obtain his nourishment by sucking instead of its being supplied automatically from his mother's blood, and here also he is handicapped at first if the nerves and muscles concerned in this act are not properly co-ordinated.

The solution for such difficulties is to bring him back often as nearly as possible to his condition before birth. The closest he can come to this now is to be rocked in the arms of a loving mother while she holds him close to her breast, the source of his food. By this warmth and closeness his yearnings are partly gratified and his anxieties somewhat allayed, and by rocking and fondling him she helps his circulation and breathing.

As his brain grows he becomes more and more able to endure comfortably being away from his mother's arms, and he begins to feel more secure in the world as he understands it better. It is said that the baby who is not fondled and allowed to suck freely takes longer to develop and is more fearful than the baby who is. It is even claimed, as a result of studying the development of hundreds of infants, that the growth of the brain is encouraged if the child is truly loved. In some way or other the mother who wants her child both consciously and unconsciously does things better than the one who doesn't. No matter how careful she is to carry out the procedures necessary for the baby's comfort, it is as much love as going through the proper motions which makes a child thrive. How the child senses his mother's unconscious attitude toward him we can only guess.

We should remember that the baby is afraid of the world and is probably yearning for a place to which no one can ever return. He cannot think and has no effective inner way for coping with his fears and desires. While his stomach can be filled from a bottle, his feeling of security and his urge to growth can best be nourished from a mother's heart.

## 3

## The emotional development of the nursing child

In order to understand the child's emotions during the suckling stage, one must be careful not to make the "homunculus" error by asking: "How should I feel, with my mental equipment, if I were a suckling?" One must inquire instead: "How does an infant feel, with his mental equipment?" We must remember that the child does not have any political views, nor any ideas of modesty, cleanliness, or courtesy, nor any experience of adult pleasures. The sole guides of his conduct are his primitive anxieties and yearnings.

What is the child's image of the world at this stage? It is a changeable place where "anything can happen" and where terrifying things do happen. Somewhere is something which is warm and loving and makes him feel secure. It also allays his hunger and strokes his skin so that he falls into a sweet sleep. His greatest security comes from being close to this warm and loving influence. When he is deserted, or his mother's conscious or unconscious lack of love makes him feel deserted, he is unhappy. When he is in the arms of his loving mother or can hear her loving tones, he is happy and feels secure.

His strivings at first seem to be mainly along the lines of absorbing, resembling those of the adult endomorph: he wants to absorb heat, milk, and love. His image of the world is so vague that these are almost interchangeable. If he can't have milk, he needs more love. If he can't have love, he may want more milk.

Sucking is his first "social" activity, that is, the first activity after birth which involves another person for the best results. It almost seems as though each child was born with a need to do a certain minimum amount of sucking, and if he doesn't do it earlier he will do it later. (The same applies to the pecking urges of young chicks and the sucking of pups.) Sucking the breast seems to satisfy more of this need in a given time than any other kind of sucking. If feeding fails to satisfy completely this desire, he may try to make up the difference in some other way, such as sucking his thumb between feedings. If that is not effective, this very early and strong mouth desire may remain active in later years, though as he grows older he may no longer be aware of this tension.

Conscious or unconscious, it continues to strive for satisfaction, and continues to affect his behavior through this striving. He may try to stay "on the bottle" whichever way he can that society and his own self-respect will permit, whether by sucking on a pipe or by drinking out of another kind of bottle. He may be able to keep this desire entirely out of sight in normal times, realizing deep within himself that he should have grown out of it, until something disappoints him. Then, if he is unable to do anything about the disappointment of the moment, he may turn back and try to make up for the first great disappointment of his life, his unsatisfied infantile desire for using his mouth. So when disappointed, many individuals turn to excessive smoking, drinking, eating, or some other mouth activity, preferably one which relieves many other tensions besides the one we are discussing.

Under good conditions, after a certain time, the minimum infantile sucking desire is more or less satisfied and the infant naturally "grows out" of the breast and the bottle. This may partly depend on the fact that he can begin to control the satisfaction of other tensions as the nervous system develops. He may begin to take more pleasure in handling things with his hands than with his mouth, for example, or the development of the nerves to his bowels and bladder enables him to experience new and strange delights from his mastery of these organs, which give him more pleasure than sucking.

We can see that the desire to put things into the mouth and suck them is an "approach," and sucking is therefore the first manifestation of libido. The infant largely gratifies his libido through his mouth which is also the organ he has greatest control over. We can understand that the breast makes him happier than the bottle because the more personal a relationship is the more directly it gratifies libido. The same tensions that are gratified by being close to his mother at this stage of life will play a part in his desire to be close to other women later.

In both infancy and adult life, direct gratification of libido is accompanied by swelling of certain spongy tissues. During the first few months of infancy there are sponge-like masses present in the mouth which become swollen after breast-feeding (and rarely after bottle feeding). Physically as well as mentally there are resemblances between the libido satisfaction of the suckling and that of the adult.

Let us now see what effect the nursing situation has on mortido. If his mother, instead of helping him gratify his libido, stands in the way of complete gratification by taking away the nipple or the bottle before he is contented, the infant cannot think things out, nor stop to ask: "Is this trip necessary, or should she have stayed here with me?" Being thwarted, and being an infant, he immediately seeks other methods of satisfying his tensions, and if he fails to obtain libido satisfaction he seeks mortido relief. (The same applies to other frustrations.)

Lacking control of his limbs, he has few ways of doing this, and no subtlety. Whereas the adult can either run or fight, the infant can do neither. His chief possibility for passive reaction is to lie still and refuse to suck. Sometimes he may even give up trying to digest his food, leading to a dangerous state of malnutrition, even to the often fatal condition known as "marasmus." Many older physicians before the days of modern psychiatry knew by intuition and experience that the best treatment for the kind of "sulking" that caused marasmus was loving, mothering, and breast feeding.

If he reacts actively, he has to do it with the muscles at his disposal, and in the early months the chief ones he can control besides the muscles of sucking are those of breathing and stretching; so when he is "angry" he holds his breath until he gets blue, and stretches his muscles out until they are rigid, to such an extent that he may form an arch with his back.

At a slightly later age, the child may express his anger in a more aggressive way by biting. He may bite his mother's breast hard enough to make it bleed. Here mortido, just as in the case of the man who murders the woman he loves, uses the same object as libido to obtain gratification. The most satisfactory way the infant can "eliminate" things at that age is by eating them. Thus, when he wants to make the offending breast disappear, he tries to bite it off (always with the idea that when it has been punished in this way it will reappear again and feed him properly). Fortunately his dental equipment does not usually allow him to get very far.

It is no accidental coincidence that a study of savage tribes justifies us in thinking of this nipple biting as a kind of cannibalism. We find that adult cannibals too eat with the greatest gusto those things which they feel have given them their greatest satisfaction and yet which have in the end frustrated them. There is more to cannibalism than just dressing a missionary in a salt and pepper suit and boiling him in a pot.

The same fateful compulsion that applies to sucking applies to this infantile cruelty. A definite amount of frustration seems to awaken a definite amount of cruel desire, and if this is not satisfied at the time, it may remain with the Id instincts continually striving to obtain satisfaction throughout the individual's life. Such buried desires hanging over from infancy partly explain why some people can put so much time and energy into being cruel. They have an enormous ungratified mortido tension which is striving for release, and since it can never be fully gratified in civilized society it is drained off from time to time through partial satisfactions.

The prevention of such unhappy personality formations, which bring misery in later life to the individual and those around him, may lie partly in allowing him plenty of sucking satisfaction during the sucking age. Only if he repeats frequently certain forms of objectionable behavior after there is pretty good evidence that his nervous system is ready for something more advanced, should the parents begin to worry about where they might have made a mistake that is holding the child back.

While biting due to frustration presents a definite problem, there may be other reasons for biting. For example, the infant may bite as a sign that his biting muscles are ready for action so that he is prepared to give up sucking. It is up to the mother or the doctor to figure out in each case to what extent biting is due to resentment.

Free feeding and late weaning promote generosity and optimism; deprivation and early weaning may encourage stinginess and greed. Richard Wright, in his autobiography *Black Boy*, tells how after a childhood of grim poverty he used to hoard food even after he was sure of getting enough. Early fears haunt and early satisfactions give perpetual confidence and gratitude.

The things mentioned in the last two sections are more fully discussed, in simple terms, in Dr. Margaret Ribble's book *The Rights of Infants*, published in 1943 by the Columbia University Press in New York. This is a book which every expectant mother and every mother (and father, too) of a young infant should read.

## 4

## How does the child learn to behave himself?

As the child's nervous system develops he seems to have an urge, which in our way of speaking is based on Physis, to abandon his old ways of gaining pleasure and use new ones as they become available. In addition, those about him make it necessary that he do whatever he is capable of, since they leave him more and more to his own devices to cope with the problems which life places before him in ever-increasing profusion as he grows older.

If the developments described in the last section proceed normally, the child satisfies his sucking and biting urges and is ready to go on to something else. One of his most important jobs if he is to survive is to learn about the physical universe around him. He has to begin by analyzing the four dimensions of the "space-time continuum" into certain important elements, namely time, space, and gravity.

He learns about these from hard experience. Since gratifications are no longer automatic as they were in the womb, he first has to learn how to wait, and his ability to do this without distress will depend, as we have supposed, upon the efficiency of his brain as a storer of energy. His brain carries him through time.

He later learns that things which should be together in space in order to gratify his wishes are often found apart; he therefore has to learn to walk in order to gratify such wishes. His body carries him through space.

Waiting and walking (or crawling) are two of his most important lessons in the Reality Principle, with speech as a kind of short cut which helps to shorten both space and time by making his wants known to others.

Meanwhile he is also learning about gravity by continual experiment. He finds that if he knocks something over it always falls down, and never up; but sometimes he doesn't appear to accept this as the necessary order of things for quite a while. He may behave as though he thought it possible that sooner or later he might find something that would break this rule.

His parents are delighted when he learns to walk and talk; there is usually no serious emotional problem here, and his progress along these lines is a matter of encouragement. It is when he is learning to control his bowels and bladder that real trouble begins. He soon realizes that whereas up to this time his parents have had the upper hand, now he is "in the saddle." He discovers that they value his bowel movements, or feces. This is no surprise to him, since he thinks quite highly of them himself. They are the first things which he himself has been able to produce, his very own creation, and therefore very, very important. And how does he know that his parents also value them highly? Simply because they beg for them.

When he sits on his little pottie, he knows that his mother will be impatient if he doesn't produce, and delighted if he does. He also knows that she is beginning to get upset if he produces at the wrong time or in the wrong place. So now for the first time he has effective methods for controlling not only people's actions, but their feelings as well, and very important people, too. He can annoy them by producing these valuables at the wrong time or withholding them at the right time; and he can cause them delight by producing them at the right time. If we only try to put ourselves in the infant's place, remembering what he knows and does not know, we can realize how powerful he must feel. It is very much as though he had handfuls of gold and his mother needed money. He likes the look of the gleaming metal himself, and he observes the great pleasure she too shows when it appears. We may compare him at this stage to a mischievous man who has control of his family's fortune in cash. He can cause them distress by throwing money away or withholding it, and delight by giving it to them when they want it.

So we have the infant on his throne indulging his feelings of the moment: either playing the open-handed monarch and giving his mother what she beseeches, or punishing her for some real or fancied slight by withholding it or depositing it in the wrong place.

At first the situation is in his favor: he receives much enthusiasm for producing and little punishment for withholding. As he grows older he loses this advantage. Instead of winning love and approval and an increased feeling of security by producing, and losing nothing by not producing, he finds that his generosity and efforts are, alas! beginning to be taken for granted, while any withholding meets with increasing disapproval (the fate of all generous monarchs). Instead of winning by producing, he now loses by not producing. How many times throughout his life is this shift to occur! Thus for the first time, at a tender age, he meets with ingratitude.

In the beginning the child complies because his mother, whose love he wants to hold, is standing over him. Later occurs one of the most amazing things in all nature. He behaves as he thinks his mother would want him to behave, even if she isn't there!* In other words, he begins to act in accordance with her beseeching image, so that the reality is no longer necessary to guide his behavior. At first this image may be conscious, but as the years go by it sinks deeper and deeper into the unconscious so that the bowel habits become more and more automatic.

This image of the mother beseeching for the feces, which the infant gradually incorporates into his unconscious personality and which has the rest of his life the same effect as though his mother were not too far away, is one of the first items which goes to make up the Superego. It is accompanied by an image of himself as a good boy, that is, a boy who behaves in such a way to gratify his mother and his own growth urge, or Physis, and this is one of the first items which go to make up the ideal self he would like to be, or the Ego Ideal.

The establishment of bowel habits thus depends on the growth of the nervous system and the development of the Superego, including the Ego Ideal. Lapses will occur mostly when resentment is aroused and mortido tension becomes strong enough to overcome the regulating forces of the Superego, usually on account of some real or fancied hurt or deprivation of love. Mortido satisfaction may then be gained either actively or passively. He may be

* It is noteworthy that other mammals besides humans seem to have the ability to form a "Superego" by a similar process of introjection, especially certain house pets. Other animals can be "trained," but not trusted.

a stubborn little fellow who will actively withhold the gifts and refuse to move his bowels for days on end unless the frustration is removed or the love restored; or he may give up trying to control himself and passively allow accidents to happen. He gets an additional satisfaction from "accidents" when he comes to know the meaning of "dirty," because he then realizes that his mother is humiliated and punished by having to clean up after him.

These two patterns of revenge and mortido satisfaction are often carried into later life by people who do not completely grow up emotionally and remain partly fixed at the bowel level of behavior, or as it is called, the "anal stage." Of course their self-respect and Ego Ideals, underdeveloped though they are, do not allow them to act as crudely as they did when they were infants, but their behavior shows the same characteristics. Such people show spite and resentment in one of two ways: either by messing things up, literally or figuratively, which is a rather easy way requiring little apparent originality, control, or determination; or by being stubborn, withholding things, and trying to control the situation in a petty, unrealistic way which is more annoying than threatening: as though to say, "Things will happen in just the order which I determine, even if you win in the end."

If "anal mortido" is not able to get complete satisfaction in childhood, it may remain as the main driving force of the personality, instead of showing itself only on special occasions. This results in two adult types of "anal" personalities which may occur in pure form or mixed with each other: the "passive" or messy type, exhibiting untidiness and apparent lack of determination, and often suffering from diarrhea or colitis; and the "active" or orderly type, showing stubbornness, stinginess, too much fussiness about details in thought and action without regard to what is actually being accomplished, and usually suffering from constipation.

If we compare the anal way of gratifying mortido with the "oral" way of earlier days, we can see how different are these two stages of development. "Passive" oral resentment is shown by not eating and getting sick, "passive" anal resentment by messiness; "active" oral anger expresses itself by cruel biting, "active" anal spite by stubbornness and withholding.

The reasons why some people fail to grow up emotionally and

show thinly disguised anal or oral ways of reacting in adult life are not clearly understood. While such checks in development can usually be connected with unsatisfied tensions hanging over from infancy, constitution also seems to play a part. This is most obvious in the case of anal personalities, who are typically of a decided ectomorphic build, and perhaps it is significant that ectomorphs often suffer from fallen stomach and intestines. (Oral types, incidentally, are often endomorphic.)

Old Mr. Krone, with whom we are already acquainted as one of Nana's victims, was almost a pure anal type. A decided ectomorph, he was tall, thin, and gangling, with long awkward legs and a long face. His neck was scrawny, his ears stuck out, and the corners of his mouth turned down. His posture was stiff, his movements were jerky, and his skin was thin and gray. He never had any friends because he was more interested in his bowels and his budget than he was in other people.

Mr. Krone had a good income, but he was miserly and lived on crusts in a tiny room on Railroad Avenue. Every day he had the same meals at the same time in the same corner, and every day he put his dishes back in exactly the same place. His mornings he spent fussing about in the bathroom, his afternoons calculating his expenses for the previous day, and his evenings going over his old ledgers from former years and looking through his collection of magazines.

Twice a week for the last thirty years, old Mr. Krone, who was nearly seventy, had visited Dr. Nagel to complain about his bowels. He had been constipated all his life, and in his cupboard was a shelf containing rows of laxatives. The only variation in his life before Nana came to live with him was changing over to a different medicine every few days. One was too powerful, the next was not powerful enough, and another took too long to act. On each visit to the doctor he described his bowel movements in great detail, sometimes proudly and sometimes regretfully, depending upon how original and powerful he thought they were, while the physician, as the well-known medical writer Dr. Harry Beckman remarks, was supposed to be comparing them mentally with the standard bowel movement kept under glass with the standard meter stick in the archives in Paris.

Mr. Krone had a hobby, which was sorting out and mutilating with a pencil pictures of naked women in his magazines, and an amusement, which was pinching very precisely the buttocks of prostitutes. The cost of these diversions, including carfare, he noted in his ledger along with his other expenses, and at a moment's notice he could open his cupboard and look up the exact amount he had spent on pinching in 1917. When Mr. Krone became ill, he was too stubborn to let Dr. Nagel examine him, and he finally died of cancer of the rectum.

Mr. Krone illustrates clearly the characteristics of an anal personality: stubbornness, stinginess, orderliness of a fussy kind, cruelty, and an undue interest in his bowels which gave him his greatest pleasure.

He shows us that the bowels can be used to gratify libido as well as mortido. The infant takes an unsophisticated pleasure in his bowel movements. He enjoys his mastery of his own body and he enjoys his "creating," since this is his main "creative" activity and he can see the results. Sometimes he even likes to play with what he has created. In adults we see such frank bowel joys mainly in the mentally ill, when the unconscious mind reveals itself more clearly, and in dreams, where the same thing occurs. Psychoanalysis enables normal people to detect such tendencies in their everyday activities in disguised form. Accompanying the anal characteristics we have already described we often find certain other interests: buttocks, backs, rears of all kinds, including rear doors, and a preference for bathroom jokes rather than bedroom jokes. There also seems to be some connection at times between anal interests and homosexuality, and possibly lefthandedness.

The important things in this section are, first, the possibility of something going wrong during the anal stage of development in the second to fourth years of life which may affect the character of the individual when he grows up; and, secondly, the connection of the anal stage with the formation of the "unconscious conscience," or Superego and Ego Ideal, by acceptance of the mother's image as a guide in place of the real mother so that the child continues to behave as his parents would have liked long after they have vanished from his life. (Since it is usually the mother who gives the child his toilet training, we have spoken mostly of her. If it is the father who has this job, or if both parents take part, the same general ideas apply.)

## 5

## The little boy and the little girl

It now behooves us to transport ourselves to Brschiss, an eastern land full of giants, dwarfs, troglodytes, astomi, caprimulges, cynocephali, camelopards, and other wonderful creatures described by Pliny, sSanang sSetsen, Alcofribas, and Cyprian St. Cyr in his book "Letters to my Wife's Maid."

The Brschissians are a warlike people who have slaughtered all the foreigners for a hundred miles around, and they are so inbred that their people suffer from strange afflictions. As a result of this, says St. Cyr, both sexes have the same sexual organs, but they differ in that the males have long noses and the females have no noses at all. Because of this, their religion makes much account of noses, which have become sacred objects and sacred parts of the body. For this reason, every Brschissian from earliest childhood wears a sort of half mask over the nose and cheeks, called a "cashney." People, even small children, are never supposed to see the opposite sex without their cashneys until they are married.

If the little children of Brschiss ask about cashneys, they are told that they will understand this when they grow up. Meanwhile they are taught not to pick their noses or fiddle with them, and are sometimes severely punished if they do. The little boys are even threatened with having their noses cut off if they pick them.

Naturally, the children are curious about what is under the cashneys of the opposite sex. Some of them also take a special delight in breaking the rules which the adults are trying to teach them, though they feel guilty and a little afraid when they finger and pick their noses. And eventually, no matter how strict the supervision, they get to see the difference between the two sexes. When the little boy discovers that girls have no noses, he wonders what has happened to them, and the only explanation he can think of at that age is that they have had them cut off for some misdeed, in the same way that his parents may have threatened to punish him. This gives him a good scare, especially if he has been breaking the rules. The girls on their part feel injured and envious, and may blame their parents for their inferior status in life. Just as a savage has to imagine that a hurricane is the result of something he has done to bring on the wrath of the gods, so the child explains things in terms of his relationship to the powerful beings around him, his parents, and feels that his situation depends upon their good will or ill will. At any rate, that is what St. Cyr says.

This description of the sacred nose-lore of Brschiss has a kind of parallel in our own country where little boys and girls have the same kind of noses, but different sexual organs. When they discover this difference, their feelings are often much the same as those described in the children of Brschiss. The boys may become frightened and the girls envious. Usually, they do not discuss these reactions with their parents, especially if they have been brought up from earliest months to hide their feelings about such things; and if they are shocked this adds to their reluctance to mention the matter. Just as a soldier who suffers from a great shock received in battle cannot remember without the aid of a psychiatrist the details of what affected him or how deeply he felt at the time, so children, if they are shocked deeply enough by their discoveries about the sexual organs, tend to push the whole incident out of their minds, particularly the emotions connected with it. Only if they are brought to a psychoanalyst when young, or come to a psychoanalyst when they are older, do they learn the power of the buried fear or envy which, without their being aware of it, has been influencing their conduct. The little boy may have begun to act as though his penis might be cut off if he did not behave or was too daring, while the little girl may have felt resentful, as if she had once had a penis which her parents had cut off for some misdeed when she was a little baby.

Of course the boy's pride (and fear) about his penis, and the girl's envy (and resentment) vary in different individuals. But if we dig down deeply enough into the unconscious mind of a man we generally find some anxiety about the sexual organ left over from childhood, usually a fear that if he does certain things, especially things his father or father-image would not like, he may lose his penis and become like a girl; while in the woman's mind we find traces of her penis-envy—sometimes quite conscious—or perhaps of resentment against her parents.

It is evident that if there is such a tension as penis-envy in certain women, it can never be satisfied directly, and therefore has to be satisfied indirectly by getting something else that boys don't have. The most natural way to do this is by having babies, which, after all, are things boys cannot have; furthermore, a boy can have only one penis, while a woman can have many babies. Some women, however, avoid such feminine acquisitions as babies, and try to beat the man at his own game in order to assuage their envy, which brings them into a business or profession where they will be in direct competition with the opposite sex. If a woman's choice of occupation is based on such penis-envy, she will eventually become unhappy, because she will be frustrating the tension of her Physis, which is urging her toward a feminine line of development.

In many individuals, especially timid men and aggressive women, such fears and envies may play an important part among the many strivings of the personality. The discovery of sex differences is another problem for the child to work out in his or her own mind. If the experience leaves little or no permanent wound it will cause no trouble in the future. If it is an emotional problem which he or she cannot solve at the time it may cause troubles in later life.

# 6

## Getting along with people

The child is not born with a knowledge of how to get along in the world but must learn this from others. Up to the age of two or thereabouts he is so much concerned with controlling his own body that he has little time or energy for paying attention to how his behavior affects other people—just so he gets what he wants when he wants it. At about that age, however, he begins to see that getting satisfaction is no longer merely a question of asking for it, but depends partly upon whether his parents are pleased with him or not. In order to find out how to handle them, he watches how they handle each other. What he learns in the next three years, from two to five, will largely determine for life how he uses his energy to handle people (unless he goes out of his way later to take lessons from his teachers, friends, wife, or psychiatrist). Though his brothers and sisters play an important part also, we shall not speak of them here, in order to keep things as simple as possible.

His parents are the handiest teachers and they are the ones the child is most anxious to get along with, so he learns most from them. If he has no parents, or only one parent, he is handicapped because later he will be competing with people who have had two parents to learn from. That is one important reason why it is a great advantage for the child to be brought up by his two parents. A child who starts to learn a foreign language at the age of two will feel more at ease with it later than one who starts to study it at the age of fifteen. Similarly a child who is brought up with a good man in the house will usually get along better with men when he grows up than a boy who is raised fatherless. The latter may make up his disadvantage later, but he has had a bad start.

The baby is innocent of the ways of social behavior, and his fate lies with his family. If he sees them continually quarreling and grabbing, he soon notes that the more aggressive one gets what he or she is after. This encourages him to be aggressive and selfish likewise. He says to himself, so to speak:

"I see that the way to get along in the world is to be aggressive, fight and grab, and the toughest one always wins." So he tends to grow up to be contentious, selfish, and grabbing. The result is that he is disliked, often does not get things easily, and blames the world for this, thus reinforcing his grabbing tendency; and so things go from bad to worse.

If, on the other hand, he sees his parents get along by loving, generosity, and consideration, his own generosity is nourished, and he says to himself:

"I see that the way people get along in the world is by love, consideration, and generosity." So he tries it out, and if it does not work at first, he says perhaps: "Maybe I have not been careful enough of others' feelings," so he becomes even more careful, kind, considerate, and beloved.

Although the child's own personality tendencies in the end determine how much he imitates his parents, nevertheless they have it in their power to reinforce or discourage his various possibilities. They can encourage his possibilities for greedy competition, or his possibilities for considerate kindness, and his capacity to be agreeable, or his capacity to be disagreeable. If they do their best to encourage the ones they choose, and the child does not take the way they have pointed because of other factors, at least they have done their duty and their conscience is clear.

The little child is the center of his own universe. If one watches him carefully one cannot help seeing that most of his affection goes to people who satisfy his immediate needs for him. This system of returning affection only for immediate favors cannot go on forever if he is to carry out in the most desirable way his adult function of procreating and raising children. In order to win and live happily with the prospective mother of his children in years to come, and raise his offspring in a happy household, he will be obliged to learn to give his greatest love without hope of immediate reward. Instead of regarding people as sources of satisfaction to himself, he is going to have to love them "for themselves alone." This applies equally to both sexes. We call such unselfish love "object love," while the love which people have for things that give them immediate satisfaction is very much like self-love.

In this latter way of thinking the child behaves like a person in love with himself. This reminds us of the Greek legend of Narcissus, who fell in love with his own image when he saw it reflected in a pool of water. We therefore call libido directed inwardly toward the self, *narcissistic* libido, and libido directed outwardly toward outside objects, *object* libido. We can then say that the task of childhood should be to turn narcissistic libido into object libido. This is necessary if the adult is to be happy living among other people, and is especially necessary for successful marriage and parenthood since in these situations the individual is going to have to love, cherish, and take care of outside beings before he thinks of himself. His Superego helps him in this unselfish task.

Thus the formation of the Superego in infancy, with its feelings of "duty" and responsibility, lays the groundwork for the later job of marriage and parenthood. After the Superego is pretty well under way there is a period from about six to about ten years of age when the child has more or less learned to control himself but does not as yet have much responsibility toward others because his body is not ready for it. These years he spends in learning more about the people and things around him, so that when his muscles are strong and his glands begin to work full blast at puberty, he will be more ready to cope with whatever arises.

## 7

## When does sex begin?

There are so many people who can remember distinctly sexual feelings from the age of three or earlier that there can be no doubt in the mind of anyone accustomed to judging such feelings that infants can have sexual experiences in the ordinary sense of the word. Those who say that sex does not begin until the first orgasm will have a hard time explaining such childish feelings, or attributing to mere curiosity the incidents between little boys and little girls which take place behind barns and in haystacks which they find so thrilling at the time, and often also in looking back.

The affectionate relationships of early life have much of the quality of such relationships in later life. We can call the love relationships of the infant "sexual" even though there is no erection or orgasm. The normal voluptuous feelings of an adult are only the fourth stage in a lifelong development.

The two earliest methods of direct libido satisfaction we are already acquainted with: they consist of sucking pleasure and bowel pleasure, which we call for the sake of convenience "oral" and "anal" satisfactions. During the third stage, gratification consists of pleasure derived from the sexual organs without the real participation of another person, that is without real object libido, and takes place commonly through masturbation, which can frequently be seen in children between the fourth and sixth years. Many adults remain fixed at this stage, merely "using" their partners to obtain pleasure rather than sharing pleasure with them. Thus we have promiscuous men who merely use women as "seminal spittoons," and women who use men as "vaginal tampons"; in both cases the individual is not concerned, except from vanity, with how much pleasure the partner obtains.

In lucky or wise people, the adult fourth stage of sexuality is reached, which consists of a mutual sharing of pleasure with another person, and not merely in using a partner for the purpose of having one's sexual organs stimulated. The infant loves himself most and wants only to get pleasure for himself; he is not much concerned with giving pleasure to others except in order to get what he wants from them. Adult sexuality involves a real unselfishness. Adult male sexual feeling consists of a desire to penetrate in order to give as well as get pleasure. Adult female sexuality is based on a desire to accept and be penetrated so that pleasure can be given as well as received. This applies also to giving and accepting material things as well as to "emotional penetration."

The difference between the third and fourth stages is more clearly shown in women. In the third stage they get their pleasure chiefly from the little penis that they have on the outside of their bodies, called the clitoris, and are mostly interested in having that organ stimulated. In the adult stage they get their greatest pleasure from the vagina, which can be used much more effectively to give pleasure to a male partner.

We also find through psychoanalysis that in some ways the sexual act gratifies mortido as well as libido. In the male, penetration suggests not only getting as close as possible, which is libidinous, but also destruction, which is mortidinous. In the female being penetrated also gratifies both drives.

Sometimes the mortidinous satisfactions in the sexual relationship become more important to the individual than the libidinous ones, so that he gets an abnormal amount of pleasure from inflicting or suffering pain before and during his sexual activities. If his mortido tension is on the active side he will consciously or unconsciously find excuses to inflict mental or physical punishment on his sexual partner. If his mortido tension is passive, he will consciously or unconsciously get himself into a position where she has good reason to make him suffer mentally or physically, and then he will consciously or unconsciously encourage her to do it. If an active, sadistic man or woman meets a passive, masochistic partner, they will each have a golden opportunity to relieve their infantile mortido tensions through consciously planned physical suffering or unconsciously encouraged mental suffering. While it is not so common to hear of whipping parties, it is only too common to hear of men and women who unconsciously arrange their love relationships so that again and again they can obtain active or passive mortido gratification through emotional cruelty or suffering, without having to experience the painful realization that they are asking for it.

Alecta Abel was the daughter of Prete Abel, who owned the slaughterhouse down by the Olympia freight yards. Her father had such bad luck with his marriage, his children, and his business, that Mr. Weston, the Episcopal minister, told him he must have "the mark of Abel" on his forehead, since the Lord seemed to have chosen him to be a born victim like his Biblical namesake. Mr. Abel's ill fortune, however, was always due to outside circumstances.

Alecta's life seemed to follow the same pattern, but with one important difference: she brought most of her trouble on herself. Her first husband was a steady man and a good provider, but when she began to be unfaithful to him, he left her. Alecta was devoted to her little daughter; but in spite of the harm it did her child, she continued to live a dissolute life. One day a friend informed her that her husband was having her watched by detectives so that he could get custody of the child. Alecta was panic-stricken, but nevertheless that very night she went home with a man she picked up in a bar. When the divorce came to court, the child was taken from her until she could prove her fitness to have its custody.

Her second marriage followed the same pattern except that this time she chose for a husband Don Chusbac, a drunkard who beat her regularly. Again she had a child, and again she became devoted to her. This time it was her mother-in-law, Mrs. Chusbac, who had her followed and took the custody of the child from her. She then married another drunkard, a hypochondriac of evil reputation from whom she caught syphilis, even though she knew before their marriage that he had the disease and was not following his treatment. She now spent her time either nursing him or drudging to supply him with money for liquor. In spite of the repeated warnings of Dr. Nagel that they must not have children until they were both cured of the disease, she allowed herself to become pregnant and now had the additional burden of caring for a child with congenital syphilis.

Alecta Abel was by no means a stupid or evil woman, and both her reason and her ideals were in violent and continual protest against her conduct, but they were helpless against the forces of her inwardly directed mortido. Fortunately Dr. Nagel, who was a friend of her father's and had known her since she had been an infant, finally prevailed upon her to go for psychiatric treatment; and she now lives quietly in the neighboring town of Arcadia with her third child, who is cured of his disease and is developing normally, though he is somewhat scarred by the neglect of his condition during infancy.

This is an extreme and horrifying example of "moral masochism" and self-punishment on the part of a woman, and of both physical and "moral" sadism or cruelty on the part of two of her husbands, which in milder forms make thousands of men, women, and children miserable throughout their lives. In Alecta's case, her desire to punish herself was based partly on a desire to be like her unlucky father; that is, she "identified" herself with him. A careless observer might have said that she "inherited" her bad luck.

## 8

## How does the child react to his parents' behavior?

There has been much study of the boy's preference for his mother and the girl's preference for her father. The subject is complicated because the mother is usually gentle and the father sterner, the mother indulgent and the father firm, and because the mother gives nourishment to both sons and daughters in the early stages of life and often in the later stages also. In order to understand clearly the child's true feelings toward his parents, one has to probe deeply into his mind, or into the adult's buried memories of his emotional development. Fortunately, the people of Brschiss live in such a way that they offer us a less tedious way of studying this problem.

As we remember, there are giants and dwarfs in Brschiss, and this makes strange households, for the women are all of normal size, and each family consists of a giant, a dwarf, and a woman. Each dwarf lives with the woman he loves, who returns his affection, but there are no direct sexual relationships between them. He spends most of his time in her company; he has nothing else to do, as their giant takes care of all the responsibilities.

During the day, the dwarf's happiness is quite undisturbed as he follows the woman about while she does her housework, petting her occasionally and being caressed and jollied in return. In the early evening, the trouble begins. Every day at 5:17 P.M. their giant, about nine feet tall and wearing size 24 shoes, comes tramping into the house. The lovely housewife (all women are beautiful in Brschiss) immediately "deserts" the dwarf and runs to meet the newcomer, embracing him warmly while the dwarf looks on. From that moment, the woman gives the giant most of her attention. The dwarf is sent to bed right after supper; and as he lies there he can hear the other two in the next room, billing and cooing for a couple of hours, until finally they too go to bed together—(sometimes even in the same room where the dwarf is if they are poor or unwise) and he can still hear them talking and giggling for a while until other sounds begin.

In some cases the poor dwarf is sadly confused by all this. He loves the woman, and he loves the giant as well, since the latter takes care of all his material needs for him and treats him with consideration and affection in most things; nevertheless he may be unable to help feeling resentful at the setup. In spite of his good intentions and his feeling that he is wicked for doing so, he gradually comes to feel more and more jealous of the giant and wishes that he would permanently forget to come home. There isn't a thing he can do about it, really, because that is the way people live in Brschiss, according to St. Cyr, and there is nobody he can talk to. They would just laugh at him. He is so ashamed of himself for resenting what everybody knows is a perfectly normal and happy household, that he daren't even discuss it with the dwarf next door. He wouldn't know how to begin talking about it. He almost feels at times that the giant would be justified in cutting his nose off and making him look like a girl for having such shameful feelings.

Knowing that his feelings are wrong doesn't relieve them, however. In spite of himself, as the months go by and he realizes that he isn't getting any younger, he begins to get sulky and loses his appetite. The other two don't understand this. To them, of course, the arrangement seems perfectly natural, and it wouldn't occur to them that the dwarf could be jealous. They wouldn't believe he was capable of feeling that way toward them, even if St. Cyr explained it to them in person. The woman says to the giant: "I don't know what on earth has come over the dear boy lately." They try to persuade him to eat, but he stubbornly refuses. After a while they give up and ignore him, letting him eat or not, as he pleases. This only makes him feel worse. He begins to go off by himself and brood. His heart starts to pound every evening when 5:17 approaches. He manages to contain his feelings for quite a while, but one Saturday they explode. He begins to shout and scream, trips and falls to the floor, and lies there thrashing his arms and legs around violently, screaming at the woman, the giant, and his own helplessness and shame. Then he weeps bitterly at his own undignified behavior, and that night he doesn't go to sleep until dawn, lying there listening to the other two. From then on he has trouble sleeping. He frequently has nightmares and also begins to walk in his sleep, usually ending up in the other bedroom.

This dwarf is obviously letting his feelings run away with him. The dwarf next door has the same problem, but he manages to accept things much more gracefully. Instead of kicking up a rumpus, he "adjusts" to the situation. While we are not sure just what "adjust" means, we know that it means something, since those who adjust to unpleasant situations are happier, healthier, and more agreeable people than those who don't. Perhaps it has something to do with the flexibility of the individual's images. Adjustment is another of those things in nature, like electricity, which we know more about from its effects than from understanding what it actually is.

Since the dwarf is so dependent on the woman for his comfort and affection, his reaction to the nightly home-coming of the giant is the most important event in his emotional life, and certainly has more to do with his happiness, says St. Cyr, than money, the other dwarfs he plays with, or what he learns at school, and in the end will have more to do with his behavior and his reactions to other events, than any of these things.

The average American child in the average American home reacts in much the same way as the dwarfs of Brschiss to what goes on in the household. The fact that the American giants are a little smaller, usually under six feet, and the dwarfs a little younger, only three or four years old, doesn't really change the situation much from the dwarf's point of view. He will either have to adjust, or he will begin to lose his appetite and sulk, have temper tantrums and palpitation of the heart, and suffer from anxiety, insomnia, nightmares, and sleepwalking.

If he reacts in a neurotic way to this early problem, we may suppose that sometimes he will react poorly to later problems, perhaps with the same pattern: loss of appetite, irritability, palpitation, insomnia, and nightmares; his reactions to the father-giant and the "deserting" mother may persist and leave traces in his behavior for the rest of his life. If he succeeds later in changing his images of his parents, so that the father-image ceases to be that of a giant-rival, and his mother-image is altered from that of a deserting woman, he will be able to grow beyond these problems and become interested in other things. But if he is unable to change these childhood images, and spends the rest of his life acting in accordance with them and trying to solve the situation they present, they will take up much of his energy. He may spend his time eternally seeking a woman who will not look at another man; or eternally seeking feminine conquests, like Don Juan, in order to prove to himself and to his mother-image which he carries within himself, that she missed a desirable fellow when she deserted him every night in favor of the giant; or perhaps if the image of the father-rival is stronger than that of his unappreciative mother, he will react by beating up strangers on the barroom floor, to prove to himself and his father-image that he could have licked his father if he hadn't been such a coward as a little fellow.

We can see that there is object displacement of libido and mortido in these cases, since it is really his mother whom he wants to win and his father whom he wants to beat up. In any case, being so intently interested (without being aware of it) in proving himself, he will have less time and energy left for the world's work.

In the case of girls, though the situation is more complicated, a similar period of emotional adjustment or maladjustment has to be lived through, and the results of their solution of the turmoil show themselves in adult life in similar ways, allowing for the difference in sex. Girls spend less time with their fathers than boys do with their mothers, and therefore the problem of growing up to become interested in the opposite sex is different in the two cases. Boys associate closely with the opposite sex from infancy, while girls usually do not (leaving out the question of sisters and brothers, who add more complications). In addition, in a typical case, the boy receives nourishment from the opposite sex and stern reprimands from the same sex, while with girls the situation is not quite the same. In the long run, however, the results of bad management on the part of the parents are not too dissimilar in the two sexes so that there are girls who flit about from man to man and girls who despise all women. Another complication has already been mentioned: boys get their chief sexual pleasure from the penis from earliest infancy, while somewhere along the line the girl not only has to transfer her affections from the same sex to the opposite one, but also has to shift her ways of gaining sexual pleasure from the clitoris to the vagina if she is to obtain complete relief of her libido tensions.

By the time the child is four his main patterns of reacting have begun to take form: he has already shown how he is going to behave when something makes him unhappy. Normal children may be upset by their home life for a while, but eventually they adjust. In neurotic children the awakened mortido may be turned either outward or inward, so that the child either makes trouble for others when he is unhappy or else keeps his unhappiness inside and bothers only himself. Some express their unhappiness mostly during the day, others chiefly at night. So we have the "nasty" child who sleeps soundly, and the docile child who suffers from nightmares, bedwetting, and sleepwalking.

The earlier a pattern is established, the harder it is to change afterward. Though later adventures can make some changes in the personality, much of the child's happiness as he or she grows up depends upon how well his parents handled the ticklish "Oedipus situation" between the beloved baby and the beloved giant. *If* the child can be made to feel that he is one of a threesome, rather than the third wheel on a two-wheeled bicycle, he will usually make a happy adjustment. One should no more be affectionate in front of a child without including him than eat in front of him while he remains hungry.

After childhood, the next period of strain is during adolescence. When the boy gets socially interested in girls his troubles begin anew. If he doesn't have the personality or the physical requirements to attract run-of-the-mill girls, they will desert him for other fellows who do. If he resented deeply his mother's nightly "desertion" when he was an infant, the new desertions will make him more unhappy and bitter. He may be too easily discouraged. But if his parents kept him feeling happy and emotionally secure when he was a baby, though his new troubles may cause him disappointment, they will not embitter him; nor will he give up easily, for he has a good foundation. The feeling that his mother loved him will give him more confidence with the girls and he may try to develop himself in some way which will overshadow his drawbacks, particularly with girls of more than average good sense. The same applies to the relationships between a plain girl and the boys she meets later in life.

On the other hand, there is the case of the boy who grows up to be very attractive. In this instance, infantile bitterness at "losing" his mother may be diluted, though perhaps never washed away, by his later successes. But if both his mother, in infancy, and his girl friends, in adolescence, are won too easily, he may find it difficult to accomplish anything which requires effort. Many beautiful women are of this type. They easily "won" their fathers from their mothers when they were babies, and they easily win boy friends when they grow up. The result is that they are content to sit back and let good things come to them as a consequence of their beauty, so that they never try to develop their personalities in a healthy way and have no genuine interests outside their own bodies. When they grow old and lose their beauty, they are surprised and hurt if life begins to pass them by, and their old age becomes a period of frustration and failure instead of one of mellowing maturity and perfected accomplishments.

Another period of stress occurs when the individual has to begin to earn his own living and make an economic adjustment. Here again, early attitudes can be reinforced or weakened, though it is doubtful if they can be fundamentally changed. Easy money does not make truly kind men out of resentful ones, nor does hard work easily embitter loving people. But the man who was embittered in childhood by his parents or foster parents can grow more bitter if he does not do as well financially as those he envies, while the man whose parents made him feel secure and happy in his infancy, if his later efforts are rewarded justly, will continue to be happy.

The bitter infant who later rises through chance or talent may use his money in a bitter way, to make others envious, and his power in a cruel way, to make others suffer for his own pleasure and satisfaction, while the happy infant who later cannot make a living wage, through mischance or lack of ability, may use his hardship as an example of unnecessary suffering, and seek just security not only for himself, but for all humanity.

Marriage and parenthood are severe tests of emotional strength and of the effectiveness of the individual's early upbringing. In wartime, military situations of various kinds will reveal hidden weaknesses of emotional development which have remained covered up under the ordinary strains of civilian life. The change of life in women, and the decline of power and efficiency in men in later years, are further periods of stress when a sound infancy will stand the individual in good stead.

Thus are secure and insecure infants strengthened and weakened as they go through life.

The clever and beautiful need not be proud, since they did nothing to earn their advantages. The ignorant and ugly need not be ashamed, since they did nothing to deserve their fate. The hateful need not be blamed, since they did not make themselves hateful; nor need the loving be praised, for the same reason. But the hateful can be blamed for not restraining their hatred, and the loving can be blamed for not expressing their love.

## Footnotes for Philosophers, Chapter Three

1. *Adult and Child*

An account of what is to be expected in the behavior of the child at different ages is given by Gesell and his associates from the Yale Clinic of Child Development:

*Infant and Child in the Culture of Today*, by Arnold L. Gesell. Harper & Brothers: New York, 1943.

2. & 3. *Newborn Infant and Suckling*

Some ideas concerning the inner tensions of the infant, and the beneficial effects of suckling, loving, and rocking, are modified from Ribble's article in:

*Personality & the Behavior Disorders*, edited by J. McV. Hunt. The Ronald Press Company: New York, 1944. Chapter 20.

4. *Oral and Anal Erotism*

The classical exposition of the psychosexual development of the child is Freud's "Three Contributions to the Theory of Sex," which can be found in *The Basic Writings of Sigmund Freud*, already referred to. For many interesting ideas about the psychology of space, time, geometry, and physics, consult:

*Mind*, by Paul Schilder. Columbia University Press: New York, 1942. Chapters 12, 13, 14, and 22.

For didactic reasons, I have again taken some liberties with terminology in the matter of "active" and "passive."

3, 4, 5, 6, & 7.

The processes of libido development outlined in these sections are summarized in more orthodox and systematic form in:

*Introduction to the Psychoanalytic Theory of the Libido*, by Richard Sterba. Nervous & Mental Disease Monographs, No. 68. New York, 1942.

There is disagreement as to the instinctual meaning of infantile nipple-biting, but the viewpoint presented here is useful didactically.

8. *The Oedipus Complex*

The development of the Oedipus situation and the child's relationships to his parents and siblings were beautifully described years ago by Flugel.

*The Psychoanalytic Study of the Family*, by J. C. Flugel. The Hogarth Press: London, 1939. (First printed in 1921.)

For a study of the later psychological development of the female, Deutsch's two books should be read.

*The Psychology of Women*, by Helene Deutsch. Grune & Stratton: New York, 1944 and 1945.

Volume 1, 1944, deals with the mysterious epochs of girl-hood, puberty, and adolescence. Volume 2, 1945, deals with motherhood in a variety of aspects, including adoptive mothers, unmarried mothers, and stepmothers.

For a long time I have been using the esoteric Brschiss legend in expounding the Oedipus complex. Recently I discovered that a surprisingly similar tale of a child, a giant, and a woman is a part of the Norse folklore, in the story of "The Blue Belt," which can be found in many children's books of fairy tales.

### CHAPTER FOUR

# DREAMS AND THE UNCONSCIOUS

---

## I

## What is the unconscious?

WE HAVE HEARD a good deal about the "unconscious." Let us now try to set down in one place how we can think of it.

First of all, the unconscious is an energy center, where the Id instincts begin to take form. It will help to understand it if we compare it to a factory. This factory is full of dynamos which supply energy to run the machines. Into the factory come all kinds of raw material brought from the outside. These raw materials go through the machines which are run from the dynamos, and the finished product results.

There are two important things to notice. First, the products which come out are quite different from the machines which make them. Secondly, the parts of the product look different from the finished product. We may use automobiles as an illustration. The presses, punches, and furnaces which are used to make an automobile are quite different in appearance from an automobile. Also, any part of an automobile, such as a carburetor, looks different from a finished automobile. One would never be able to guess what an automobile looked like by looking at a carburetor. On the other hand, one would never be able to guess what either a punch press or a carburetor looked like by watching automobiles.

In the same way, the individual cannot guess how his thoughts are made by watching them go through his mind. Thoughts are the finished products, and observing them will not give anyone but an expert an idea of what their parts look like or what the "machines" look like that made them.

If, however, we allow a specially trained engineer to observe an automobile, he will probably be able to tell what parts are in it and what machines were used to turn them out. Similarly, if one lets a trained psychiatrist listen to one's thoughts, he can make a pretty good estimate as to what parts go to make them up and where they come from. Strangely enough, untrained people are often more confident that they can explain a thought than that they can explain an automobile, although a thought is much more complicated. An automobile has an end to it, that is, there are only a certain number of parts in it and a certain number of machines that are used to make it. There are a lot of them, it is true, but there is an end to them eventually. A thought, on the other hand, is made up of parts without end by processes without end. No matter how many parts one breaks it up into, one can always find more by looking farther. The thought that made Midas King have high blood pressure is a good example. Regardless of how much Dr. Treece studied it, there was always more to be learned by studying it longer. We shall demonstrate this more clearly later when we study the thought that made Rex Bigfoot lose his hair. The study of any thought stops only because the time is up and not because we know all about it.

Let us return to our factory. The dynamos in the factory correspond to the energy of the unconscious, which comes from the Id instincts. These dynamos supply their energy to machines, which correspond to the images in the unconscious. The machines in the factory look different and work differently from their product. Similarly, the images in the unconscious look different and work differently from their product, which is conscious or thought images. This can be seen by thinking about dreams, which are halfway between conscious and unconscious images in form, and are a little like both and a little different from both. The conscious mind arranges things and uses logic, while the unconscious mind "disarranges" feelings and doesn't use logic. A dream, which is a glimpse of the unconscious, may look as strange to the dreamer as a huge punch press in an automobile factory might look to a taxi driver.

The unconscious, then, is a source of energy and a part of the mind where thoughts are "manufactured," but the way the unconscious works is different from the way the conscious mind works.

Secondly, the unconscious is a region where feelings are stored. This is not "dead storage," but very much "live" storage, more like a zoo than a warehouse, for all the feelings stored in the unconscious are forever trying to get out. Feelings are stored by being attached to images, just as electricity is stored by being condensed in something. One cannot store electricity by itself; it has to be stored in something. In the same way, a feeling has to be stored about something. When a feeling is stored in the unconscious, or "repressed," it either detaches itself from the representation which awakened it and attaches itself to an image already in the unconscious, or else it takes its own representation down into the unconscious with it. In the first case, the representation remains conscious and the feeling becomes unconscious, so that the individual is not aware of the latter; in the second case, the representation is also forgotten, since it also becomes unconscious. Thus forgetting depends on repression rather than on "wearing out." The storage of an image, that is, a feeling plus a representation, by repression, is always connected with forgetting something. This can also be said the other way round; forgetting means that a representation is being repressed. We have previously mentioned another variation of this, where the representation is repressed and the feeling remains conscious.

We remember that when Mr. and Mrs. King were planning their party, Mr. King remembered what Mr. Castor, the horseman from Hawaii looked like, but couldn't remember how he felt about him. In this case, the feeling detached itself from the representation and was repressed into the unconscious, where it attached itself to another (and unpleasant) image concerning horseback riding. Thus the representation remained conscious while the feeling became unconscious, so that Mr. King was not aware of his dislike for Mr. Castor.

Later on, after their conversation, Mrs. King repressed her feeling about Mrs. Metis, whom she was angry at, and in this case the feeling took the name of the person down into the unconscious with it, so that she forgot that Mrs. Metis even existed. When it came time to do the inviting, Mrs. King had a feeling she was leaving out someone important, but couldn't think who it was, and committed the social error of not inviting Mrs. Metis, who was the banker's wife, to her party.

Mrs. King never did recollect the name of the "marvelous Mr. What's-his-name"; in this case the feeling was not repressed, but the name was forgotten, since the representation was repressed. In all these cases we can see that repression means forgetting, and that the forgetting was due to repression.

During psychoanalysis and in dreams many demonstrations occur of the fact that forgetting does not mean "wearing out"; during such processes the individual often remembers things that he thinks he has "naturally" forgotten years ago, such as a fragment of a child's poem or an incident that happened in early infancy. Mr. King, for example, had frequent dreams of horses, and during his treatment with Dr. Treece he suddenly remembered an incident that had taken place during a visit to Hawaii when he was only three years old. His father, who was a great horseman, had bought little Midas a saddle. One day when Midas was disagreeable to his mother, the father had taken the saddle away from him and sold it, which had thrown the child into a fit of rage and grief. He had "never thought of the incident since," until he recalled it for the doctor.

One reason people do not remember much of what happened to them before the age of three is that most adult thinking is done with words or at least with images of things that have names. Before that age the individual doesn't know many words or the names of many things, so feelings have to be stored on "unnamed" images, which he has no way later of easily explaining to himself or someone else. All that can come to mind under such circumstances is an "unnamed" feeling about some "unnamed" thing. People all have unnamable feelings about unnamable things, and usually don't understand where they come from. These may refer to the period of life before the individual could use words. It was a long time before Mr. King was able to explain to the doctor an unnamable feeling which he had had, and which from certain circumstances he mentioned must have dated back at least to his second year of life. He finally realized that it referred to the fact that his mother used to take his food away before he had finished eating it if he didn't eat it as fast as she wanted him to. It was this feeling which played a large part in his adult desire to get rich in a hurry and hold on to what he had, and which caused him to rush, and to get upset when things went wrong, so that his blood pressure was high by the end of the day's work.

There is a good reason why some storage place is necessary to human beings for their unsatisfied libido and mortido tensions. If every ungratified affection and every ungratified resentment which a person felt from the day of his birth were present in his conscious mind at all times, he would be unable to carry on his life. His mind would be in such a continual confusion and turmoil that he could give no attention at all to practical affairs. (Something like this actually happens in some forms of mental illness.) In order that he may be free to deal with important matters of the moment in accordance with the Reality Principle, his Ego has the ability to repress undesirable piled-up feelings into the unconscious, where they may stay out of the way.

As we mentioned, however, storage in the unconscious is not "dead" storage. It is not like putting a pile of books in the basement, where they will remain dusty but otherwise unchanged until the time comes to use them. It is more like storing a flock of rabbits. These "rabbits," fed by the feelings of the moment, breed and grow more powerful and would soon overrun the mind completely if they were not let out. But just as letting out some of the baby rabbits, without touching the father and mother rabbits, would not stop the rabbits once and for all from overrunning the house, so indirect relief of Id tensions will not give permanent results, and will have to be repeated again and again, to prevent the Id from overrunning the Ego. No matter how often the tension is drained off indirectly, the original "parent" tensions are still there and can breed new little tensions. Only by satisfying the original tensions directly could the Id be emptied completely (though temporarily) of unsatisfied libido and mortido. This, of course, is impossible, especially when we remember that one of the strongest tensions is the inwardly directed mortido of the Superego, which would undoubtedly be increased after an attempt to accomplish such complete relief of the other tensions. For a while after satisfactory sexual relations with a loved one, however, the complete relief of libido tension is closely approached.

The unconscious, then, is the source of Id energy, a "thought factory," and a storage place. It cannot think, any more than an automobile factory can go on a trip. It can only feel and wish, and it pays no attention to time, place, and the laws of the physical universe, as is often seen in dreams, where the dead may be resurrected, the separated reunited, and the laws of gravity may not work normally.

Everyone is familiar with the "knee jerk" which follows a tap on the tendon of the knee. This movement is outside of the will and gives some people a queer sensation, occasionally amounting to actual nausea, so greatly are they upset by their minds losing control of a part of their bodies. The knee jerk is carried out through the spinal cord without the assistance of the brain, and the spinal cord works quite differently from the brain. The brain works by movement patterns, with all the muscles working together to make a certain movement, such as kicking something. The spinal cord controls separate muscles which move without accomplishing any definite purpose. The unconscious differs from the conscious in a similar way, so that the conscious mind gets a weird impression when it observes the peculiar way in which the unconscious puts things together. A dream scene of a market place is as different from a real market place as a knee jerk is from a kick.

2

## What is in the unconscious?

The contents of the unconscious consist mainly of the "unfinished business of childhood" and matters related thereto. This includes tensions which have never become conscious, but are still capable of influencing behavior indirectly, and tensions which have become conscious and have been repressed. Together with these tensions are found the corresponding images: some which have never become conscious, and others which have been pushed out of consciousness.

Since imaginations, or fantasies, are just as real to the unconscious as actual experiences, many of the representations in the unconscious have little connection with reality, and yet are just as influential as realities. A "good" representation of Father may be based on memories of what he was like, fantasies of what he was like, or present experiences of his goodness, and both the memories and the fantasies may be equally important in determining the individual's attitude toward him.

The tensions in the unconscious are "unfinished business" because they have not yet been relieved, do not disappear until they are relieved, and are continually seeking complete or partial relief through their true aim and object or through substitutes.

The chief tensions present in the unconscious minds of most people are unsatisfied oral wishes, unsatisfied anal wishes, and unsatisfied wishes of the later period of life after the fifth year. They are usually both libidinous and mortidinous, loving and hateful. They are both inwardly and outwardly directed. The outwardly directed tensions take the form of affections and hostilities. The inwardly directed ones take the form of a need for affection and approval, and a need for punishment. Their aims range from sexual intercourse and murder to merely looking at or knowing that the object exists. The objects range from parents and relatives to casual acquaintances and inanimate things. Any one or more of the tensions, even contradictory ones, can become conscious if circumstances are right, and seek direct relief through the proper aim and object, or indirect relief through aim or object displacement. As many tensions as possible, conscious and unconscious, seek relief in everything the individual does or imagines.

The unconscious (as well as the conscious) tensions of the individual may be divided into two groups: those relating to the Id, and those relating to the Superego (remembering that the Superego is only a split-off part of the Id, so that in the last analysis both groups spring from the Id instincts). What he actually does and how much he expresses himself is a compromise between these two groups of tensions, under the control of the Ego (which in turn, in the last analysis, is also a split-off part of the Id). (These splits need not be confusing. All that we need to remember is that in the adult the Id is split, and in the very young infant it is not.)

If everyone tried to gratify all his Id wishes, anarchy would result. The gratification of Id wishes often involves suffering on the part of others, and free Id expression would mean the pleasure of the mighty and the misery of the less mighty. Many political situations in the course of history have demonstrated this.

The Superego wishes, if normal, tend to bring happiness to others. They help to make people generous and considerate. Our civilization is largely based on the triumph of the Superego over the Id, and if civilization is to continue, this triumph must continue. The growth force or Physis which we see evidence of in the individual and in society, if properly nourished in infancy, works along with the Superego, so that the individual has an urge to grow up and behave "better," that is, in accordance with the principles of the adult stage of sexual development which takes the happiness of others into consideration. Both Superego and Physis, if normal, oppose crude and childish expressions of Id wishes. They start the individual off in not soiling his diapers, and end up in the noble ideals of the United Nations.

If the development of the Superego is hindered, or takes place in an unusual way, there is likely to be trouble, as we shall see later. If the feelings and representations stored in the unconscious through the forces of repression become disturbed, the consequences may also be undesirable.

3

## Why do people dream?

By this time, the reader should have little difficulty in understanding what a dream is. It is an attempt to gain satisfaction of an Id tension by hallucinating a wish fulfillment. Awake or asleep, the Id continues to strive for gratification. During the waking hours it is prevented from asserting itself directly by the Superego, with its stern ideas of what is right and wrong, and by the Ego, with its realization of what consequences may follow unwise gratification of impulses. During sleep, the Ego relaxes its repressions and the Reality Principle by which it attempts to govern is out of commission. Thus the contents of the Id are partly freed from control. The Superego, however, does not relax much during sleep, and its effects are still felt when the Id tries to assert itself. This means that even during sleep, the Id must still conceal the true nature of its strivings for fear of offending the Superego. Therefore, these strivings only dare show themselves in disguised form, so that the dream is rarely frank, but usually presents the Id wishes in a distorted way. The task of the dream interpreter is then to penetrate this disguise and reveal the true nature of the Id wishes which are striving for expression.

Since the individual is asleep, he cannot move about and actually obtain the gratifications he desires. All he can do is visualize them in his mind. Because the Ego with its ability to test reality is no longer in action he is able to believe that his visions are real, and at the time they content him almost as much as the reality would. A sexual dream may be as satisfying to the sleeper as actual sexual relations would be in waking life. When the Ego is awake, it prefers that satisfactions be real. When it is asleep, the mind may be content with imagined gratifications.

Two apparent exceptions to what we have said in the last paragraph will help to make it clearer. First, at times the individual does move about during sleep. If we analyze an example of sleepwalking, we find that it is related to the individual's dreams, and that it is an attempt to realize the satisfactions that the dream strives for. The dwarf of Brschiss who walked into his "parents'" bedroom while he was asleep is a good instance. During that period his wish was to separate his "parents," and his sleepwalking was a kind of attempt to accomplish this. Secondly, at times during waking life, the individual may believe in his own imaginings. This occurs in certain forms of mental illness. The example we have already given is that of the alcoholic who believes in the reality of his terrifying, mortidinous hallucinations. This means that one way alcoholism may affect the mind is by suspending the operation of the Ego's reality testing so that imaginings seem real; when this happens, they are called hallucinations.

What is the effect (or "purpose") of dreaming? A dream is an attempt to keep the sleeper from being awakened by the shamefulness or terrifying nature of his own Id wishes. The dream is the preserver of sleep.

When the Ego is asleep, repressions are partly lifted, and the Id tensions are released. We know that the Id is ruthless and has no morals. What would be the effect on the individual if he felt these tensions in all their power? He might immediately want to get up and bring death and sexual violence to those around him, no matter how close their relationship; the Id in the raw does not believe in moral discriminations and halfway measures, as we often see in criminal situations, when the repressions break down and deeds of horror are committed. It happens that the sleeper does not have to get up and carry out his desires since he can be content with imagining their fulfillment. The reality to him of his hallucinations (dreams, that is,) make action unnecessary, so he can have his Id pleasures while he continues to sleep.

But even in sleep, if the true aims and objects of his Id tensions became known to him, the indignant reactions of his Superego would awaken him. The distortions of the dream fool the Superego so that it sees no need for indignation, and thus sleep can continue. An apparent exception again makes the situation clearer. If the Id tensions are so strong that they threaten to break through frankly in spite of the Superego and what little repression is left during sleep, the Ego half awakens and a terrific struggle follows to keep the Id from expressing itself openly. If this struggle cannot be won by the Ego in its sleeping state, the alarm is sounded and the sleeper awakens, with his heart pounding and his skin drenched with sweat, panic-stricken by his narrow escape from becoming aware of the power and ruthlessness of his own Id tensions. A nightmare is a dream which has failed in its attempt to preserve sleep. If the individual senses, or learns from experience, how dangerous it is for him to relax his repressions by going to sleep, he sometimes prefers to lie awake all night rather than run the risk of becoming aware of his unconscious desires. Insomnia often results from such a fear of going to sleep. Sometimes this fear is conscious, but usually it is unconscious, and in the latter case the sufferer, not being aware of the real reason for his wakefulness, may find all kinds of other excuses such as worry, noise, etc., which satisfy him and usually his family as well.

Not only does the dream attempt to keep the sleeper from being awakened by his own Id tensions, but it also attempts to keep outside stimulations from awakening him. A familiar example of this is the man who sleeps through his wintry alarm clock. If his sleeping Ego interpreted the bell correctly, he would have to wake up, get out of his comfortable bed, put his feet on the cold floor, and go to work in the dark and shivering dawn. By "dreaming away" the sound of the bell he fools his Superego and Ego into letting him sleep on and avoid this unpleasant experience. The Id, ever alert to use all kinds of opportunities for its own gratification, seizes upon the sound of the bell to use in gratifying some of its tensions. In this case, for example, it may transport him in a dream back to the happy days of his infancy, when he did not have the duty of controlling and postponing his satisfactions, and when life was more charming and pleasant. He may dream that he is hearing church bells, which is a way of saying:

"What a beautiful sound I hear. 'Tis the church bells of Olympia. How comforting it is to know that I am back there living again my carefree childhood days!"

Upon getting the subject's reaction to this dream, the interpreter may find that the church bells of Olympia remind him of his long dead mother. Thus the dream satisfies three wishes. First, the wish to continue sleeping: since the dream allows him to believe that he is hearing church bells, and not an alarm clock, there is no need to get up. Secondly, the wish to be a child again: if he is hearing those particular bells, he must once more be a child, since that is exactly the way they sounded to him in childhood. Thirdly, the wish that his mother were alive again: in the days when he heard those bells, his mother was at his side; now that he is hearing them again, she must also be here.

In this case, the fraud he is practicing on his Superego, with its sense of duty, and his Ego, with its desire for him to keep his job, may eventually be exposed, so that in spite of the comforting dream he begins to stir uneasily in his sleep and suddenly springs wide awake with the realization that he is going to be late for work if he doesn't hurry now. Reluctantly he abandons his dream world and plunges into the cold reality of the morning.

People often say that dreams are "due to" outside stimulations. This is not so. The truth is that the Id *uses* outside stimulations as handy material around which to weave its wish fulfillments. In expressing itself, the Id takes the line of least resistance, using the channels most readily available. This may be called a law, or even *the* law, of the Id. It applies not only to dreams, but also to neurotic symptoms. Thus we have wish-fulfilling dreams based on, but not "caused by," indigestion, and wish-fulfilling neuroses based on, but not "caused by," old bodily injuries. For example, the pain of indigestion may be used by the Id in forming a dream of "anal" satisfaction. Since anal satisfactions are often horrifying to the adult mind, the type of conflict may follow which we have described in connection with nightmares, and such a dream therefore may take the form of a nightmare.

In addition to attempting to fulfill the anal wishes, such a dream attempts to gratify the wish to go on sleeping in spite of the pain and the increased tension which it activates in the Id. By using the pain as material in a wish-fulfilling dream, the same soothing effect is obtained as in the case of the alarm clock. If the alarm were perceived as an alarm, the subject would waken; if the pain were perceived as a pain, the subject would waken. But if the pain is "dreamed away" by being used, for example, in a pleasant hallucination of the subject having his abdomen massaged by a woman resembling his mother, just as his real mother used to do when he was constipated as a child, then the dreamer can go on sleeping blissfully in spite of the pain. If the idea of such a massage offends the adult Superego, then the dream will be turned into a nightmare, and will fail in its purpose, so that the dreamer will awaken anyway. The following is an example of such a nightmare.

Wendell Meleager dreamed one night, after eating a large and fancy dinner, that an ugly woman giant was chasing him with a blazing object resembling a rubber roller such as is used in massage parlors. The dream was so terrifying that he awoke in a panic.

Mr. Meleager had come to the psychiatrist because of the symptoms which followed his uncle's death. When the treatment began, he complained of shakiness, palpitation, insomnia, nightmares, exaggerated fears, depression, inability to concentrate, and impotence. Throughout his life he had suffered from lack of confidence and constipation, both of which he felt were relieved by frequenting massage parlors.

Mr. Meleager's "associations" to his dream were as follows: the woman giant did not look like his mother, but somehow she reminded him of her. Then he remembered that she had the same kind of hands as his mother and wore the same kind of wedding ring. Then he recounted some of his pleasant experiences while he was being massaged. Suddenly he remembered something he had not thought of since early childhood: that when he was constipated as an infant, his mother used to massage his abdomen. More than that, he recalled something which startled him even more, and that was the *feeling of pleasure* he had had on such occasions. At that moment, in the doctor's office, he went through the tremendous experience of reliving that feeling in all its meaningfulness.

The dream can be reconstructed as follows: the underlying dream was that his mother was massaging his abdomen, which would have brought his Id much gratification. Such a dream was quite unacceptable to his adult Superego, since it revealed too plainly how much he formerly enjoyed and still desired physical contact with his mother, and how much this procedure and the satisfaction it brought had encouraged his tendency to be constipated in childhood. In the work of "manufacturing" the dream, therefore, his mind had disguised the nature of the Id wish it fulfilled. First, it had disguised his beautiful mother by turning her into an ugly giantess, so that his Superego would not recognize the real object of the dream. Secondly, instead of visualizing the actual massage in the dream, he had "symbolized" it by the picture of the blazing rubber roller in the giantess' hand. This meant instead of "She is massaging you," rather "She is going to massage you," which, though less satisfying, was at least a fair substitute and might have brought some gratification with less guilt if the deception had worked.

Unfortunately for Mr. Meleager, however, his Superego was in this case not fooled by the indirectness and the disguises of the dream, and began to protest violently, resulting in the panicky feeling of the nightmare. When the Id threatened to break through completely and let the giantess catch him and perform the massage (as is not unusual in nightmares, he was unable to run despite his fear, so that she was in a fair way to catch him), his Superego was in danger of losing control. The alarm was sounded, and he woke up. His Ego also probably felt this dream as a threat.

This dream and its interpretation by means of Mr. Meleager's associations marked a turning point in his treatment. It opened up such a rich mausoleum of long-buried feelings and memories that rapid progress was made from that time on. The important thing to notice about the process of interpreting this dream is that without Mr. Meleager's associations it could not have been done effectively. The interpretation hinged on the sudden memory of his childhood pleasure, which had been unconscious for nearly forty years and was only recalled during the "free association" of psychoanalysis, which we shall discuss further in a later chapter. Without this association, the dream would have meant little to either Mr. Meleager or the psychoanalyst. The doctor might have guessed its meaning in a general way, and his guess might have helped him understand Mr. Meleager better, but it would not have helped Mr. Meleager understand himself better. Only when he recalled by free association the actual *feeling* of the experience upon which it was based, could he profit greatly from the interpretation.

It should be said that this profitable opening up of his childhood emotional life, which gradually led to a beneficial reorganization of his personality, began to be effective only after almost six months of daily visits to the analyst, and that it required many more months to work it out completely. As Mr. Meleager told his friends, however, his increased efficiency in the end enabled him to earn more in his law practice, so that his eventual freedom from symptoms and the new-found happiness of himself and his family were almost free dividends on his investment.

In this section we have learned that the function of dreams is to preserve sleep, and that dreams are wish fulfillments in disguise. We have seen that it is necessary to obtain the dreamer's associations in order to interpret a dream properly, and that such interpretations reveal the dreamer's unconscious wishes to such an extent that dreams have been called "the highroad to the unconscious."

It is probable also that dreams have another function, and that is to assist in healing the mind after emotional wounds and distressing emotional experiences. As the reader will see later, the terrifying battle dreams of Si Seifuss probably represented an unsuccessful attempt to accomplish this healing after his damaging war experiences.

4

## Interpreting dreams

We have just given an example of the method used in interpreting dreams. Briefly, the material used in the interpretation is obtained as follows: after relating the dream, the subject tells exactly what comes to his mind when he thinks of what he has dreamed without any attempt to censor his thoughts or to put them in order.

The purpose of the interpretation is to find out which Id tensions are trying to find expression in the dream, their true aims and objects, and their meaning for the individual. These factors are called the "latent content" of the dream. The dream itself, as the dreamer experiences it and tells it, is called the "manifest content." The interpretation is an attempt to trace back from the manifest content to the latent content. Without the subject's associations, an experienced dream interpreter might be able to guess from the manifest content alone which Id tensions were trying to find expression in the dream and even what their true aims and objects were, but he could not tell the most important thing of all: the significance of these things for the individual. And until the dreamer realizes significances by *feeling* them, the interpretation is of no immediate value to him except as an interesting scientific study. Only by making associations to the dream can he experience these all-important feelings.

It is a common error to suppose that *finding out* the meaning of the dream is the important thing. This is not so. The meanings must be *felt*, not merely understood, for the interpretation to have any effect in changing the underlying Id tensions, which is the purpose of the procedure.

The interpreter has to remember that a dream is a disguised attempt to picture a feeling during sleep. Factors which influence the formation of the manifest dream from the latent content are as follows:

1. During sleep, the Ego is largely out of commission. Thus the dream is formed without much help from the Ego in "arranging," and without the full benefit of the Ego's experience in learning from reality. Therefore the dream may appear strange to the Ego after the dreamer awakens. It may seem absurd, unarranged, and even disorderly, nor is it bound by any of the demands of reality: Time, space, gravity, death, and other basic relationships which the Ego has to take account of in waking life, may have no effect on the content and action of the dream.*

2. During sleep, the Superego is partly out of commission. Therefore the dreamer does things in his dream which he would never dare to do nor perhaps dare even to think of doing in waking life.

3. Among the unconscious influences which the Ego keeps more or less inactive or at least under control during waking life, but which have freer expression in the dream, are the three "absolutes." In his dreams, the individual is always immortal (if he pictures his death, he always survives as a spectator); his charms are irresistible (he can and does make love to any woman he wants to); and his thoughts are omnipotent (if he thinks he can fly, he jumps, and lo! he flies).

4. The task of the dream is to show complicated feelings in pictures. A feeling cannot be shown directly in a picture. Only the act which signifies the feeling can be shown. There is no such thing as a picture of fear, but an expression of fear, or the act of running away can be pictured. There is no such thing as a picture of love, but approaching, giving, adoring, or a sexual act can be shown. There is no such thing as a picture of hate, but destroying, casting out, or injuring can be visualized. Sometimes the dream has the task of condensing all three feelings into a single picture and, in addition, disguising the feelings so that the Superego will not know what the picture represents. Furthermore, the aims and objects of the feelings may also be condensed and disguised. That is one reason why sometimes the analysis of a single feature of a dream may take a whole session.

* In the experience of the author, a slow-motion picture is the nearest thing in dynamic reality, and the paintings of Salvador Dali are the nearest thing in static reality, to the unreality of a dream.

In Mr. Meleager's dream, the principle of "disguise by opposites" was very active, as well as "disguise by symbolization." When Mr. Meleager finally *felt* the meaning of his dream, *he* told the *doctor* (and not vice versa) that it expressed a long-forgotten desire to have closer physical contact with his mother. The disguises were then revealed. His beautiful mother was disguised on the principle of opposites as an ugly woman; instead of running to her, on the same principle, he ran away from her; instead of his having the male organ, she had it. The male organ was symbolized in disguise by the rubber roller, and the heat of his passion even as a child was symbolized in disguise by the flame.

The figure of the giantess was a good example of "condensation" of several items. First, she represented his mother. Secondly, she represented two large and ugly masseuses who held a strange sexual fascination for him. In addition, her ugliness represented the ugliness of his desires, her fearsomeness represented the fear they aroused in him, and her enormity represented their enormity. He told the analyst these things with great feeling, the sweat pouring off his face and his heart pounding as he talked.

5. Above all, the interpreter bears in mind that the dreamer writes his own scenario. The dream is the sole product of his individual mind. Like the author of any scenario, he can put in any characters he pleases and do with them as he will. He can take his heroine and marry her, kill her, impregnate her, set her up in business, enslave her, beat her, give her away, or do anything else with her which his fancy dictates and his sleepy Superego will permit. If he feels passionate he can caress; if he feels envious he can plunder; if he feels guilty he can punish himself; if he feels angry he can kill; and if he has unusual desires he can gratify them. But whatever he does, or to or with whomever he does it, and whatever disguises he cloaks them in, it is his own desires he is gratifying and not anyone else's. The manifest dream will be a compromise between the tensions of the Superego and the unsatisfied wishes of the Id, and the analysis of the dream will lead back to the latent thoughts which arise from these two forces. It may be said that the influence of the Ego can also be noted in "secondary" arranging of the manifest dream elements.

## *Footnotes for Philosophers, Chapter Four*

1. & 2. *The Unconscious*

Korzybski's influence may be seen here. An account of the unconscious suitable for the lay reader is given in:

*Facts and Theories of Psychoanalysis*, by Ives Hendrick. Alfred A. Knopf: New York, 1944.

3. & 4. *Dreams*

There is no substitute for Freud's work "The Interpretation of Dreams," which can be found in *The Basic Writings of Sigmund Freud.* Part II of his *General Introduction to Psychoanalysis*, and the revision of his dream theory found in the first chapter of *New Introductory Lectures on Psycho-analysis* may also be read.

Freud's study of dreams is so subtle that some trained psychoanalysts reread "The Interpretation of Dreams" periodically, each time gaining further enlightenment.

# PART
# II

---

# Abnormal Development

---

### CHAPTER FIVE

# NEUROSES

## How can emotions cause physical disease?

THERE ARE millions of unhappy people all over the world who suffer from headache, backache, stomach-ache, loss of appetite, excessive belching, nausea, heavy feeling after eating, pain in the chest, pounding heart, dizziness, fainting spells, breathlessness, weakness, and pains in the joints, without ever finding out what is the matter with them. Year after year they go from one doctor to another, getting X-rays, urinalyses, gastric analyses, electrocardiograms, and blood sugars, and taking vitamins, hormones, electric treatments, elixirs, and tonics, and sometimes undergoing one operation after another. If they have been in the army or navy of their native land, they have been labeled "psychoneurotic," and many a man who faced machine-gun fire calmly has quailed at the sound of this word. Some of them hate doctors and love chiropractors, osteopaths, Christian Science practitioners, and naturopaths, because they feel that doctors think their troubles are imaginary.

When a doctor, after doing all the tests and examinations and finding them negative, says that these troubles may be caused by emotions, he does not mean that they are imaginary. Everyone has heard of people getting headaches from worrying, which gives us the expression "This job is a headache!" Those who have had such headaches (as many doctors have) know that they are not imaginary. The happy little Gremlin who is driving red-hot rivets into the backs of the victim's eyes may be imaginary, but the pain isn't.

Anyone who has seen a robust man or woman faint at the sight of blood knows that such fainting spells are not imaginary either, and whoever has seen a child vomit from excitement after coming home from the circus knows that such vomiting is real enough. In these cases, the headaches, fainting spells, and vomiting are all caused by emotions. There is no disease of the head, heart, or stomach, but the trouble happens just the same. There is nothing to get angry about if the doctor says that the patient's symptoms are emotional. He does *not* mean that they are imaginary. Emotions can cause mild illnesses, serious illnesses, and death.

A hundred years before there was any scientific psychiatry, there was a famous doctor in England by the name of John Hunter. Dr. Hunter had a heart attack which nearly killed him. Being a good physician, he knew even in those days the importance of the emotions in affecting the heart. When he recovered, he said: "My life is in the hands of any rascal who chooses to annoy and tease me!" He was unable to keep his temper, however, and one day he became angry and dropped dead. Though his death was caused by his emotions, it was not imaginary. His temper brought on a very real blood clot in the wall of his heart.

If we examine the inside of the chest of an animal or human being under an anesthetic, we can understand how the heart can race and cause pounding, or slow down and miss a beat, without anything being wrong with the heart itself. There are two nerves of different kinds which go to the heart. These nerves can actually be seen with the naked eye and picked up with the fingers. They are like pieces of white string which run from the heart to the lower part of the brain. We can call one kind the S nerve (for sprinting) and the other the P nerve (for plodding). If the S nerve is touched with an electric battery, a current goes down the nerve and the heart begins to sprint. If the P nerve is touched with a battery, the heart slows down and begins to plod. This can be repeated again and again. Anybody can do it because the nerves are right there for anyone to see. Thus one can make a perfectly normal heart pound or slow up without even touching it.

There are similar nerves which affect the blood pressure. If electricity is sent along one of these, the blood pressure goes up; if it is sent along the other, the pressure goes down. We have only to remember that fainting is caused by a fall in blood pressure to understand how a person can faint without anything being wrong with the heart.

Normally, of course, there is no electric battery in the chest, but there is something similar in the lower part of the brain where the S and P nerves end. There is some "electric" tissue there that can send a current down the S nerve to speed the heart up, or down the P nerve to slow it. This can be tested easily by putting two wires on the S or P nerve and connecting these wires to a galvanometer, which is something like the ammeter in an automobile. It has a needle which shows when an electric current passes between the two wires which run out from it. In this way we can show that when the heart speeds up from excitement a current goes from the brain down the S nerve to the heart; and when the heart slows down for an instant from fear (many people faint when they are afraid because slowing contributes to a sudden fall in blood pressure) current is passing down the P nerve.

If one uses a tomcat in this experiment, and a dog is shown to the animal after it comes out of the ether, the current can be demonstrated passing down the S nerve. If the cat's feelings are stimulated in a different way, the current passes down the P nerve. This shows that the cat's emotions can determine which way the current flows, and the heart can be seen accordingly to speed up or slow down without anyone touching it. It is the same with a human being. When a man gets angry, his heart speeds up; when he is afraid it may slow down for a few moments. The rate of his heart at such times depends on his emotions and has nothing to do with the condition of the heart itself. When his mind grasps what is happening, an electric current goes from the upper part of his brain to the lower part of his brain. If it passes by way of the anger or "pounding" complex, it will arrive at the S nerve center, and a current will then go down the S nerve. If it passes by way of the fear or "fainting" complex, it will reach the P nerve center, and a current will then go down the P nerve.

What determines whether the current goes by way of the anger complex or the fear complex? The same thing which determines the path of any electric current. It follows the path of least resistance. If the person is irritable and aggressive, the anger path has a lower resistance; if he is timid and fearful, the fear path has a lower resistance. Thus the things in early life which determine whether a person's attitude toward the world is a belligerent one or a timid one determine which nerve the current will pass down and how the heart will react when emotions are aroused.

We can see that the reactions of the heart to emotion are important and often useful to the individual. It is important and useful for an angry man to have a strongly beating heart, for he may get into a fight with a man or a lion and his muscles will then need plenty of extra blood pumped into them. If the heart slows down in a tight spot, on the other hand, this is important, but hardly useful, as the person may then faint and be at the mercy of whatever danger threatens. We can recognize here two old friends, "active" and "passive." The brain uses the S nerve in connection with active, fighting mortido, and the P nerve in connection with passive, fainting mortido. The theory that the brain can store energy explains how a person can remain calm while things are happening and only faint or feel his heart pound after the excitement is all over. In such a case the energy is not immediately released down the S or P nerve, but is stored until the situation has been taken care of.

We notice then that emotions can cause electric currents to go through the nervous system in various directions. These currents can be studied without exposing the nervous system, by means of various electrical devices, including the brain-wave amplifier, which we shall hear more about later.

The patient who comes to the doctor complaining of palpitation may have one objection to all this: he may say that it is all very well for such things to happen to people who are angry or afraid, but that his heart begins to pound when he is lying quietly in bed at night and doesn't feel either emotion.

The answer to this, of course, is that the fact that he is not aware of the nature of his tensions does not mean that they do not exist. The very fact that his heart, though normal, pounds when he is lying quietly is one of the best proofs that they do exist. There is no reason to suppose that people are aware of all the tensions of their libido and mortido. Quite the contrary. We know that it is perfectly possible for a person to have ungratified tensions without being conscious of them. Many people are in love, or angry, or afraid, for ten, twenty, or thirty years without being aware of it until they come to a psychoanalyst. They may not know that they are angry, but their hearts know it, and act accordingly. The reason such feelings are called unconscious is that the person is not aware of them. Therefore, it is not logical for a person to say that he has an unconscious feeling, or to deny that he has it. If he knew that he had it, it would no longer be unconscious.

Some doctors and psychologists, it is true, maintain that we must be conscious of all our mental energy imbalances, and claim that if we are not conscious of a libido or mortido tension, it does not exist. So far they have not been able to prove their point effectively enough to convince those whose business it is to study Id tensions, namely, the psychoanalysts.

After all, we breathe because of energy imbalance, but no one would say that the wish to breathe did not exist because the individual was not always conscious of it. By a simple procedure he can become conscious of it. It is a little more complicated to become conscious of unrecognized libido and mortido tensions, but it can be done. Because an individual is not aware that he is acting affectionately does not mean that he has stopped loving.

What has been said about quickening or slowing of the heart applies also to rise and fall of blood pressure, which can cause pounding sensations or fainting spells.

In the case of the stomach, the story is even more interesting. From time to time one finds a man with a wound of the abdomen which will not heal properly, so that for years he has a little window in his belly which looks in on his stomach. Some of these men, for money or for the sake of humanity, have let doctors watch their stomachs in action. The most famous case of this kind occurred in the 1820's, when a man named Alexis St. Martin was hired and observed by Dr. William Beaumont, and to these two we owe much of our early knowledge as to how the stomach works. Other examples have been observed since that time.

From such studies we learn that as in the case of the heart, many of the stomach's reactions depend upon the emotions and in much the same way. There are two kinds of nerves going to the stomach, the S (for Sponge) and the P (for Pale) nerves. If a battery, or the nerve center in the lower part of the brain, sends a current through the S nerve, the blood vessels in the wall of the stomach expand and soak up blood like a sponge; if the current passes down the P nerve, the blood vessels shrink and squeeze most of the blood out, so that the organ looks pale. It happens that when an individual gets angry, the current goes down his S nerve. His face gets red and so does his stomach. Though the individual does not know that his stomach is red, he often notices that it feels heavy. This is perfectly natural. It feels heavy because it *is* heavy, just as a sponge is heavier when it has lots of water in it than when it has only a little bit.

If a man is afraid, on the other hand, whether he is conscious of it or not, the current goes down the P nerve and the stomach turns pale. At the same time the nerve current slows it up so that it squeezes less efficiently than usual and takes longer to digest food, which lingers in the stomach and begins to ferment. This causes belching and loss of appetite, since, for one thing, no room has been made for more food by the time the next meal rolls around. So people with unsatisfied mortido tensions, which may be expressed at times through the S nerve and at times through the P nerve, often complain of heavy feeling in the stomach, excessive belching, and loss of appetite, for ten, twenty, or thirty years.

In addition to becoming congested if the mortido current goes down the S nerve, something more serious may happen to the stomach. The digestive juices may become too powerful and burning. It is one of the great mysteries of life why the stomach doesn't digest itself. If a man eats a piece of tripe, which is cow's stomach, his digestive juices will digest that piece of dead stomach, but they don't usually digest his own live stomach. If his digestive juices get more powerful than usual, however, while at the same time the stomach wall gets congested and soggy, it may happen that he *will* digest his own stomach, or at least a little piece of it. This has been seen in the cases referred to above. So sometimes when a man has an unsatisfied tension over a long period, conscious or unconscious, a little of the inside layer of his stomach wall may get digested off and leave a raw place. What do we call such a raw place, whether it be on the leg, the gums, or the stomach? It is called an ulcer. The man's tension may partly relieve itself by discharging electrical impulses down his stomach nerves until he digests himself off a stomach ulcer. A long way back we said that the necessity for the human energy system to postpone the relief of certain tensions had a connection with why some people get burning pains in the stomach, and we also said that repressed Id energy may affect the individual's body adversely so that some bodily illnesses are disguised expressions of Id wishes. We now see how such things come about.

Diet will do little to prevent a stomach ulcer, but it does help ulcers heal more quickly. The idea behind this applies to ulcers anywhere on the body. If a man had an ulcer on his leg and put salt and pepper into it three times a day, together with some coffee and hamburgers, it would take quite a while to heal up, whereas if he covered it carefully with milk poultices it would heal pretty quickly. In the same way a milk diet helps a stomach ulcer. If in addition to the milk we pour in some alkaline powders to neutralize the overly powerful acids of the stomach, that helps it along too.

How long does it take a stomach ulcer to heal? It may take only a few weeks.

Mr. Edgar Metis, president of the First National Bank of Olympia, became very angry when Dr. Nagel told him that his latest X-rays showed he didn't have a stomach ulcer.

"You local doctors," he muttered, "don't know one end of the intestine from the other, especially that X-ray man. I had X-rays taken two months ago at the University Hospital in Arcadia, and they definitely showed an ulcer."

"Let me tell you a parable," said Dr. Nagel. "A man once came to me and said: 'Doctor, I cut myself while shaving and I have an ulcer on my left cheek. Can you cure it for me?' I looked at his cheek and found it smooth and healthy. I told him so and he got very mad. 'I know I have an ulcer there,' he insisted. 'In fact I have a picture of it.' He pulled a photograph of himself out of his wallet, and there on his left cheek, sure enough, was a large ulcer. 'There!' he said. 'The picture *proves* I have an ulcer.' 'Yes,' I said, 'but when was this picture taken?' 'Oh,' said the man, 'about two months ago!' "

An ulcer in the stomach under favorable conditions may heal just as quickly as an ulcer anywhere else.

The moral of all this is that psychiatry can prevent many stomach ulcers by keeping the stomach from getting red, soggy, and overly acid due to unsatisfied Id tensions, and can help ulcers heal quickly by making the stomach wall a nice healthy pink instead of an angry red. This ceases to be true after a certain length of time, because sooner or later an ulcer will go deep enough and get dirty enough so that it cannot heal by smooth repair like a shaving cut, but will have to heal by means of scar tissue. Scar tissue is permanent, and furthermore it contracts. Many people know how in a bad burn of the face, as the months and years go by, the scar tissue contracts and pulls the face over to one side, sometimes interfering with chewing, speaking, and turning of the head, so that the scar has to be cut away by a surgeon. The same thing happens in the stomach. Once scar tissue begins to form in an ulcer, healing will be slow, and later the scar may contract and deform the stomach to such an extent that food cannot get through the passage leading into the intestine. Then the individual has to have part of the stomach cut out, or a new passage made, by a surgeon.

Psychiatry can often prevent or cure certain kinds of heart trouble, stomach trouble, and high blood pressure, as well as some kinds of asthma and eczema, as long as no scar tissue has formed, but psychiatry cannot ever change scar tissue. Once the scar stage is reached, it can only attempt to prevent the condition from going further. The time for psychiatry in such conditions, therefore, is before any scar tissue has a chance to form. In other words, a man is wiser to bring his unconscious tensions under control and keep his stomach than he is to have his stomach taken out for the sake of believing that he does not have any unconscious tensions. Unfortunately for them, many people would rather lose their stomachs than their aggressions, so they find excuses not to go to a psychiatrist, and in some cases, alas! their family doctors or surgeons encourage this pathetic attitude. Every American citizen feels that he has a "constitutional" right to give up his stomach if he so desires.

Thus we see that physical diseases may result from emotional tensions because the various organs are connected to the brain by means of nerve cords. Some methods for the partial discharge of repressed Id tensions through the body organs may not result, even over long periods, in such serious conditions as those we have described, but they may cause milder afflictions which result in embarrassment and a waste of time and energy. Diarrhea is rarely an asset in any practical situation. Neither is an urgent desire to urinate or the sudden onset of a menstrual period or menstrual cramps. All these conditions may result from conscious or unconscious tensions.

## 2

# How can emotions cause physical pain?

We have seen that emotional tensions over a long period may play an important part in diseases of the stomach and heart, and that there is nothing imaginary about such diseases. Now let us look at some of the more common and less sinister types of pain.

How can an emotion cause a headache? This can be studied during a spinal tap. A spinal tap is in many ways similar to a blood test. In a blood test, a needle is put into a vein in the arm and some blood is withdrawn. If it is desired, a harmless measuring instrument called a manometer can be attached to the needle to measure the pressure of the blood in the vein. In a spinal tap, or lumbar puncture, a needle is put into the spinal canal in the back and some of the fluid which surrounds the brain and spinal cord is withdrawn for study. This fluid acts as a cushion and as a nourishment for the nervous system, and is not much different from tap water or mineral water. There is so much of it that it is quite harmless to remove the few drops required. Usually measurements of the pressure of the spinal fluid are made in the meantime with a manometer.

Let us take an individual who has many unsatisfied libido and mortido tensions. When the needle is inserted into his back, the pressure of the fluid shows in the glass measuring tube. If the patient is lying down and is fully relaxed, the fluid will rise up normally about five inches, or 120 millimeters, and that is the pressure of the fluid as it surrounds the brain inside the bony skull, just as the pressure of the air in the atmosphere as shown by a barometer is normally about 30 inches, or 760 millimeters.

We now watch the water level in the tube and ask the individual some simple question which will not make him emotional, such as,

"What is four times four?" or "What does the Fourth of July celebrate?" As he answers, we see that the pressure in the tube hardly changes. Thus, answering a question does not in itself change the pressure around the brain. Now let us ask him a more personal question, particularly one which hits a sore spot, such as: "Do you love your lawyer?" Usually there is a pause before he answers such a question, and as we watch the pressure gradually rises to 150, 180, or 200 millimeters. After he answers the question, the pressure may slowly fall again, or it may stay up for an indefinite length of time, depending upon how much the individual is stirred up.

Thus we can show that emotional disturbances can increase the pressure of the fluid around the brain. If this increase in pressure is maintained, the contents of the skull will be squeezed by the fluid and a headache may result. So we can see with our own eyes how an emotion might cause a headache. On the other hand, if an experienced psychiatrist is unable to get a rise in pressure by asking personal questions, he may be justified in assuming that the individual does not have emotional headaches.

It is possible that some low back pains are also caused by emotional tensions. The back is a balanced mechanism, more delicate in some cases than in others. In some people this balance probably has to be kept just right for the back to be able to perform the tasks imposed upon it.

In such individuals, if the female sexual organs or the male prostate become congested with blood like an angry stomach, the soggy organs may affect the muscles and ligaments of the back so that they begin to ache. This often occurs when the congestion is caused by inflammation due to disease. There is also a normal cause for such congestion, namely, sexual excitement. Since people are not aware of all their unsatisfied libido tensions, it could happen that an individual's sacroiliac would be painfully conscious that he was sexually excited without his realizing it himself.

Ambrose Paterson, the electrician, began to have backaches when he was fourteen years old. At the same time he began to have a discharge from his penis which was not due to venereal disease. For years, whenever he became excited, sexually or otherwise, his backache and his discharge would both get worse. The worst backache Mr. Paterson ever had occurred on the day he married Barbara Dimitri, but during the following week it gradually got better and then he was free of both backache and discharge for a long time. Eventually, however, both symptoms returned.

The day after he went looking for Loki Farbanti with his gun (an incident which we shall hear about later), Mr. Paterson had not only a backache and a discharge, but for the first time in his life he had the hives, and a few days later, hay fever. He was now going to three doctors: one for his back, one for his discharge, and one for his hives and hay fever. The doctors all got together one day at the hospital and decided that the best thing to do was to send Mr. Paterson to Dr. Treece, the psychiatrist. Dr. Treece liked difficult cases, but for a long time he shook his head whenever he thought of Ambrose Paterson. After a long course of psychiatric treatment, however, lasting almost two years, all Mr. Paterson's symptoms cleared up. After all this is not so astonishing. Although his symptoms sound very different from each other, actually, they were all due to the same thing: changes in the blood vessels in various parts of the body: the prostate, the skin, and the nose; and we know how easily the emotions can affect the blood vessels, as in blushing, sexual excitement, and anger. It will be noticed that before he went for psychiatric treatment, Mr. Paterson's symptoms got worse whenever there was an increase in his ungratified libido or mortido tensions.

Another painful condition which may sometimes come from unsatisfied Id tensions is arthritis. This may be due to disturbances in the blood supply to a joint. In this case we have to know that the blood vessels which supply the muscles around a joint also supply the joint itself. If the blood supply to the muscles is altered over a long period, so is the blood supply to the joint. The tissues in the joint are then affected accordingly. (A good example of how the blood supply to a limb may affect the growth of the bones is seen in cases where a child has a large birthmark full of blood vessels on one leg. The bones in the affected leg may grow longer than those on the other side because of the increased blood flow.)

Well, how can we suppose that the bood flow is altered in the muscles and joints of an arthritic arm?

The body is always kept in readiness to gratify conscious and unconscious tensions. The stronger the tensions, the more prepared the body is kept to gratify them. A person with strong ungratified mortido tensions, such as often hang over from childhood, may always be in a condition of readiness to gratify those tensions, even if he is not aware that they exist. Direct satisfaction of mortido tensions involves mainly the muscles of the arms, legs, and back, which are used in running and fighting. We may suppose, therefore, that a person with strong repressed aggressions and hostilities might keep one or more of his limbs tense as though in readiness to satisfy these unconscious mortido tensions. In other words, he might not know that he was angry over a period of years, but his arms might, and be kept tense as though always in readiness to hit someone; or his legs might, and be kept tense as though ready to run away. Because certain muscles were tense, their blood supply might be altered, and this might affect the bones and other tissues of the joint, resulting in the painful condition we call arthritis.

In connection with arthritis and other conditions where a combination of infection and emotional tension might be the cause of a disease, the following medical principle should be kept in mind: disease germs tend to settle in those parts of the body where the blood vessels are abnormally widened. Since we know that the chief changes which are caused in the body by the emotions consist of widening and narrowing of blood vessels in various places, we can see how an emotion, especially one which lasts over a period of years, might make disease germs especially apt to settle in the particular part of the body concerned, be it the stomach, the prostate gland, the neck of the womb, or one of the joints.

We have tried to show some of the ways in which emotions might contribute to the occurrence of physical pains in various parts of the body. In connection with headaches we have described some actual observations concerning the spinal fluid, and in connection with backache we have mentioned some facts concerning infections of the organs contained in the lowest part of the abdomen. The rest of what we have said is half speculation, supported by what facts are known. There is no doubt that certain cases of headache, backache, and painful arthritis can be benefited by psychiatric treatment. Suggestions for further reading on this important subject are given in the notes at the end of the chapter.

## 3

# What is psychosomatic medicine?

The things we have discussed in the two previous sections, that is, the connection of the emotions with physical disease, together with the effects of physical disease on the emotions, are often spoken of as "psychosomatic medicine." This term often means thinking of a human being as consisting of two separate parts, a mind and a body. The idea is then that a sick mind may affect a healthy body, and a sick body may affect a healthy mind.

If we think of the whole human being as a single energy system, we can understand that anything which affects the body will always affect the emotions as well, and anything which affects the emotions will always affect the body. In other words, all diseases are "psychosomatic." There is no such thing as a disease of the body which does *not* affect the mind. Even such a simple thing as an ingrown toenail is related to the tensions of the Id, as may be seen in some of the dreams of people with this condition. The same applies to a cold in the head. The simplest operation, such as squeezing a blackhead, also has its effect on the Id tensions and may influence the subject's dreams, while the emotional effects of having a tooth pulled may be quite consciously perceived. Similarly, there is no emotional disturbance which does not affect the body, and all mental illnesses are accompanied by some physical effects.

Thus there are not three kinds of medicine, as the word "psychosomatic" might lead one to think. It is not a question of mental medicine, in which only the psyche is involved; or somatic medicine, in which only the body is involved; and "psychosomatic" medicine, in which "sometimes" both are involved. There is only one kind of medicine, and it is *all* psychosomatic. Medicine is just medicine. It is not either psychosomatic or non-psychosomatic. It is true that some doctors are more interested in the mental aspects of disease, and some in the physical aspects, but every disease is both "mental and physical." The diseases don't care whether the doctor knows this or not, they go ahead just the same. The real problem of the doctor is whether a certain patient who is experiencing a certain illness in a certain way at a certain time will be more easily cured by psychiatric methods or physical methods, or by a combination of both.

The harmfulness of the word "psychosomatic" lies in the fact that it may mislead some people into thinking that in certain cases one doesn't have to treat the mind aspect of the human energy system, but only the body aspect, as though to say: "Let some doctors go ahead and practice psychosomatic medicine, but let some stick to non-psychosomatic medicine." There is no non-psychosomatic medicine.

# 4

# What is neurotic behavior?

We have seen how mortido tensions which have not been able to find relief through their natural objects may accomplish their damaging aim by turning inward upon the individual himself and causing physical pain or disease. Libido tensions also seem to be naturally intended for outward expression, and if they are turned back upon the individual, they too may cause unhappiness. In addition to their physical effects, long unsatisfied Id tensions may cause mental difficulties, such as insomnia, inability to concentrate, restlessness, irritability, sadness, sensitivity to noises, nightmares, unsociability, and a feeling of being talked about. Besides such symptoms of chronic anxiety from which anyone may suffer at times, there are particular individuals who have special kinds of symptoms, such as the hysterics, who suffer from paralysis, blindness, inability to talk, and a host of other afflictions which imitate physical diseases; and the compulsives, who complain of continual doubts, inability to make decisions, strange fears, persistent thoughts, and inability to keep from doing certain things over and over, such as counting, washing their hands, stealing, and retracing their steps.

All these abnormal ways which the human mind has of partially relieving Id tensions when they overflow have certain things in common.

1. They are all inappropriate; that is, none of them uses energy in such a way as to give final relief to the tension. The energy is used for some purpose which does not satisfy the Id instincts in the way they want to be satisfied, and which in the end may result in harm or unhappiness to the individual.

2. They all waste energy. Instead of the energy being put under the control of the Ego, it is spent to no good purpose in spite of all the Ego's efforts to prevent this. The Ego, guided by the Reality Principle, normally uses energy to change the individual's surroundings in such a way as to make possible the satisfaction of libido and mortido. In these abnormal conditions, from stomach ulcer to compulsions, the Ego has lost control of part of the mental energy.

3. They all result from too long unsatisfied Id tensions, "the unfinished business of childhood."

4. They are all disguised expressions of Id wishes, so well disguised that in all the history of human thought, it was not until sixty years ago that they were first clearly recognized for what they were.

5. They all employ over and over again the same useless or damaging methods for this disguised expression. This is called the "repetition compulsion." The individual seems to be compelled to use the same patterns of reaction again and again when the Ego loses control.

6. They usually result from inwardly directed Id energy which really requires an outside object for complete satisfaction; in any case, there is always object displacement, whether the false object be the individual himself or merely something closely related to the real object.

Any *behavior* which has these earmarks is called neurotic. A neurosis, or psychoneurosis, is an *illness* due to an attempt to satisfy Id tensions which is inappropriate, wastes energy, results from unfinished business of childhood, expresses the wish tensions in disguised instead of direct form, uses the same pattern of reaction over and over, and employs object displacement. A little later we shall discuss at greater length the difference between neurotic *behavior*, which is simply a method all members of the human race use for getting rid of their excess wish energy in disguised form, and an actual *neurosis*, which is a *sickness* characterized by *too much* neurotic behavior.

Normal behavior uses energy efficiently in a way which is appropriate to the situation of the moment to satisfy easily recognized Id tensions by effective behavior toward the proper objects in the surrounding environment. Planning for future financial security, family life, or the conquest of nature are examples of this. Neurotic behavior uses energy inappropriately and wastefully to satisfy old disguised Id tensions—which should long have been outgrown—by means of old patterns of behavior directed toward substitutes for the real object or toward the individual himself. Examples of this are gambling, overconcern about bowels, diet, and appearances, sexual promiscuity and a compulsion to "conquer" members of the opposite sex, a hunger to collect possessions and objects which have no practical value, smoking, and drinking. From these examples it will be seen that in a mild form much neurotic behavior is harmless, socially acceptable, and "normal"; only when it becomes damaging to the individual and those around him is it called "a neurosis."

We have to consider with special care those cases where the neurotic use of energy involves one of the individual's body organs as a false object. If the patient has complaints which seem to come from his stomach, heart, thyroid, or one of his other organs, but nothing can be found wrong with that organ by physical examination, X-rays, or laboratory tests, such complaints are called "functional" because they are due to the way the organ functions rather than to any change in its structure which can be demonstrated. If there is evidence from physical, X-ray, or laboratory examination that the organ has been changed in appearance by physical, chemical, or bacterial action, such changes are called "structural," and the complaints "organic."

A good many people use "functional" to mean the same thing as "neurotic," and "structural" to mean "not neurotic." This is not strictly correct because there are many functional changes which are normal. Any emotion, such as sexual desire or anger, will cause functional changes throughout the body in preparation for the gratification of Id tensions. In such cases, the reactions do not have the characteristics of neurotic behavior described above; they are appropriate and efficient preparations for the gratification of immediate, undisguised Id tensions in accordance with what the Reality Principle calls for in different situations with the proper object. "Functional," therefore, does *not* mean neurotic; nor does "structural" mean "not neurotic," since, as we have seen, neurotic reactions often lead to structural changes in various organs such as the skin or stomach.

## 5
## What is a neurotic symptom?

The fact that a certain amount of energy finds expression in a neurotic manner does not by itself make a neurosis. People who suffer from functional disorders such as headaches, stomach upsets, or constipation are not necessarily "neurotics" if, aside from the actual pain or inconvenience caused by the symptom at the time it occurs, they feel well and are able to carry on their everyday lives efficiently. Certain types of migraine and hay fever are particularly good examples of this. These conditions may result from piled up Id tensions, and during the attack the individual may be uncomfortable, but between the attacks he may feel perfectly well; even during an attack he may carry on with his affairs, though not as efficiently as usual.

It is only when the battle between the Id instincts and the other forces of the mind takes up so much time and energy that the individual feels poorly for long periods, or is unable to make full progress in his personality development because of this struggle, that we have a true neurosis. This is the distinction between neurotic behavior and an actual neurosis. As we have mentioned, smoking is neurotic behavior according to our standards, but this does not mean that everyone who smokes suffers from a neurosis. Smoking may be beneficial from the point of view of mental efficiency, since it drains off small amounts of tension which might otherwise hamper the individual. A true neurosis is accompanied by a lessening of efficiency and a slowing up or cessation of emotional growth.

Neurotic symptoms are complicated to unravel because they result from not one, but four tensions striving for relief, and the symptom tries to take care of all of them at the same time: inwardly and outwardly directed libido, and inwardly and outwardly directed mortido. This means that each symptom must meet the following specifications: it must in some way gratify the individual's self-love, as by attracting other people's attention; it must give him some external libido satisfaction in disguised or symbolic form, as by making him dependent on people; it must punish the patient, as by causing physical pain; and it must harm others, even if only in a disguised or symbolic way, as by making them tiptoe around the house.

The unconscious, being a natural system of forces, automatically takes care of all these tensions at once without having to do any figuring; just as a cloud floats through the sky without thinking, its course being determined by a number of factors: wind speed and direction; rotation of the earth; altitude; temperature; density of the cloud; etc. If we stop to think about all these factors, and use them to try to figure out where the cloud is going or where it came from, it looks complicated, but it isn't complicated to the cloud; it just goes where the resultant of the acting forces carries it. Similarly, the forces in the human mind act together to produce a symptom and that symptom is the automatic outcome of all circumstances acting at any given moment; if the circumstances change, so may the symptom. If we try to figure out the forces behind a symptom we have the same trouble as in the case of the cloud, but because something is complicated to explain does not mean that it has trouble happening. It *has to* happen.

There is one more specification which the symptom must meet: it must disguise the Id wishes sufficiently so that the Ego does not recognize their true nature. If the Ego should recognize their true nature from the symptom, the symptom may disappear because it no longer meets this requirement; that is one way in which analysis of a symptom may cure it. If the treatment does not find another way of handling the tensions behind the symptom, however, they may simply find another and better disguise, and a new symptom arises.

We may state these requirements of a symptom in another way

by saying that a symptom is a defense against certain urges becoming conscious, while at the same time obtaining some gratification through the symptom. Thus, a symptom is (a) a defense (b) a symbolic or indirect expression of an Id wish. Anything which has to do with the mental image concerned in gratifying the wish can serve as a symbol of that gratification. For example, we have already indicated that the infant's image of comfort has at least three clear elements: love, warmth, and milk. If a symptom should arise from a wish relating to this early stage of life, it might take the form of an unquenchable thirst for milk. This would symbolize the individual's difficulties in coping with adult life, and his wish to return to the early stage of comfort and freedom from responsibility of the nursing infant.

Lavinia Eris was Ludwig Farbanti's secretary when he owned the Olympia Cannery. Lavinia's three sisters were all married by the time she was thirty, but she stayed on at home and took care of her mother. Every time Lavinia got serious about one of her boy friends, her mother would have a "heart attack," and then Lavinia would have to give up any idea of marriage so that she could stay home and take care of her ailing parent. When Lavinia was forty, Midas King bought the cannery. She stayed on at her old job, but she had a hard time at first. Mr. Farbanti was quiet and never showed that he was excited, but Mr. King was irritable and was always shouting at Lavinia, who was very sensitive.

About this time Lavinia's mother had another heart attack and took to her bed for good, so that Lavinia had to stop going out with Mr. McTavish, who owned the drygoods store and whom she had hoped to marry. Lavinia began to feel a nervous strain, and suddenly acquired a great desire for milk. She drank several quarts of it every day, and began to put on weight. The doctors could find nothing wrong with her physically, nor did injections of calcium and vitamins have any effect. After a few months, the desire gradually diminished. It was not until she had a nervous breakdown seven years later that she went to Dr. Treece and found out the meaning of this symptom.

Her neurotic craving for milk satisfied her tensions in the following symbolic and indirect ways:

Inwardly directed libido: Up to that time it was always her

mother who got all the attention, with her heart attacks. Now that Lavinia was "sick," she got some attention too.

Outwardly directed libido: In a symbolic way, it brought her close to the comfort of infancy and her early loving relationship with her mother.

Inwardly directed mortido: By getting fat and less attractive she punished herself.

Outwardly directed mortido: Since she was sick, she neglected her mother for a while; and not entirely unconsciously, she had the satisfaction of blaming her mother by taking the attitude: "See, it is you who have made me sick and unattractive to men with your demands!" (Which was true enough actually, since her mother literally took great pains to keep Lavinia from getting married, so she would not lose a good provider and nurse.)

At the same time, her symptom successfully concealed most of these tensions from her conscious mind. Nearly all of them would have horrified her if they had become fully conscious, because of her pride, hope, and charity. The symptom was a defense against the strength of these desires.* At that time the defense was successful. After the tensions had been partially relieved through the mechanisms described above and she had succeeded in making a readjustment to her situation, the extra defense was no longer necessary and her craving gradually diminished. Later, under the new added stress of her approaching fifties, she was unable to defend herself successfully by means of neurotic symptoms and broke down completely into a psychosis, when the Id took over control of the personality from the Ego. (In the next chapter, we shall learn what a psychosis is.)

It is easy to see why this illness was called a neurosis rather than merely "neurotic behavior," since while she was suffering from this symptom, Lavinia's efficiency was lowered and her emotional development went backward instead of forward.

* The more complicated tensions manifested by her craving we need not go into here.

## 6

# The different kinds of neuroses

We are already familiar with some of the results of the neurotic use of energy and the damage it can do. We saw how Nana Curtsan's neurotic drive for seeking affection eventually led her to become a prostitute. Nana suffered from a "character neurosis," that is, a neurosis which did not cause any obvious symptoms, but weakened her character so that she was unable to get along in the ordinary way of life. Midas King's inwardly directed Id instincts affected his circulatory system, so that his blood pressure went up and down from time to time, until at length it remained constantly at an abnormally high level. Edgar Metis's inwardly directed tensions laid the foundation for an ulcer of the stomach. Ambrose Paterson's neurosis also affected certain special organs, including his skin, back, and prostate gland.

While these are good examples of the neurotic use of energy, the types of neuroses most commonly spoken of by psychiatrists are somewhat different and fall into several groups the best known of which are compulsion neurosis, conversion hysteria, anxiety neurosis, hypochondriasis, and neurasthenia. Let us study examples of some of these, starting with compulsion neurosis.

Ann "Nan" Kayo, the only daughter of Enoch Kayo, the chief of police of Olympia, had a hard time going through college, especially after she broke her engagement with Hector Meads. Her asthma interfered with her studies, but worse than that was her feeling that she never did anything right. Even when she went for a walk, she was beset by doubts. She had to step on all the cracks in the pavement wherever she went, and often upon getting home, she would begin to wonder if she hadn't missed one somewhere. On several occasions she had even got out of bed late at night, after lying awake worrying for an hour or two, to go back over her route and do the whole walk again to make sure she didn't miss a crack.

At times when she went out she felt as though there were a rope tied to her which she paid out as she went along, and if she didn't return the same way it seemed as though this "rope" had gotten tangled. Even if she did return the same way, she would sometimes doubt her own memory of the journey, especially if she was feeling bad for some other reason, and would lie awake wondering if she should do it over in order to make quite sure that the imaginary rope was untangled.

The problem of doorknobs also took up a lot of her time. She could only permit herself to turn doorknobs to the north or west. If a room faced in the wrong direction, she would not go in unless the door were open. This phobia changed after she fell in love with Josiah Tally. Then she had a compulsion to turn all the doorknobs she could find. She was obsessed with the idea that every time she turned one, she was transmitting "love power" toward Josiah, and making their relationship more secure.

This brought on a new difficulty, however, since now, every time she touched a doorknob, she felt that she was getting her hands full of germs, and that the only remedy was to wash and dry them four times. Furthermore, she often doubted her memory of her counting after this cleansing process was finished, and then she would have to do it all over again. If she didn't, her doubts would bother her for hours until they became unbearable. She was passionately jealous of Josiah, and was obsessed by the idea that if she omitted to do things the way she "had to," he would go out with some other girl. She often lay in bed imagining that he was making love to some other woman, fascinated by torturing visions she could not get out of her mind.

If everything was going well, she got along better. But the minute things went wrong, or if she had to worry about some change in her routine, even such a small thing as going home for the weekend, her doubts would become worse and then also her asthma was likely to come on. At such times she was unable to make up her mind about anything, and it would take her hours to get dressed for the twenty mile drive to Olympia.

It should not be supposed that Ann was unintelligent. She realized only too painfully how unreasonable her phobias, obsessions, and compulsions were. Her Ego exerted every ounce of will power to conquer them, but to no avail. It was a problem to eat, sleep, and concentrate on her studies, and only by letting her compulsions have their way was she able to accomplish these things.

Such compulsion neuroses are very difficult to cure, but after a few weeks of treatment Dr. Treece made her life easier to a certain extent so that her studies improved. She got so much confidence in him that she no longer had to retrace her steps after going somewhere. She felt that if she had come home the wrong way, or neglected to step on a crack, somehow the doctor would take care of it for her. As she told him:

"I feel as though you will fix it up personally with whomever or whatever it is that threatens to punish me if I don't make sure of carrying out the compulsions to the letter, and then I am able to go to sleep without worrying about it any more."

At the bottom of Ann's troubles, including her asthma, were a terrible hostility to her mother and some mixed feelings toward her father, whom she loved dearly but also despised for his weakness of character. In spite of his aggressive occupation of police chief, at home he was the weakling and leaned heavily on Ann's mother, letting her decide even things relating to his office. Ann's mortido tensions, together with the three "absolute ideas" we talked about in a previous section, were the important factors in her illness, and when these things were made conscious and she learned how to handle them properly, she improved. Her belief in the "omnipotence of thought" showed plainly in her feeling that through doorknobs she could influence her lover and strengthen their love, while her belief in the "irresistibility of her charm" expressed itself in a twisted way through an unconscious wish that all the other women in the world would die so that she could have all the men. In the main, her symptoms were connected with powerful death wishes.

Apparently people have the same difficulty nowadays in handling their death wishes that their ancestors of the Victorian era had in handling their sexual wishes. Since it is not considered proper to admit to oneself that such wishes exist, they are repressed into the unconscious, whence they continually strive for release and gratification, sometimes causing symptoms which are quite out of the control of the Ego, since the Ego has banished the tensions which give rise to them. We may compare such death wishes to the death-dealing Nihilists whom the Czar of Russia banished from his Empire. Once they left the country they were out of his control and were able to carry on their work unhampered, though they could only express themselves indirectly. Since the unconscious is outside the boundaries of the conscious Ego, wishes which have been banished to the lower regions are out of the Ego's control, and if they make trouble there is little the Ego can do about it.

Compulsions such as hand washing, phobias such as fear of germs, and obsessions such as self-torturing jealousy are very commonly found together.

Conversion hysteria is a different type of neurosis, and usually has its most dramatic effects on some part of the body rather than on the emotions.

Horace Volk hated his father, but he never said anything about it to anybody. His father was a hell-fire Baptist minister who raised Horace and his three older sisters very strictly. Their mother died while they were all still small children, and their father from then on did not spare the rod.

Horace was eighteen when his oldest sister Mary became pregnant. When she came to her father for help, he ordered her never to come into his house again. When Horace came home from work that night and heard what had happened he started to protest, but one look at his father's fiery eyes, and he was struck dumb. He remained unable to speak above a whisper for about six weeks, and then his voice returned.

When his second sister ran away from home two years later, Horace again lost his voice. After a few weeks, it came back as it had the first time.

When his third sister found out she was pregnant, she took the precaution of getting married before she told her father about it. She and her brand-new husband came to the house on the evening of their marriage and announced what had happened. Reverend Volk listened to their story, and then raised his hand slowly and pointed to the door. He ordered them never to enter his home again. Horace tried to say something, but again his voice had gone.

This time it did not get better. After about two months, Horace went to the family doctor, who tried to cure him by injecting sodium amytal. While he was under the influence of this drug, Horace was able to talk, but as soon as its effects wore off, his voice sank to a hoarse whisper again. After three trials of this treatment over a period of a month, the doctor sent Horace to see Dr. Treece.

Dr. Treece was able to "cure" him without using drugs or hypnotism. Horace had been in quite good spirits while his voice was lost, but after it returned he became depressed and was unable to sleep. When the doctor removed his symptom of dumbness, which was the only way his repressed Id tensions had of expressing themselves, they had to find a new way, which was accomplished partly by forming an overly emotional attachment for the doctor through the mechanism we described in the section on "images," and partly by making Horace depressed and keeping him awake. Dr. Treece had expected both these new symptoms and proceeded with the second part of the treatment which consisted in dealing with the underlying Id tensions which caused all the different symptoms. During this period, not only Horace's inner difficulties were studied but also the origin and nature of his childish worship of the doctor. Eventually, after a year of treatment, Horace grew up enough emotionally to get married himself and make a success of it.

In this case we see that the mortido tensions which were connected with the illness were conscious, while the libido tensions were unconscious. Horace was perfectly aware that it was his hatred of his father, suddenly fanned into new life, which had caused him to be struck dumb. What he did not realize was that each time he had lost his voice he had not only had new reason to hate his father, but had also lost one of his beloved sisters; that is, he had lost a libido object, leaving a large amount of libido with no outside object for release. This libido had turned inward, and for certain reasons which came out later, had affected his ability to speak (rather than his stomach, or his arm or leg muscles).

Such sudden cripplings of special parts of the body are characteristic of hysteria. Hysterics suffer from inability to use the arms, legs, or vocal cords; they may suffer from wry neck or spasms of the body muscles which keep them bent over; they may lose one of their senses, such as smell, taste, sight, or hearing, or they may lose the ability to feel in one part of the body such as an arm or a leg. In fact, almost any medical condition can be imitated by hysteria. While it can be imitated, however, it is not duplicated, so that the doctor can nearly always tell that the symptom is functional. As we have previously remarked, hysteria is accompanied by a change in the individual's image of his own body, and since he acts and feels in accordance with his images instead of in accordance with what his body is really capable of, the symptoms correspond to the altered body-image rather than to any change in the body itself. The task of the psychiatrist, then, is to change the altered body-image back to normal, rather than to change the body. The change in body-image which causes the illness is due to a suddenly awakened rush of unconscious libido or mortido which cannot for various reasons find outside relief. It therefore turns inward and distorts the body-image in the manner described. Because such a neurosis depends on the conversion of mental energy into a bodily symptom, it is called conversion hysteria. There is always a special reason why one part of the body is affected rather than another. Horace, for example, remembered since early boyhood a desire to shout his defiance and tell his father he wanted to kill him. His dumbness was a perfect mask for this frustrated mortido tension, which is why he "chose" this symptom rather than any other.

Because individuals who are overly dramatic in their behavior and overly emotional in their responses are especially apt at some time or other to suffer from hysterical conversion symptoms, such people are commonly called "hysterical."

Let us now turn our attention to anxiety neurosis. Septimus Seifuss ran a bookstore and artists' supply shop on Thalia Lane. His son Simon, or Si, was the oldest of his five children, the other four being girls. Simon worked in the postoffice until the war began, and then he enlisted in the army. Simon had always helped his sisters with their lessons and done other things for them that a good big brother should do, so he was used to looking after people. This soon became apparent to his captain, who gradually promoted him until he was a sergeant in charge of a platoon.

When his outfit went into combat on a little island in the Pacific, things happened in a hurry, and Simon didn't have as much time as he would have liked to see that each of his men dug his foxhole in the proper place and in the proper way. A big shell landed on their position and killed ten soldiers. It also knocked Simon out, but luckily he was only on the edge of the blast. When he came to he was in the hospital, and somehow he heard about the ten men who had been killed.

Simon wasn't wounded, and he might have been discharged from the hospital almost immediately if he hadn't become a "nervous wreck." The slightest sound would make him jump and set his heart racing. He couldn't eat, he had hot and cold sweats, and he slept poorly. Everything got worse at night. He had nightmares about battle—almost the same nightmare every time. He would go through all the events of the attack until he could hear the fatal shell coming over. Then he would wake up screaming, shaking, in a cold sweat, and with his heart pounding.

Simon had to be moved back to the United States where he spent some months in a general hospital before he was fit for duty again. For a long time he had the same dream every night, and just as the shell came over he would wake up screaming. This not only frightened him but worried him because he woke up some of the other men in the ward every time. Under proper treatment, however, he recovered from this part of his illness and as treatment continued he calmed down more and more.

With the psychiatrist's help, Simon began to understand the feelings at the bottom of his neurosis. He was a conscientious man and as so many conscientious people do, he blamed himself for things that weren't his fault. It soon appeared that he felt that if he had been more careful to watch where his men dug their foxholes, they wouldn't have been killed. He had a strong feeling of guilt about this which he was unaware of until it was brought out during the treatment. Of course, this feeling was unreasonable, for if the men had dug their foxholes elsewhere the shell might have landed elsewhere too, and actually there was nothing he could have done about it.

Simon was the victim not only of his feeling of "guilt," but also of a blocked fear tension. He had been so busy taking care of other people that he had had no time to prepare himself for the shock which followed. He was knocked out so quickly by the shell that he hadn't had time to feel the fear which it aroused when he knew it was coming. In other words, he didn't have time to "feel through" and "act out" his natural fear. With the doctor's help, under hypnosis, he was able to go through with this "acting out" and relieve the intense, unconscious, pent-up fear tension. He and the doctor crawled on their hands and knees under the table, pretending it was a foxhole. When Simon "saw" the shell coming over, he screamed again and again:

"Oh, God! *Get* in your foxholes! Oh! God! Hit the dirt, for *Jesus*' sake. Oh, God! *Get* in your foxholes!"

This was the way he would have relieved his fear tension at the time if he hadn't been knocked out before he could do it. After a few sessions of this, ending with Simon putting his face in his hands and weeping as he "saw" the men being killed, his dreams stopped.

Why did Simon have this dream? It was apparently an attempt to "act out" his fear in his sleep. If he had been able to carry the dream through to completion naturally, as he did under hypnosis, it might have stopped by itself. One reason why he couldn't do this was that he blamed himself so much for his "carelessness" (as he thought of it) that he felt he should have been killed by the shell instead of his men. To have carried his nightmare to completion might have meant being killed in his dream. For some reason which we do not understand, inwardly directed mortido is rarely if ever allowed to express itself completely in dreams. The terrified dreamer who falls off a cliff always wakes up before he hits the ground; the panic-stricken girl who cannot move while the giant with the big knife rushes toward her always wakes up before she is caught; or if she is caught, it turns out that he is not going to kill her after all. This is in contrast to dreams of outwardly directed mortido or libido, which often go on to completion in murder or orgasm. Since Simon couldn't finish himself off in his dream, that was one reason he had to stop dreaming at the critical moment. With the doctor's assistance, however, the business he could not finish in his natural dreams was completed; the dammed-up energy was released, and he became a free man again.

The psychiatrist did not stop at this point. On further study he and Simon both became aware that the whole situation had been a repetition of some unfinished emotions of childhood, regarding some similar supposed "carelessness" while he was taking care of his young sisters, when one of them had been slightly burned during the big fire in Olympia many years before. By the time the treatment was finished, this had also been worked out, and Simon was relieved of this additional tension which had been in his unconscious mind for years, and which even before he went into the army had caused some nightmares and palpitation.

Milder forms of this neurosis occur even in people who lead an apparently quiet life and have suffered from no known emotional shocks, the symptoms consisting of jumpiness, restlessness, excessive sweating, fast heart, insomnia, nightmares, and a haggard feeling and facial expression. These symptoms resemble those of hyperthyroidism so closely that some doctors feel that in any case where there is any possible doubt whether the thyroid gland is actually diseased or not, the gland should not be removed until a psychiatrist is consulted. A further resemblance is the fact that an emotional shock often marks the beginning of thyroid disease, as in the case of Polly Reed, whose father ran a music store next door to the Seifuss Book Store. When she was twenty-six, her father died, and immediately afterward her thyroid gland began to enlarge and she acquired many of the symptoms described above. These symptoms disappeared after the diseased gland was removed. Thus it is sometimes very difficult to distinguish between a disease of the thyroid gland and an anxiety neurosis, since the two may resemble each other in many respects.

While it is possible to say in a general way that there are different types of neuroses, such as those we have been discussing, actually there are as many neuroses as there are patients, so that it is really artificial to speak of compulsion neurosis, hysteria, anxiety neurosis, etc. The dreams of Simon Seifuss were obsessive in a way like Ann's thoughts, while Horace's hysteria turned into a mild anxiety neurosis after his conversion symptom was taken away from him. To be accurate, one should really speak of Simon's neurosis, Ann's neurosis, and Horace's neurosis, instead of calling them by the names of different diseases. For convenience, however, since most patients seem to favor a certain type of symptom over a long period, classifications are made so that psychiatrists will understand each other when they say that a patient's symptoms "fell mostly into the compulsive group," or "mostly into the hysterical group," or "mostly into the anxiety group." But psychiatrists always remember in dealing with a patient that they are not dealing with an example of a disease, but with a certain individual who has gone through certain experiences which caused certain tensions, resulting in certain measures to get partial relief of the tensions; and that each individual has his own special way, which may change from time to time, of handling his tensions.

Hypochondriasis and neurasthenia are two other classifications which should be mentioned. Anyone who complains unduly about his health is commonly called a hypochondriac, but a true hypochondriac is relatively rare. A true hypochondriac not only complains about his health, but uses his complaints in a shrewd way to control his environment. These patients suffer from an excess of inwardly directed or narcissistic libido. They use their energy to "love themselves." They continually observe the reactions of their bodies and take alarm at the slightest irregularity, much in the manner of Mr. Krone or Mrs. Eris. They call a doctor or visit their favorite quack on the smallest pretext. Their rooms are full of strange medicines and weird contraptions for giving themselves treatment; many a quack makes his whole living from feeding the fears of these people and flattering their self-love. Their households are run entirely for their own comfort no matter what sacrifice this means for the other members of the family, and they will cause an upheaval for the most trivial reasons. Hypochondriacs are very difficult to treat, since they are so much taken with themselves that they bridle at any suggestion that they are neurotic, and if anyone dares to suggest that they go to a psychiatrist they become infuriated. It will be seen, however, that their behavior fulfills the requirements of a neurosis. Even if they *appear* to co-operate, they are almost incurable. It would have been easier to cure Romeo of loving Juliet than to cure a hypochondriac of loving himself.

Neurasthenia is an old term which is often still used to describe people who are tired, depressed, lackadaisical, slightly irritable, and who cannot concentrate on anything and like to lie around without much responsibility. A good many psychiatrists nowadays prefer to classify such cases with either the anxiety neuroses or the neurotic depressions.

In this section we have discussed different types of neuroses, but it should always be remembered that each neurotic has to be treated as a separate individual and not as an example of some special form of disease. Symptoms change from time to time, and each individual experiences his symptoms in an individual way.

# 7

## What causes neuroses?

A neurosis depends, first of all, on the strength of the Id impulses and their opportunities for expression either directly or by healthy methods of displacement. A person with uncommonly strong Id drives may simply not be able to handle them all by the methods available and the pent-up tensions will then interfere with normal functioning. Some people, on the other hand, cannot handle even normal or weak drives without getting into trouble, because of a strong Superego, a weak Ego and storage capacity, or unfavorable outside circumstances.

If a person has trouble in handling his piled-up tensions, a change in any of the factors mentioned above may bring on a neurosis. He may get along all right until circumstances either increase his Id tensions (increased love or resentment), weaken his storage capacity (physical disease), increase the severity of his Superego (guilt feelings), or deprive him of ways for healthy expression (poverty), and then a breakdown results.

The Superego is very important in determining how much tension the individual allows himself to relieve and how much he must store up. If it is easygoing, it will permit free relief and little storage will be required; if it is strict it will allow little relief and much tension will pile up, putting a strain on the individual's storage capacity. This does not mean that the way to avoid neurosis is to give free expression to one's impulses. In the first place, such behavior may lead to so many complications with outside energy systems, such as nature and other people, that further relief will become impossible and in the end more tensions will pile up than ever before. For example, a man who scolds his wife whenever he feels like it may lose her, and then he will be left without anybody who will permit herself to be used as an object for either mortido or libido, and he will suffer accordingly.

In the second place, it is wiser to exercise restraint than to risk offending the Superego, since the latter is a jealous master whose punishments are difficult to avoid. For example, a woman may decide that her Superego will permit her to have an abortion without punishing her for it afterward. At the time, because of her inability to judge her true feelings properly in her highly emotional state of mind, it may seem all right to go ahead; but if she has misjudged herself, as is often the case, she may begin to feel guilty many years afterward, and perhaps break down when she is forty or fifty under the long-continued reproaches of her Superego.

Another important factor in neurosis is the amount of unfinished business left over from childhood. The greater the amount, the more likely a neurosis is to occur in a given situation, and the more severe it is likely to be. Thus among three patients exposed to the rigors of army life together—whose fathers had died when the patients were two, four, and eight years old, respectively—the first man had the most severe breakdown, the second had a less severe one, and the third had the mildest. The first man had the most unfinished "father business," the second man had less, and the third man had least of all. The severity of their neuroses corresponded to the degree of their emotional development in relation to older men, this relationship being an important factor in army life where the officer takes the place the father held in infancy. A man with few emotional hangovers from childhood can stand much more strain in later life without breaking down than a man with many unsolved infantile problems.

It is very common among neurotics to say: "My mother and father were nervous, so I am nervous. I inherited it."

This is not true. Neurosis is not inherited; but its foundations may be laid in early infancy because of the neurotic behavior of the parents. Neurosis depends upon how the individual uses his energy. Some of his *tendencies* in this direction may depend upon his inherited constitution, as we saw in the first chapter, but his actual development is influenced mostly by what he learns from watching his parents. As an infant, whatever his parents do seems like "the natural thing" to him, since he has few chances to compare their behavior to other people's. We have already described how he imitates them by being agreeable and affectionate or hateful and selfish. If he sees that they meet difficulties by flying off the handle instead of coping with reality according to the Reality Principle, he will imitate this behavior. If they use their energy in a neurotic way, he will have a tendency to do likewise, since whatever his parents do seems "right" to an infant. Thus, if his parents are neurotic, he may grow up to be neurotic also, but not because he inherits neurosis, any more than they did. They also learned it from their parents.

It is true that the strength of the Id drives, the ability of the mind to go through the processes required to form a stable Superego, and the storage capacity of the mind may be inherited, but what the individual does with his natural endowments depends upon his early training. It is a fact that some children by nature find it more difficult than others to develop a normal personality, which is an added burden for their parents, who in such cases have to be particularly careful to set a good example of the patient and reasonable use of energy. If the parents fail, it is then up to the psychiatrist to go through the tedious process of correcting the neurotic behavior patterns of twenty or thirty years' standing, with due regard to whatever assets and liabilities the individual came into the world with.

## Footnotes for Philosophers, Chapter Five

### 1. & 2. *Emotions and Disease*

In this exposition of how noxious emotions, as well as noxious physical, chemical, and bacteriological agents, play a part in those readjustments of the human organism which are called disease, precision and detail have been sacrificed somewhat for the sake of clarity, particularly in regard to the workings of the sympathetic and parasympathetic nervous systems. The explanations for backache, arthritis, and "stomach ulcer" are offered more as paradigms than as scientifically proven theories, although there is literature to support them. The observations on the spinal fluid under emotional stress are not difficult to verify. The fact that microscopic particles collect in areas of vasodilatation has been well demonstrated by H. Burrows (1932). For an amazing exposition of the so-called "psychosomatic" viewpoint more than a hundred years before the advent of modern psychiatry, the contemporary biographies of Dr. John Hunter are unique.

The following easily obtainable references are suggested for those who wish further information on the subjects covered in these sections:

*Emotions and Bodily Changes,* by H. Flanders Dunbar. Columbia University Press: New York, 1938, 2nd ed.

*Human Constitution in Clinical Medicine,* by George Draper et al. Harper & Brothers: New York, 1944.

"Physiological Effects of Emotional Tension," in *Personality and the Behavior Disorders,* op. cit., Chapter 8, by Leon J. Saul.

3. *Psychosomatic Medicine*

The problem of the psychosomatic approach in relation to the general philosophy of "etiology" is discussed by Halliday:

"Principles of Aetiology," by James L. Halliday, in *The British Journal of Medical Psychology,* Vol. XIX, 1943, pp. 367-380.

Among those who question the term, Iago Galdston of the New York Academy of Medicine is an articulate example.

"Biodynamic Medicine versus Psychosomatic Medicine," by Iago Galdston, in *The Bulletin of the Menninger Clinic,* Vol. VIII, 1944, pp. 116-121.

4. *Neurotic Behavior*

See: *The Autonomic Functions and the Personality,* by Edward J. Kempf. Nervous & Mental Disease Publishing Company: New York, 1918. Monograph No. 28.

5. *Neurotic Symptoms*

For further reading on this subject see: *General Introduction to Psychoanalysis,* by Sigmund Freud, op. cit. Especially Chapters 17, 18, 22, and 23.

6. *Nosology*

One of the most readable and easily understood formal descriptions of the different kinds of neuroses can be found in the textbook of W. A. White.

*Outlines of Psychiatry*, by William A. White. Nervous & Mental Disease Publishing Company: New York, 1935, 14th ed. Monograph No. 1.

While the case of Si Seifuss is descriptively an example of anxiety neurosis, some clinicians might prefer to call it technically a "traumatic neurosis." For more cases similar to his and their fuller explanation, the reader may consult Grinker and Spiegel's study of war neuroses:

*Men Under Stress*, by Roy R. Grinker & John P. Spiegel. Blakiston: Philadelphia, 1945.

7. *The Causes of Neurosis*

I have selected here those items and that point of view, especially about inheritance, which seem most useful and enlightening to the layman. For a better understanding of modern ideas about neurosis, the reader should consult Fenichel.

*The Psychoanalytic Theory of Neurosis*, by Otto Fenichel. W. W. Norton & Company: New York, 1945.

# CHAPTER SIX

# PSYCHOSES

---

## I

## What is insanity?

IN MOST PEOPLE the Ego is able to keep the Id reasonably well controlled, so that mental energy can be applied to useful purposes and emotional growth proceeds normally. In some individuals, if the Ego is weak or the Id is strong, energy is wasted because the Id instincts manage to obtain partial gratification in a disguised form, in ways which do not promote welfare or emotional development. Such defenses against the unconscious becoming conscious are called neurotic behavior; and if they seriously hamper the individual's efficiency, they constitute a neurosis. A few rare and unfortunate individuals have such weak Egos that the Id is able to break down the Ego's barriers completely. The unconscious Id images then become conscious and lead to strange forms of behavior which are called psychoses.

In order to make clearer the actual effects of such a complete breakdown of the defenses, let us examine a case of one of the commonest forms of psychosis, namely, schizophrenia, in which the illness went through four different stages of development before the healing process began.

There was a young fellow in Olympia living down on the mud flats by the river who should have been a shepherd. Alone with his sheep, he could have lain on his back in the grass, arms outstretched, dreaming his dreams as he gazed at the cerulean skies. He was full of heavenly aspirations. With his sheep for subjects and audience, he could have played at being a king and philosopher. Unfortunately, Cary Fayton worked in the Meat Department of

Dimitri's Grocery, where he had to take care of dead sheep instead of living ones. When he lay on his back, all he could see was the cracked ceiling of his room in a cold-water flat near the Olympia Cannery.

Cary spent a good deal of time lying in his room. He was never able to get along with other young people, and girls, whom he wanted to be with badly, found him too strange and silent. Most of his life was wrapped up in his daydreams, and he couldn't bring himself to talk about those; and since he didn't have much else to talk about, conversation was difficult.

One time he did tell a girl named Georgina Savitar about his daydreams: how he would be a great man when he grew up and would save her life sometime when some man got too fresh with her. But the next day Georgina whispered to the other girls in school what she had encouraged him to tell her; after that, they always giggled when he passed by, and he felt so small that he couldn't bear to come near any of them and would cross the street to avoid meeting them. He once walked home with Minerva Seifuss, a kind and intelligent girl, who tried to tell him in a helpful way that she thought he was a nice boy but because he was so shy people and especially other girls thought he was funny, and why didn't he try to get interested in sports and things so he could be like other boys? Cary knew she was trying to be kind, but what she said only made him feel worse and more helpless. He always avoided Minerva after that, though at home he secretly wrote poetry about her.

When Cary was lying on his bed in the evening while his divorced mother was entertaining her boy friends, such as old Mr. Krone, he often thought about the various women who came to the butcher shop during the day and how some day they might get into trouble and he would come up and rescue them and then they would fall in love with him. There was one woman especially whom he liked to think about because she had very long thin legs and he was particularly fond of that kind of legs. He always watched her carefully when she came into the shop to see if she gave any sign of noticing him particularly. One day she smiled at him in a friendly way and then he decided that she must be in love with him. He figured out that she had been in love with him for a long time and that she had been afraid to tell him about it because her husband would beat her if he knew her secret thoughts about Cary.

Cary learned that the woman was Georgina Savitar's sister and the wife of Alex Paterson, the druggist. He found out where she lived and began to loiter on the corner, hoping that some time she might come out and then he could speak to her alone, which he could not do in the store. He wanted to tell her how much he loved her, and also that the butcher shop was beginning to worry him and that he wanted to leave it. He hoped that she might run away with him and leave her husband, whom Cary imagined to be treating her cruelly. One time she did pass by but when the big moment came he couldn't say what he wanted to and lowered his eyes so that he didn't even say hello to her. Finally he decided that the only way to tell her he knew about her suffering was to write her a note. He wrote the note and kept it in his pocket for weeks before he had the courage to put it in the parcel when he wrapped her meat.

When Mrs. Paterson got home that day she found the note, which read as follows:

"Dearest:
"I love you. I would like us to go away together. I know how you are suffering. I will kill the beast. I am tired of the butcher shop. When I look at the meat I feel dizzy and don't know if I am alive or dead. It all seems like a dream. I have been here before. My face is changing. They will get us both if we don't watch out. They will make your legs change. Good-by darling. I'll meet you at the usual place.

"Cary"

Mrs. Paterson didn't know what to make of this note. She and her husband talked it over. They thought of going to Cary's mother to tell her about it, but they were both timid people and she had a reputation for drinking, so they went to the police instead, or, rather, Mr. Paterson did. When he walked into the police station he was surprised to find Cary there too. Cary was asking for protection. He said people could read his thoughts and that they followed him down the street making signals about him which caused his face to change. He wanted to have someone arrested. He said it was a plot, though he didn't know who was at the bottom of it. Mr. Paterson walked out of the police station without saying anything and came back later. When the police sergeant read the note, he called Chief Kayo. They decided that it was a case for Dr. Treece, so they went down to Mrs. Fayton's house and brought Cary to the hospital.

Dr. Treece found that Cary had had some strange experiences. The Lord had appeared to him and told him that he was to be King of the World. He had given him a certain sign, a cross with a circle under it, which was to be his sign. Voices kept talking to him, telling him what to do. Sometimes when he went to do something like lifting a quarter of beef, the voices would tell him just what he should do. They would tell him to bend down, put his hands under the beef, raise his arms, put the beef on his shoulder, and so on. When he went out in the street, the voices would warn him that everybody was making faces about him and that they were out to get him.

Everything seemed like a dream. The people who were after him used mental telepathy to change his appearance. He would spend almost an hour sometimes in front of his mirror wondering just how much his face had changed in the last few hours. Everything he did seemed to have happened before. All these feelings got worse when he was around the butcher shop and sometimes they were so bad when he was actually handling meat that he got sick to his stomach. He said that his only hope was in Mary. Mary was what he called Mrs. Paterson, though her real name was Daphne. He said that they were after her too, and that he was the only one who could save her, by using his magic sign. When he was asked about his mother, he replied: "I don't have any mother."

When his mother came to visit him, she was weeping and sobbing. He didn't even say hello to her. He just smiled at her and asked: "Do you like porridge?" He didn't seem to recognize her, and paid no attention to her weeping or to her statements that she was his mother and could make him better. He looked at her as haughtily as an ancient king might have looked at a peasant, gave her a piece of paper with his magic sign written on it, and then walked away and stared at the tips of his shoes with a puzzled frown.

The next day began a period during which Cary just lay in his bed and didn't move. This lasted for more than two weeks. He didn't talk, open his eyes, or show any signs of recognizing anybody. He refused to eat, and in order to keep him from starving to death food had to be put into his stomach through a tube which the doctor slid gently down his gullet. He didn't take any care of himself at all. He didn't care what happened in his bed. If the doctor took his arm and raised it in the air, it would stay there for a long time, sometimes a few minutes, sometimes over an hour. His arm and hand could be bent into any position and they would just stay that way, as though he were a wax image that could be bent into any shape.

One day Cary came out of this state and began to speak again. He didn't complain any more about the people who followed him. Now he said they couldn't touch him. He would sit in a chair in a corner and tell how he was King of the World and the world's greatest lover. All the children in the world were fathered by him. No woman could have any more babies without his help.

He still didn't recognize his mother. No matter what she said or how she behaved, he showed no response. He went right on telling her what a great man he was, just as he did with the doctors and nurses, without any emotion, as though the whole world knew it except the person he was talking to. If anyone tried to argue with him about this, or ask him how he could be a king if he was sitting in a corner in a hospital, he would just listen and then go right on telling what a great man he was as though no one had spoken to him.

Dr. Treece didn't try to argue with Cary nor did he give him any special treatment at that time, because he had a feeling he would eventually get better by himself, which he did after seven months.* Only when he seemed to be well again did Dr. Treece begin to talk things over with him.

Two years have passed since he was discharged from the hos-

---

* A good percentage of such cases, with the passage of time and without any special treatment, recover sufficiently to return to their former occupations. See Section 7, Chapter Eight.

pital and he is still getting along well, and seeing Dr. Treece about once a month. Because Dr. Treece is taking care of him Mr. Dimitri has given him a job again, but not in the meat market on Main Street. Mr. Dimitri also owns the Depot Market on Railroad Avenue North, and Cary works with the grocery stock there. Mr. Dimitri thinks he is taking a chance with the customers by having him work there, even though Cary never has to serve anybody, but he says the boy deserves as much of a chance as anyone else and as long as he does his work well he is going to keep him, providing Dr. Treece says it is all right. Dr. Treece worries about Cary though he never lets on to anybody that he does. He just keeps close tabs on him. He knows that if Cary has any funny feelings he won't hesitate to come right to the doctor and tell him about them before he even goes home that night.

What has happened in this case? It is evident that Cary was different from the other boys and girls around him. He never formed any friendships or attachments for anybody. He was not even close to his mother, which may or may not have been mostly her fault for leading the kind of life she did. Certainly if he *had* any ability to form human relationships she did not make it easier for him. On the other hand, neither did he ever actively express enmity or resentment against anyone. All his expressions of both mortido and libido took place in his daydreams. In real life he neither kissed nor punched anybody, while in his fantasies he had intercourse and killed people.

He was so little experienced in the realities of human contacts that on those rare occasions when he tried to approach another human being he always bungled it. He had no opportunity, and perhaps little ability, to learn to form accurate and useful images of human nature in accordance with the Reality Principle by experimenting from childhood as people with normal parents do. He didn't have a very good image of Georgina or of his schoolfellows, or he would have known how they would respond to the kind of thing he was telling her; and his image of Daphne Paterson's feelings was definitely warped.

Finally, for some reason which we do not know, things came to a head. His completely ungratified object libido and mortido became so strong that they overwhelmed his Ego; his mind gave up the Reality Principle entirely and his Id took over all his images and changed them according to its own desires and its own picture of the universe. We remember that the Id feels that the whole universe centers around the individual who, in the eyes of his own Id, is immortal, all-powerful in matters concerning both libido and mortido, and able to influence anything in the world by merely wishing or thinking about it.

The changes in Cary's images became more and more obvious as the Ego lost control. His image of his face changed, as well as his images of the people around him, of his place in society, and even of the meat in the butcher shop. Instead of being something he handled, the meat became something personal that frightened him to the point of nausea. During the struggle between the Id and the Ego's reality testing, his images became so confused that he could no longer tell the difference between a new image and an old one, and between the images of his daydreams and those based on reality. The result was that he didn't know whether or not he had seen things before; he felt as though things were happening for the second time when they were happening for the first time; and he couldn't tell half the time whether he was dreaming or not.

At the same time, all his tensions, which so far had received only make-believe relief through daydreaming, suddenly exploded outward, but in a very unrealistic and unreasonable way. Instead of expressing them through healthy loves and hates toward other people, he put his own wishes into the minds of others and felt as if they were directed toward himself. It was like projecting his feelings on a screen so he could sit back and watch them as though they were someone else's. It was as though his feelings were made into a movie called: "Love and Hate, starring Cary Fayton," and he was watching that movie. After all, that is what he had done all his life anyway in his daydreams, which consisted of movies of "Love and Hate" inside himself, with himself as the star, in which he made love to beautiful women and killed his wicked rivals. In a way, the only difference now was that he was projecting these movies outside himself.

Because he was a sick man, however, he didn't recognize his own feelings in these movies. He thought that they belonged to the other actors, and didn't realize that he was the author of the scenario. Because he didn't recognize this strange movie as his own creation, it frightened him with its powerful and dramatic libido and mortido drives, just as it might have frightened anyone else who saw it as plainly as he did. But no one else could see it and that is why no one else could understand his agitation. Perhaps if the desk sergeant saw the world as Cary saw it at the time he was in the police station, he too would have asked for protection.

Cary's sickness at this stage, then, consisted in not being able to recognize his own feelings when he saw them, so that he imagined that they were other people's feelings directed toward him. Psychiatrists call this "projection," just as in the example of the movie. It might also be called "reflection." Instead of his mortido and libido being directed toward other people in the normal way, they were projected toward others and reflected back toward himself. Instead of admitting that he wanted to kill someone, he imagined others wanted to kill him; instead of loving someone, he imagined that she was in love with him. Thus he avoided the guilt which would have arisen if he were the aggressive one in either case. It got to the point where his Id instincts had to express themselves outwardly somehow, and since he couldn't express them directly (for some reason which we don't know), he had to "get permission" from his Superego by a false belief that others had made the first move. Projecting love and hate, and then returning the imagined feelings in kind, is an interesting way to avoid guilt, but what a price he had to pay for adopting such a roundabout method of expressing his libido and mortido! It resulted in his being hospitalized for the better part of a year, until with Dr. Treece's help he was able to stuff his Id instincts back into the unconscious and put his Ego in control again. As long as things stay this way, Cary will be able to live a normal life.

A neurosis, as we have said, consists of a troublesome but successful defense against the Id wishes becoming conscious. When the defenses break down and the conscious Ego is overwhelmed by the unconscious Id, we call the condition a psychosis. In Cary's case, the first defense was a general paralysis of all outward expression of the Id instincts, so that they were permitted to obtain relief only in daydreams. In the first chapter we have already mentioned this type of "inhibiting" personality, with a weak "barrier" between the unconscious and conscious parts of the mind and a brittle "barrier" between the conscious mind and outward action, and have noted that these people wish that the world would change to correspond to their images while they do nothing to bring about such a change. It is evident from Cary's case why the barrier between daydreams and action in such individuals was described as "brittle." When it breaks, it does not give way gradually but shatters completely and suddenly so that the Id pours out copiously and unhindered.

As long as his unconscious only broke through in daydreaming, nobody was harmed except Cary, who lost time and energy in this profitless occupation, which did not make his spirit grow stouter or increase his usefulness to himself or society. But when the barrier between fantasy and action broke down, he became a danger to himself and to others and had to be kept where he could not harm himself or others socially or physically. He had to be protected by society from the scandalous desires of his Id until he was once more strong enough to protect himself.

At the beginning we mentioned that there were four stages in the development of Cary's illness.

1. First of all, during most of his life, he suffered from a "simple" inability to make human contacts through either libido or mortido. He neither loved nor fought. His tensions were locked up inside of him. He never got to love any of his jobs. He never got so he could master any situation or person. He just drifted through life, through jobs, and through people, without showing any outward feeling for any of them. Such a way of experiencing is called "simple schizophrenia." We might say that he acted as though he had neither libido nor mortido to spare for anything outside his daydreams. He appeared to suffer from an insufficiency of mental energy, just as an anemic person seems to suffer from an insufficiency of physical energy. This appearance was partly false since we know that, underneath, his feelings were piling up. What appeared to be a "simple" insufficiency was partly at least a complicated inability to express his feelings in a normal way.

2. When his acute breakdown arrived, heralded by many strange feelings, both libido and mortido were projected in large quantities. He saw his own feelings reflected from others, and just

as a light reflected from a mirror might appear to a confused mind to come from the mirror itself, so he thought that he was loved and hated by people who hardly knew him or knew him not at all. He heard voices and saw visions which confirmed his projected feelings. An important part of his illness besides his delusions, or false beliefs, was a tendency to misjudge "significance." He would think that the slightest careless movement on the part of another person had great personal meaning for him and was connected with the way he felt. Everything about him had too much "significance." The meat in the butcher shop looked more significant than usual, so significant that it made him nauseated. A person lighting a cigarette or licking his lips in a restaurant seemed to be doing it for the purpose of conveying to him a significant personal message or threat. All these new significances confused him.

Such a mental state, involving projection and reflection of feelings, and increased significances, we call "paranoid," especially when the person feels that people are doing everything they do for mortidinous reasons, that is, to warn, threaten, insult, or harm him. A "paranoid schizophrenic" feels persecuted and usually hears voices, as did Cary, confirming his feelings. The voices, of course, were only another kind of projection and reflection: they were his own thoughts being spoken back to him. That somehow he vaguely knew that he himself had written the scenario is shown by his feeling that his mind was being read, that other people could see his thoughts, and so on. We should note that during this stage both his libido and mortido were in action. One person loved him, others hated him.

3. In the third stage he lay for a long time almost as though dead. In such a state patients often show sudden, unpredictable outbursts of great violence. They will appear to be completely uninterested in their surroundings and then suddenly lash out murderously at someone standing nearby. There is practically no outward sign of libido activity in such a state and everything that can be observed seems to come from inwardly and outwardly directed mortido. What is called the "tone" of the muscles is also changed, since the limbs can be placed in any position and will stay there indefinitely without tiring, as though the individual had been given a tonic which made him stronger than usual. At the same time, his

interest in what happens to him and around him seems to have cataracted away. This cataract of indifference and the tonic state of the muscles help us remember that this condition is called a catatonic state of schizophrenia.

4. In the fourth stage there was no more evidence of mortido. Cary seemed agreeable and docile. Everything, he said, was fine. He was now the greatest man in the world, the procreator of all children, and the source of all sexual energy. He appreciated himself to the fullest as a benevolent king and a great lover from whom all gifts came to men and women. At times he passed out scraps of paper to the other patients and to the staff as tokens of his generosity; at other times, when he fancied some insult, he withheld his gifts. Once or twice he wrapped small pieces of his feces in the paper as a sign of special favor. He loved all the world and especially himself. His libido was going full blast, and now no longer projected, but mainly turned inward. The similarity of his behavior at this stage to that of the infant who sits king-like on his throne and donates or withholds his gifts of feces is evident.

During this stage, Cary would want and do opposite things from one minute to the next, without seeming to notice how contradictory he was, as though one part of his mind didn't know or care what another part was up to. He acted as though his personality was split into separate pieces, each acting independently of the others. This disconnected behavior with a somewhat sexy tinge gives the impression of stupidity or hebetude when it is observed. Since these patients seem to be in a frenzy—or "phrensy," as it was formerly spelled—besides showing a lot of hebetude, they are called "hebephrenics."

Cary's mind was split in another way, besides being cut up into separate pieces each acting as though the others didn't exist. The sights which met his eyes and the sounds which came to his ears were split off from his feelings so that reality did not call forth the normal emotional responses. His mother's sobbing no longer made him feel sympathy, nor did the kindness of his nurses awaken gratitude. His feelings seemed to have no connection with what went on around him. His mind was split two ways, so to speak, up and down, and also across. These splits remind one of the up and down split in the Church during the Middle Ages, which was called the Great Schism, and of how a certain rock called "schist" splits across when it is under stress. The schisms in such frenzied minds is what leads us to call all such conditions "schism phrensies," or schizophrenias.

Schizophrenias are always accompanied by a split, partial or complete, between what happens to the patient and how he feels about it, so that his feelings have little or no connection with happenings as far as we can see. Cary showed this split very well when he smiled at his sobbing mother instead of weeping with her at his sad plight. Before an actual split occurs, it is often noticed that events do not affect the prospective patient as much as they do his normal companions. His feelings seem flat instead of being in sharp contact with what is going on. So we speak of things affecting the patient in a flat way, and call this type of response flattened or inappropriate affect. Such individuals are more interested in their daydreams than in what goes on around them, and because their emotions depend more upon what goes on inside their minds than upon what happens outside, a normal person has an eerie feeling when in their company. Schizophrenia is just an exaggerated example of the principle that people feel and act in accordance with their inner images rather than in accordance with reality.

We can now summarize what we have learned about schizophrenics. First of all, they show flat or inappropriate affect, with splitting of feelings from events and, later, splitting of the mind into little pieces which seem to act independently of one another.

Secondly, they can be put into four main classes. The patient may show all four types of behavior mixed up, or they may occur one after the other, as in Cary's case; or he may show only one kind of schizophrenic behavior throughout his illness. The first is the simple type, shown by inability to become emotionally attached to anything or anyone, so that the individual wanders about from place to place and from person to person. Many vagabonds and prostitutes, amateur and professional, who are forever changing places and people because they don't care where or with whom they are, are simple schizophrenics. This does *not* mean that everyone who changes jobs and companions frequently is schizophrenic.

Only a psychiatrist can judge properly if there is a true lack of emotional attachments in a person's life.

The second type is the paranoid schizophrenic, characterized by projection and reflection of Id wishes, reflections of thoughts into voices and visions, and feelings of heightened significance.

The third type is the catatonic, who shows stoppage of almost all muscular movements, queer changes in the behavior of his muscles, and impulsive violence.

The fourth type, the hebephrenic, behaves and talks queerly and expresses many fantastic ideas with a rather sexy and often religious tinge.

In the old days, schizophrenia was called "dementia precox," because the individual was supposed to become completely demented eventually, and the psychiatrists of that time felt that this was a precocious condition, since they thought that dementia was properly a condition of old age.

Fortunately, we know now that these patients do *not* become demented, though after being sick for a long time many of them may seem so to the inexperienced observer. In addition, a good percentage of them recover with modern methods of treatment, or even without them. To continue to employ the word "dementia" in view of our new knowledge of this condition is an unnecessary cruelty to the distressed and often discouraged families of these patients. Also, the disease does not always begin precociously; in fact paranoid schizophrenia is in many cases a disease of late middle age. The term Dementia Precox is therefore a worn-out and harmful one which had better be discarded. It is not too much to say that any state authorities who compel their doctors to use this sinister and discouraging word are thirty years behind the times in their care of the mentally ill. Such illnesses should always be called schizophrenia, meaning a split mind which we can hope often to put together again, and never Dementia Precox, which means to many people a hopeless condition of confusion.

Cary was insane. This means he no longer knew the difference between right and wrong in many matters and would have been incapable of doing right if he did know; and that he was a danger to himself and others, and likely to cause a public scandal. Therefore it was necessary to place him in a hospital under the supervision of experienced doctors, nurses, and attendants in order to protect society and to protect him from himself. Insanity, however, is only a legal term, and has no standing as a medical word, though it is still used as though it had by many people.

The proper way to describe Cary is to say that he was psychotic. It made little difference to a doctor trying to cure him, or to Cary, once he was in the hospital, whether he knew right from wrong. There are many psychotic people who need psychiatric treatment even though they know right from wrong, and there are some people who don't know right from wrong who should be treated by means other than psychiatry. Once society and the patient are protected, the doctor is not primarily interested in whether his patients know right from wrong. As far as medical science is concerned, it doesn't matter. The problem for medical science is how much the Id is overwhelming or threatening to overwhelm the Ego; and whether the specific wishes which will win control are acceptable to society or not is a side issue as far as cure is concerned.

A psychotic is a person whose Ego has almost completely lost control of his Id.

The cure for psychosis is to strengthen the Ego or diminish the amount of energy piled up in the Id; if the proper balance is reached the patient gets better. Then the doctor can help him make his recovery permanent. Anything which severely weakens the Ego, such as a prolonged high fever, or the excessive use of alcohol, may make it easier for a psychosis to occur in a susceptible person. Fortunately, in some cases, as with Cary, recovery takes place spontaneously, perhaps because the free expression of Id tensions during the illness restores the energy balance to its former state.

While "psychosis" is a medical term and refers to loss of control of the Id, "insanity" is a legal term which refers to the patient's inability to judge right from wrong. "Lunatic" is an outdated word which shouldn't be used at all. The old idea of a lunatic was an individual whose mind was affected by the moon. Mental hospitals are full of people who are not visibly affected by the moon (though some aspects of the weather do appear to affect psychotics). Any state authorities who use the words "lunatic" or "lunacy" in their law books are fifty years behind the times in their attitude toward the mentally ill and should be criticized accordingly. Psychotics are sick people and have troubles enough; it is only decent to do anything one can to make life easier for them. Certainly no one should call them names.

## 2

## The different kinds of psychoses

There are three great groups of psychoses: the schizophrenic, the organic, and the manic-depressive. The case of Cary Fayton illustrates well the different types of schizophrenia. The organic psychoses form a more varied group.

Anything which causes structural changes in the brain may weaken the Ego. If the Ego gets weak enough in such cases it may lose control of the Id, resulting in an organic psychosis. Among the things which may cause such changes are infections of the brain with certain diseases, such as syphilis, meningitis, and tuberculosis; also infections of other parts of the body which are very poisonous or cause high fevers, such as blood poisoning, pneumonia, and malaria. The picture of the delirious (psychotic) explorer lying prostrated with fever in the jungle is familiar to every boy and girl who reads adventure stories. Alcohol and drugs can weaken the brain and cause psychoses such as delirium tremens and bromide intoxication. Wounds and tumors of the brain, hardening of its arteries, old age, and *serious* prolonged vitamin deficiency such as occurred in prison camps during the war, may also seriously weaken the Ego.

In the most severe cases, an organic psychosis may take the form of a delirium in which the individual sees terrifying animals, people, or insects and is full of dreadful fears and forebodings. Most organic psychoses are curable if the condition which is damaging the brain can be remedied.

We can now turn our attention to the manic-depressive group. Janus Gay was the youngest of the five children of Alfred Gay, the Olympia real-estate and insurance agent. Jan, unlike his ectomorphic brothers and sister, was a round-faced endomorph, thick chested and inclined to be plump like his mother. He was usually much jollier and more easygoing than the rest of the family, but at times he would get sluggish and irritable. He would then stop seeing his many friends and spend his spare time reading sad philosophers.

Jan entered law school somewhat doubtfully in order to fulfill the ambitions which his father had for him. He himself would have preferred to be a salesman, but he had gradually been persuaded by his parents that he should do something more dignified than selling wholesale clothing. So he began to study hard and did well in his midterm examinations.

After the examinations were over he went out with his friends to celebrate. The others went back to classes the next day, but Jan didn't because his father was due to pass through Arcadia on business and Jan was going to meet him at the hotel. Just before he left his room, however, he received a telegram saying that his father had changed his plans and would not come after all. Jan, who was still feeling gay from the night before, felt that he should go right on celebrating. He had a few drinks and then went down town and ordered himself a new suit. After lunch, he thought he might as well do things properly, so he bought himself three pairs of shoes, four hats, and a dozen shirts. He took a fancy to the girl who waited on him in the department store, and spent the rest of the afternoon standing at the shirt counter telling her jokes in a loud voice which made her feel rather uncomfortable. He didn't have enough money to pay for everything he bought, but his father was well known in Arcadia, which was only twenty miles from Olympia, so his credit was good.

That night he took the salesgirl on a round of the night clubs, where they did things in a grand manner. They drank nothing but champagne, and at each place they came to, Jan bought drinks for everyone in the house, signing his father's name to the check. Then he and the salesgirl went to an auto court, where they spent the night.

The next day Jan still didn't go to classes. Instead, he went to each place where he had been the night before and demanded to see the checks he had signed. At each place he complained loudly of being overcharged. He finally went to a lawyer with his complaints, who told him he had better think it over. Jan went to another lawyer who said he would have to see the checks in order to decide what could be done. Jan wanted immediate action, however, so he went to the police and demanded that a policeman come with him and look into the situation. While he was at the police station, he was so jolly, loud, and boisterous that they almost arrested him for being drunk, but he challenged them to smell his breath and they had to admit that it didn't have any odor of liquor. He slapped the sergeant on the back so hard that he nearly knocked him over, and forgetting what he had come for, walked out singing loudly. He sauntered down Main Street, winking at all the girls, until he came to Harry's Haberdashery. He strode into the store and demanded to have all the gloves they had in the place. The proprietor was suspicious of Jan's manner, but he consented to let him have six dozen pairs of men's gloves if he would sign a paper saying that his father would pay for them before the first of the month.

Jan took his armful of gloves and climbed onto the back of a small truck which was parked nearby, where he began to give a sales talk. He shouted at the top of his lungs about the wonderful qualities of the gloves he was selling. A large crowd gathered, but no one would buy his gloves. After a while he began to get irritated. He made witty and sarcastic remarks about the tightwads of Arcadia.

A bird began to sing in a tree nearby and Jan stopped talking and listened to the bird. Then he began to whistle loudly in imitation. After a few minutes, a pretty girl walked by, ignoring the crowd. Jan jumped off the truck and dashed after her, thrusting several pairs of gloves at her. At this moment, a police car drove up. Jan saw the officers coming toward him and began to laugh heartily. Then, as quickly as he could, he took the gloves out of the boxes and threw them into the crowd.

At the police station they again had to admit that he wasn't drunk, so they called his father and told him the story. Mr. Gay brought him back to Olympia, where he was put into the hospital.

He quickly recovered from his exuberant state but Dr. Treece advised his father that he needed a long rest. Jan, however, was ashamed of his behavior and determined that to make up for it he would go back to college and study harder than ever. His father, who was anxious to have a lawyer in the family, favored this idea, especially since Jan appeared to him to be perfectly well. Against Dr. Treece's advice, Jan went back to Arcadia. His friends had a different attitude toward him, but he kept out of their way and didn't seem to be too upset by the way people whispered about him on the campus. He lived quietly and studied hard, avoiding night clubs and the department store where he had met the girl.

Because he had missed almost two months of the term, Jan sweated a good deal during the examinations at the end of the session. He felt uncertain as to how well he had done, and he knew that if he failed his father would find it hard to forgive him. The day after the examinations were finished, instead of packing to go home as the other students were doing, he sat in his room and brooded. Now that it was over, his anxiety began to grow worse by the hour. He had been feeling overworked for the past six weeks. He had difficulty falling asleep at night, and woke up before dawn in the morning, feeling more tired than when he had gone to bed. He couldn't eat, had no sexual desire, and no interest in being with people, who irritated him. He seemed slowed up and had much difficulty in concentrating on his studies. He didn't seem to have normal feelings about things, and wept easily. Noises made him jumpy. His eyes tired quickly, he was constipated, and he suffered from belching and heartburn. He began to think of the things he had done after midterm, and things that he had done when he was younger that he was ashamed of, and it seemed as though everybody knew about them and stared at him on the street.

That night Jan tried to hang himself with a necktie. Fortunately it broke and he fell heavily to the floor.

He didn't pack the next day either, and the second evening he tried to asphyxiate himself by plugging up all the cracks around the door and windows and turning on the gas. Luckily some gas leaked out and his landlady found him in time. He was again removed to the hospital in Olympia and this time his family agreed to everything Dr. Treece said. Jan was in the hospital for six months and continued to see the doctor frequently for over a year after that. Even though he passed the examinations, he did not go back to college but went to a city upstate and became assistant manager of a men's clothing shop. He still sees Dr. Treece occasionally, but he has been in good health for the past four years. Dr. Treece thinks he had better see a psychiatrist about once a month for a good many years to come.

It may seem surprising that two illnesses with such different manifestations could occur in the same person and be part of the same psychosis, but if we think about the two episodes we can see that they have one most important feature in common: they were both due to the sudden release of large quantities of ungratified Id tensions. During the first illness he was overly sociable, overly generous, sexy to the point of being careless, and also at times irritable, critical, and belligerent. These actions resulted from an explosion of pent-up libido with a small amount of mortido, outwardly directed and so powerful that it overwhelmed his good judgment and his reality sense.

During his second illness, there was another explosion of Id energy, but with two differences: first, it consisted mostly of mortido; and, secondly, it was directed inwardly instead of outwardly. In individuals who are subject to such explosions, we find all sorts of combinations of constructive and destructive energy. Usually the libido is outwardly directed, resulting in what is known as a manic episode, and the mortido inwardly directed, causing a depressive or melancholic episode. Since both conditions frequently occur in the same individual, this type of illness is called a manic-depressive psychosis. In some people there is a long depression without much manic phase, or a long mania without much depression. In others, manic and depressed episodes alternate without any normal period in between. In Jan's case there was a period of fairly good health between the two phases. Mixed types also occur in which the explosions of libido and mortido come at the same time instead of one after the other.

Once the explosions are over, the individual is as well as he ever was. This illness, unfortunately, tends to repeat itself as the years go by, and it was to prevent such repetitions that Dr. Treece insisted upon seeing Jan for such a long time after he was well. In this respect a psychosis is much like tuberculosis: when the individual is cured, he still has to be careful and should continue to see a doctor at regular intervals to make sure that he stays well.

In our country we are brought up in such a way as to turn most of our libido outward and most of our mortido inward. During a psychotic explosion of mortido, therefore, the patient generally attempts to relieve his tension by suicide. In some other countries, where mortido is not so strongly directed inward during the growth of the individual, such an explosion may result in murder instead of suicide. This is quite frequent among savage tribes, especially Mohammedans, where certain individuals may suddenly run amok and try to kill as many people as possible, sometimes with religious "justification," meaning that the Superego allows the person to direct his death wishes outwardly, instead of inwardly as in our culture.

It is often difficult to distinguish between schizophrenic and manic-depressive psychoses. The important thing in labeling such illnesses is not what the patient does, but how he does it. A manic-depressive may get the same ideas of persecution as a paranoid schizophrenic, and many schizophrenias begin with severe states of melancholia. To distinguish in doubtful cases between the flattened affect of a schizophrenic and the depressed feelings of a manic-depressive requires years of training and practice.


### 3

## What causes psychoses?


We know little about this, except that schizophrenia may have something to do with the chemistry of the brain cells, and manic-depressive psychosis with the glands. We know mainly the effects rather than the causes of psychoses.

A neurosis is a defense. In a neurosis, the troublesome tension is all corralled into one part of the personality, so that the rest is left free to develop as best it can in its crippled condition. By crippling himself in one respect, the patient leaves himself more or less free to develop in other respects. The psychotic, on the other hand, ceases developing. Instead of only part of his personality being affected, his whole personality returns to something resembling an infantile level. Physis, the growth force, is blocked. The Reality Principle is suspended. The individual acts in accordance with badly warped images. By good fortune he may accomplish something in reality, but his efforts are so poorly directed that it is only by luck that he can be successful. Thus in his first illness, Jan succeeded in attracting a woman of poor judgment, but a more sensible woman would have realized that something was wrong and he would have failed. Even Cary might have succeeded in attracting a sufficiently ignorant woman with his hectic note.

Psychosis, like neurosis, is the result of a conflict between the Id and the inner forces which restrain it, but in neurosis the restraining forces win by a compromise, while in psychosis the Id wins.

## Footnotes for Philosophers, Chapter Six

Factitious etymologies have been used in this section because of their mnemonic value. As for "flattened affect" and "split personality," there are some psychiatrists who question exactly how these terms apply to schizophrenics as one sees them in the clinic, but an attempt is made to present these concepts here in such a fashion as to satisfy the curiosity of those who are not required to have such technical doubts. As for "running amok," one accepted belief regards it as a manifestation of psychomotor epilepsy. The material in this chapter should be carefully digested by the layman before he attempts to apply it to his friends, otherwise he is likely to make false judgments in view of the prevalence of schizoid and cyclothymic personalities in our "normal" population, and our national hypochondriasis.

For further study, some of the most readable formal descriptions of the psychoses can be found in White's *Outlines of Psychiatry*, previously referred to. Of the many autobiographies and biographies of psychotics, the most constructive, if not the most Hollywoodish, is that of Clifford Beers.

*A Mind That Found Itself*, by Clifford W. Beers. Reprinted, Doubleday, Doran & Company: New York, 1923.

### CHAPTER SEVEN

# ALCOHOL, DRUGS, AND SOME BEHAVIOR DISORDERS

---

## I

## The different kinds of drinking

THALIA LANE was a tiny thoroughfare opposite Court House Square, one block long, running between Wall Street and Leonidas Street. There were three narrow houses on one side, and three little stores on the other. The stores belonged to Mr. Seifuss, the bookseller, who also dealt in spices; Mr. Reed, who owned the music shop; and Mr. Chusbac, the wine merchant. Everybody said that Mrs. Chusbac really ran the liquor business, and Mr. Chusbac was such a meek little fellow that everybody was fond of him. Mr. Chusbac loved his wines, and always had a small glass of something special to sip with his meals (1).* Sometimes the children, Thalia (named after the street where she was born in one of the little houses) and Don, were allowed to have a sip too, but Mrs. Chusbac didn't approve of this, so it didn't happen often.

The whole neighborhood went into mourning when Mr. Chusbac died. His brothers came all the way from Detroit to attend the funeral. They were not meek like him, but big, strapping boilermakers who, rather than have a few glasses of wine at odd hours during the day, would take a good slug of whisky in the morning before they went to work, and another in the evening when they came home (2).

After Mr. Chusbac's death, there was no more wine in the house. This didn't particularly bother Thalia or Don. When Don was old enough, however, he went to college, and there he learned to drink

* The numbers in this story refer to the discussion at the end of the section.

whisky. Don was a shy fellow who had trouble being sociable when he went to parties. He soon found that a few shots of whisky gave him a nice glow and then he could talk to the girls as well as any of his fraternity brothers could (3).

Don was a charming fellow, handsome and clean-cut, and he did not have much difficulty getting a job and a girl friend when he came back to Olympia to settle down. In spite of being naturally a quiet type, he became gay enough after a few drinks so that he made quite a good salesman (4). Mr. Gay, the real-estate man, put Don in charge of his insurance business, since the Gay boys had all left Olympia, and pretty soon Don was a partner in Mr. Gay's firm.

Don used to worry sometimes because he didn't really make friends with people. When he was in company he could hardly say a word until he had had a few drinks. Afterward, though, he would become talkative and lovable, and in this way he became good friends with Marilyn Gay and Mrs. Gay. Soon he was going steady with Marilyn. They had fine times together. Sometimes they would stay home and sit with Mrs. Gay. More often they would go to a bar or a night club in Arcadia and spend the evening drinking and talking, either alone or with some friends they would meet there.

When Marilyn became pregnant, neither she nor Don was very upset, though of course it was an accident that had happened one night when they had both had too much to drink to be careful. They quietly got married, and soon it was an open secret around town that they had been married for some time. Finally, when things looked right, they set up housekeeping.

Both of them liked good whisky and usually they had a few drinks every day. They would have cocktails before dinner, and then one with dinner, and afterward they would spend the evening sitting around, talking and drinking (5).

After the baby came, though, things were different. Marilyn couldn't nurse him and the doctor didn't want her to anyway. He thought the bottle was just as good. Nevertheless, he advised Marilyn not to drink for a few months. Don tried not drinking too, but he found it difficult to have any fun without it. He wasn't as fond of the baby as he thought he was going to be, and sometimes he got impatient with Marilyn for spending so much time fussing with him. He also began to find other things wrong with her. Above all, he found that when he wasn't drinking she bored him. Eventually they had a heart to heart talk together, but it didn't do much good. Everybody thought she was foolish to divorce him, for he was such a charming fellow.

After his family broke up, Don began to drink again. Now he drank more heavily than he used to. Sometimes he would get too drunk, and then he wasn't so charming. There were always some friends, however, to see him home when he couldn't make it. If he was shaky in the morning he would take a big snort, and afterward he would be all right for the rest of the day (6). People began to worry about him; sometimes he even worried about himself, so he tried to stop drinking. He managed to go for several weeks without touching liquor, and then, having shown himself and everybody else he could do it, he decided to celebrate his victory, and went on a terrific bender that lasted four days. He was very much ashamed of himself for having missed work, but he didn't let on to anybody that he was. He steered clear of liquor for a few weeks again after that. He didn't sell as much insurance as usual during those weeks, though, which worried him. He got so worried that one night he took a drink to cheer himself up. Then he took another, and a few more on top of that, and finally wound up on another four-day bender, during which he didn't eat and got hardly any sleep (7).

During the next three years he married and divorced Alecta Abel, and meanwhile things went from bad to worse. If he didn't drink he couldn't sell, and if he did he went off on a bender and lost out on his work altogether. He realized that drinking was becoming quite a problem to him, so he went to Dr. Treece. It didn't do much good, because Dr. Treece said he would have to come for treatment for a year or two, and Don thought the doctor was just trying to make a good thing out of it, since the treatment would have cost more than he was spending for liquor, which was a lot. So he went right on drinking, but he began to be pretty sensitive about it. When Mr. Gay would say something to him about missing time from work, he would reply: "I still sell more insurance than anyone else in town!" Mr. Gay wasn't satisfied with this, because he felt that pretty soon Don was going to slip way below par.

Other people tried to talk to Don, but it wasn't any use. He would only get angry at them (8).

One day when his mother scolded him a little bit, he said: "Dammit, everybody is against me! Can't a man do as he pleases any more, without a lot of blabbing women interfering?" This thing that he said stuck in his mind, "Everybody is against me!" He would lie awake at night sometimes and say to himself: "Everybody is against me!" After a while when his work did fall below his former standard, he didn't even feel guilty any more. He just said it was because everybody was against him. "Look at me," he would say to himself. "I'm well educated, kind of good-looking, smart, and I know the insurance game. If I don't make a go of it, it's because people are against me. No wonder I drink. Who wouldn't if he was trying his best and everybody looked down on him?" That was what he said to himself the day Mr. Gay told him he would have to go (9).

Mr. Paluto, Mr. Gay's competitor, had some misgivings about Don, but when Don promised that if he was given a break he would make good, Mr. Paluto gave him a job without telling him about his doubts. Don thought Mr. Paluto was a swell fellow and told him so. Don felt that anybody who could see that he was the best salesman in the game, if he was given a break, was a smart apple, and he, Don, admired anyone with such good judgment. He swore off liquor for good.

After he had been about three months with Mr. Paluto, not drinking, Don realized he wasn't doing so well anyway. A good many of his old friends were taking their business elsewhere. One night he got so sad thinking about the injustice of this that he decided he needed a snorter, just one (7). This time his bender lasted seven days instead of four and he ended up in the hospital with delirium tremens. Dr. Treece pulled him out of it all right, though a doctor in Arcadia had given him morphine, which Dr. Treece didn't think was a good idea. Don hadn't eaten for a whole week, and an important part of the treatment consisted of a heavy diet with lots of vitamins, calories, and carbohydrates, and absolutely no alcohol in any form. After a few days the shaking ceased, the fears went away, and Don stopped seeing things whenever he closed his eyes.

When Don went back to the office, Mr. Paluto wasn't at all agreeable. He didn't want to take a chance with his business reputation by having a man like Don working for him, and had resolved mentally when he hired him that the first time he went on a bender he would fire him, which he now did.

Don cussed him out plenty. "You can't fire me!" he said. "I resign! I knew you were a faker the first time I set eyes on you. You too! The whole world is against me. No wonder a fellow takes to drink!" That was the end for Don. Now that he was sure everyone was against him, there was no use trying any more. So he gave up and became a real bum. Marilyn and Alecta had both remarried, so they couldn't help him much, but his mother, his older sister Thalia, or Mrs. Gay always took care of him, no matter how bad his condition was. Dr. Treece's opinion that Don would kill himself with drink within two years frightened them, but it didn't scare Don, because he knew that if he got the breaks he could stop drinking any time (10). Every time he ended up in the hospital he would promise Dr. Treece and himself that that would be the last episode, but he always came back. Once in a while he would just give up and say to the doctor: "What's the use anyway? Everybody is against me and I don't get any breaks anywhere. What if I do die? Everybody will be happy when I'm gone, even my own mother!" But Don's mother was very sad indeed, and so was his former wife Marilyn, and so was Dr. Treece, when Don died a couple of winters later from delirium tremens and pneumonia which he caught from lying all night in the gutter on Cladeus Street near the abattoir.

Let us discuss the various kinds of drinking which took place in the Chusbac family.

(1) Mr. Chusbac, who was a European, liked to drink a little wine with his meals. This is a European equivalent of our American habit of drinking coffee and the English habit of drinking tea. A little wine with meals acts as an appetizer and cheers everyone up. For those who are brought up that way, it rarely becomes a bad habit. The signs of this kind of drinking are the sipping of the wine rather than the drinking of it, and the enjoyment of its taste and aroma as much as the effects of the alcohol. In this case wine is an appetizer and beverage rather than an intoxicating substance.

(2) Mr. Chusbac's brothers liked a slug of whisky before and

after work every day. The calories supplied by the alcohol and the lift it gives in the morning may help to start the day right and supply needed energy, and it may act as a pickup after a hard day's work. Physical workers with a certain attitude toward drinking can sometimes get away with this without becoming addicted to liquor in a harmful way or getting into a brawl every Saturday night.

(3) During Don's college days, he indulged in the typical American social drinking. Americans are always going to new places and meeting new people. It is important for their enjoyment of life that they learn to make friends quickly and converse readily. A few drinks in the course of an evening keeps people loosened up. For shy people, this may seem especially necessary, as otherwise they might be wallflowers a good part of the time. Such drinking, however, may be a danger for these very people. It is such an easy way out of their shyness that it is liable to become a habit and a crutch, and prevent them from undertaking the harder job of developing their personalities so that they can be happy in society by being themselves. If excesses can be avoided, this kind of drinking, in the American way of living, may be a help rather than a hindrance, although drinking would seem to be less desirable than trying to attain a sounder and more permanent foundation for social adjustment.

(4) Occupational drinking, that is, drinking to make business relationships easier, is not so good. A businessman is in business every week of the year and if he comes to rely on help from liquor he is likely to be drinking every day. He may soon come to believe, perhaps rightly, that he will lose business if he doesn't drink to help things along, and so it gets to be a regular habit; and being easier than trying to develop a sound adult personality so that he can do business by being himself, it comes to be leaned on too heavily. In addition, some people don't like to do business with a man who has the odor of alcohol on his breath.

(5) Don's drinking with Marilyn may have been a subtle form of insult. It may have meant as it so often does: "When we are sober we are bored with each other. We had better keep on drinking because then we think each other swell people." An affection for and an image of one's life partner formed in a retort of alco-

holic fumes will seldom stand up under stress, and Don's didn't. Married couples who spend their evenings drinking often end up in one of two ways because of the ever-present danger that they will find out how much they may really bore each other. If they stop drinking, as Don and Marilyn did, they may soon begin to feel this boredom, and a separation is likely to result. If they go on drinking, they may have to drink more and more as time passes, because the longer they know each other, the more strongly they bore each other and the more liquor it takes to cover it up.

(6) Nearly everybody agrees nowadays that when a man begins to take a morning drink to cure the shakes or hangover of the night before, he is well on his way to becoming an alcoholic.

(7) If a man can't stop drinking after the first one, when he has previously made up his mind to, he is an alcohol addict, since his craving now controls him instead of vice versa.

(8) When a man sacrifices more for a drink than any drink is worth, he is an alcoholic. If he is willing to lose his job, or let his children go hungry or without good clothes in order to satisfy his craving, he is a chronic drinker. We define the condition by its results. If the results of his drinking are seriously harmful or distressing to himself or to others, a man is an alcoholic (no excuses accepted).

(9) When a man loses his self-respect to the extent that he blames others for what he brings upon himself, he is ready for the final stages. He becomes almost useless to himself and is only a burden to those who love him.

(10) If he keeps on drinking in the face of medical advice that he will seriously injure his system by doing so, we see plainly what we saw less clearly before: that chronic alcoholism is a slow form of suicide. It is a way of evading the growth force of Physis, and the prohibition which normally keeps inwardly directed mortido from causing the death of the individual. (We remember from the case of Si Seifuss that this prohibition is so strong that it is effective even during sleep, and keeps the individual even from visualizing his own death in a nightmare.) Drinking is pleasanter in a way than hanging oneself and does not arouse the same kind of guilt that a conscious attempt at suicide would do. Chronic alcoholism is suicide even though the death wish remains unconscious most of the

time and the individual may protest, sincerely as far as he is aware, that he is doing his best to stop it. He thus avoids the reproaches of the Superego which might result if he simply took a rope to hang himself.

(11) There are other kinds of drinking also. People who suffer from cycles of depression may start to drink when they feel a depression coming, without realizing why they do it, using this method of trying to conceal their condition from themselves. In the old days, women who used to have depressions with their menstrual periods would take large quantities of certain "vegetable compounds" which contained a high percentage of alcohol and were really nothing more than cocktails; but because they were labeled as medicines, even the most rigid old maid, who wouldn't have dreamed of taking a "drink," could allow herself to take these wonderful "compounds" which magically made her menstruation seem so much gayer and more hilarious than it used to be.

Perhaps the few people who become nauseated from drinking before they reach the stage of intoxication are more fortunate than their fellows in the long run, in spite of the embarrassment which may result from having such sensitive linings to their digestive tracts.

## What is a drug addict?

There are certain drugs which are normally prescribed by doctors in very small quantities. The best known of these come from the juice of the oriental poppy plant. After an operation, the doctor makes the patient comfortable by giving him an injection of morphine which weighs about one quarter as much as a grain of corn. This is enough to put the average person to sleep even in the face of severe pain.

Some people find the products of the poppy plant a very pleasant thing and start to use them without a doctor's order, either to experience pleasant dreams and visions, or to calm their jangled nerves and make it possible for them to sit still. Since such use is against the law, the poppy is taken by these people in whatever form they can obtain it illegally. In some places they find that gangsters can sell them opium which they can smoke or swallow, while in other places they can get only morphine or heroin, which they inject under the skin by means of a needle.

After they have been taking these drugs for a while, two things happen: first, their Id tensions increase because of their guilt feelings; and, secondly, their Egos are weakened by the drug. They have all their old troubles, and in addition, the guilty knowledge that they are breaking the law and associating with criminals in order to get what they want.

In this way a bad circle is set up: their Id tensions become more and more frightening, and their Egos become less and less able to cope with them. The users thus require increasing quantities of the drug to make them feel safe, calm, and controlled. They become "addicts of the mind."

Not only are their minds in a turmoil when they are without the drug, but they also become "addicts of the body." An addict deprived of morphine suffers from all kinds of aches and pains, sweating, pounding of the heart, stomach upsets, shakiness, and, in general, "the screaming meemies." In order to quiet his body and his mind, he may require eight, sixteen, or even forty times the normal dose, quantities which would kill a normal person but are just enough to keep the addict from being miserable.

Such doses, obtained illegally, cost a lot of money. Without his drug, the addict is a trembling pulp of a man, and will do anything to get it. While his habit is becoming more expensive, his earning power is certainly decreasing. That is why the morphine addict is so often forced to turn to prostitution and crime. Since the gangsters know that he has to have the drug at any price, he is completely at their mercy. One may be sure that they charge him all that they can get, and cheat him at every opportunity, selling him baking soda, quinine, or any other white powder if they think they can get away with it. The drug traffic is a dirty, cutthroat business in which everybody concerned will double-cross everybody else at every opportunity.

A true addict, therefore, is a person who is miserable without his drug, who will sacrifice anything to get it, and who requires larger and larger doses to keep him comfortable, so that eventually he may take quantities which would kill several average people.

It should be said that some who have studied these matters very carefully think that there is no such thing as an addict of the body, and that all addiction is of the mind. There is some disagreement about this subject, but there is no disagreement about the drug addict being one of the most unhappy of human beings.

3

## The things people can become addicted to

The most serious forms of drug addiction involve morphine, opium, heroin, and cocaine; these are the most dangerous drugs, since it sometimes takes only one guilty dose to awaken the terrible craving which may lead to addiction. This does not occur when the drugs are taken for a short period under a doctor's orders. Occasionally people become addicted to codeine if they take it for long periods.

Marijuana does not cause a true addiction because it does not leave any craving. It is a pleasant thing to take, however, so many unhappy people who cannot get along in the world use it to comfort themselves with. Since it interferes with the individual's efficiency in most occupations, it is considered to be a harmful drug. Some doctors think it may cause psychosis; others say that those who have a psychosis after taking a lot of marijuana took it in the first place to cover up a psychosis which was already there. One reason for this disagreement may be that marijuana as sold to its users in this country varies in strength and composition. Marijuana or hashish comes from Indian Hemp, in the Orient named for India, and in this country named for our own redskins. It is difficult to know precisely from which plant illegal dealers obtain their drug unless they should happen to be deteriorated professors of botany, and even then they might argue among themselves as to whether it was *Cannabis sativa indica* or *Apocyanum cannabinum*.

Nowadays almost everybody has heard of phenobarbital, nembutal, and other sleeping powders, capsules, and pills which doctors call "barbiturates." These are being used habitually in increasing quantities, so that more and more people are going through life half "doped up." Most of the barbiturates leave more or less of a hangover the next day, and while it may be so slight that the individual isn't aware of it, nevertheless his efficiency is lowered. These drugs should be taken only for limited periods under a doctor's supervision, and people who take them on their own initiative are asking for trouble. The cure for permanent insomnia is in emotional adjustment and not in the drugstore.

Bromides are not habit forming, but people may come to rely upon them a good deal and take them too often. The trouble here is that bromide poisoning causes insomnia, the very condition the drug is supposed to "cure," and the natural reaction of most people to this condition is to take even more of the drug, resulting in more poisoning and worse insomnia. Patent preparations of bromides, such as are sold at soda fountains, often contain other drugs which may cause poisoning. Any doctor who has watched a bromide psychosis, or who has seen a man turn sky-blue all over from taking too much "morning-after," soda-fountain fizz, becomes very conservative about prescribing these preparations.

Probably the most harmless and effective sedative there is (for hermits or patients in a hospital) is an evil-smelling and foul-tasting drug called "paraldehyde," which is excreted through the lungs. People, especially alcoholics, may become addicted even to this unappetizing (but otherwise almost perfect) sedative.

We have defined an addict roughly as a person who has an unnatural craving for some particular thing and will sacrifice anything in order to obtain it. This definition leads to some interesting applications. We have already seen in the case of Don Chusbac how it applies to alcohol. It may also apply to many things which are not drugs. Some people are addicted to gambling, and some are addicted to sex. A man with such a yen for the horses that he will let his children go hungry so that he can put his money on a fancy mare, is a true gambling addict. One who habitually spends the family grocery allowance on the floating Cyprians of the cocktail lounges is a sex addict. The normal masturbation of adolescence often has all the marks of an addiction during that period.

There are other things which may become addictions, such as

reading, religion, and collecting stamps, buttons, and other small objects. In these cases, however, the results of the addiction are different because the present sacrifices are more likely to lead to future benefits. The reader may become a scholar, the religious addict may become a saint, and the stamp addict may become— well, it is difficult to go on, but stamp collecting does make many people happy. Thus we see that there are good, bad, and indifferent addictions. The important thing is that an addict is not the master of his own desires, but they are the master of him, and it seems desirable for every man to be the captain of his own soul. People sometimes do not like to be reminded that eating may become an addiction instead of merely a pleasure.

## 4

## How can an addict be cured?

Curing an addict is the easiest thing in the world—If. All we have to do is find something that will interest him more than the thing he is addicted to. We can cure any alcoholic *if* we can find something that will interest him more than alcohol does. So far nobody has found any such thing that will work in all cases. (We shall not discuss here the treatment of morphine addiction, since there is only one treatment and that is immediate confinement in a locked hospital or sanitarium).

The first thing to notice about an alcoholic is that usually he does not love anybody, not even himself. He may be a great "lover" and a very sociable person, but he rarely forms a real adult relationship with anybody. He may become attached to somebody he can lean upon, just as Don Chusbac leaned upon and was fond of Mrs. Gay, but this was the same kind of attachment an infant has for his mother. He loved her because of what she did for him and not for herself. In this way, as in many other ways, alcoholics are very infantile in their emotional behavior. They act like badly brought up little babies. In fact, it is no joke to say that an alcoholic is a person who has never been weaned from the bottle.

This gives us a clue as to one method for attempting to cure an alcoholic: by getting him to form a more adult relationship with another person. This can sometimes be accomplished by a skillful psychiatrist or psychoanalyst. The psychiatrist then uses his influence, which results from the attachment the patient forms for him, to guide the patient into improving his behavior. The psychoanalyst uses his influence to try to free the patient from his infantile fixation so that eventually he will grow up emotionally and stand on his own feet without any further help from the analyst. The analyst weans him from the bottle, while the psychiatrist gently takes the bottle away from him though he still craves it.

In a very rare case, the right woman can do the same thing as the psychiatrist by getting the alcoholic to love her more than he loves his liquor. This happens so rarely that no woman should count on it. Usually the alcoholic marries a woman for what she gives him, and not for herself. If his own mother couldn't wean him from the bottle, how does a mere wife think she can do it? Only if he marries her because of a true, adult object love will she be able to help him. But usually he "instinctively" avoids women who he feels may demand such a love. The fact that an alcoholic chooses a certain woman to marry, or allows her to "persuade" him to marry her, nearly always means that she does not threaten him with having to form an adult relationship with her. If she did, he would avoid her, since it would mean too much sacrificing of his infantile pleasures.

Another device which is sometimes successful is to make a missionary out of the alcoholic. The one thing which may interest him more than drinking is talking to other alcoholics about drinking, and helping them to stop. Organizations such as Alcoholics Anonymous help many drinkers as long as there is missionary work for them to do. The Olympia branch of A.A., however, was an example of what happens to such organizations if they cover their territory completely. When all the available alcoholics in the town had been "converted," and there was no more new blood to do missionary work with, many of the "cured" backslid. The members gradually grew stale, lost interest, and returned to their old habits. This was the first time Dr. Treece had heard of such a thing happening in the history of Alcoholics Anonymous, and by the time he realized what was up, it was too late to save the situation; this might have been accomplished earlier by joining with the Arcadia group so that there would be fresh fields to conquer.

The best hope for alcoholics lies in either individual psychiatry or psychoanalysis, group psychotherapy, or directed group activity such as is found in Alcoholics Anonymous. Two rules which have been found by experience to be wise are:

(1) Any treatment must start off "cold turkey." An alcoholic will not be cured by tapering off. If he won't stand for "cold turkey" (complete abstinence immediately), he hasn't the will power to be cured.

(2) No one should marry an alcoholic to reform him. It will not succeed. If he wants to marry badly enough, let him (or her) reform first for at least a year and preferably two. No more pathetic creatures come into a psychiatrist's office than the once gracious and beautiful young ladies who are beaten down and old before their time as a result of marrying alcoholics to reform them.

5

What about delirium tremens?

It seems strange on the surface that a disease which formerly killed many of its victims should be a subject for joking among the very people who are most liable to get it. It is not strange if we understand how the unconscious uses humor to relieve its tensions. Delirium tremens, or the "D.T.'s," is a psychosis which sometimes occurs following a prolonged alcoholic bout in people who have been drinking excessively for a number of years. It is a torturing and strenuous experience which may leave the marks of strain on the heart and brain as well as on the mind. Its victim is in a state of acute fear and trembles all over. He imagines that he sees all sorts of horrible creatures, such as snakes, bugs, and small animals, coming after him or crawling over his skin, or that he is faced with endless and desperately monotonous tasks, such as washing millions and millions of dishes. These experiences are very real to him, and he behaves accordingly. Contrary to the popular idea, the animals seen by these patients are usually small and horrible, rather than large and benevolent creatures such as pink elephants.

The fact that delirium tremens has become a joke, like much that has to do with alcohol in our culture, shows how childish and guilty is the American attitude toward drinking. Schoolgirls giggle about sex, and grown men giggle about whisky. But even nowadays with the best cold-turkey treatment, delirium tremens leads to fatal heart disease, pneumonia, or convulsions five or ten per cent of the time. Of course the dead ones don't go back to the old hangout and the ones who live do, so people see only the survivors, which is one reason they do not realize how serious the condition may become. Even if it doesn't kill, it may injure, and each attack may diminish the individual's physical and mental capacity.

Delirium tremens and Korsakow's psychosis (long-lasting confusion, sometimes with paralysis) seem to be as much the result in many cases of lack of food, as of the amount of alcohol consumed. People who are on a bender cannot seem to spare the time or money for eating. Vitamin B seems to be the important factor in this connection. A good rule for heavy drinkers, therefore, is to be sure to eat more abundantly than usual while on a spree. If they are unwilling to eat, they should at least buy a big bottle of thiamine chloride or vitamin B tablets before starting out, and keep eating them as they go along.

Among the other psychiatric effects of alcohol is its tendency to exaggerate paranoid tendencies and epilepsy. Both paranoia and convulsions may make their first appearance during an alcoholic bout. We saw how over a long period drinking brought out Don Chusbac's paranoid tendencies more and more openly. In some people this may happen quite suddenly, with an acute onset of paranoid panic and hallucinations. Alcoholic homicidal mania is another condition which sometimes results from heavy drinking, and is particularly apt to occur after drinking cheap liquor.

Alcohol weakens the Ego and Superego and allows the Id to express itself more freely. People tend to show their true emotional urges when they are drinking. If a man is disagreeable when he is drunk, beware of him in a pinch when he is sober, no matter how charming he may appear on the surface in his normal state.

# 6

# What is a psychopath?

In the common neuroses, the individual afflicts mostly himself with his neurotic behavior. His Id instincts are turned inward. We shall now consider a group of people who make others do most of the suffering in their attempts to obtain relief of tension.

If the Superego is too weak to keep the Id instincts under control, the individual can either find some outside influence to help keep the Id in check, or he can let it go ahead and express itself freely. In the first case, he may let some stronger personality guide him, or adopt an outside set of standards, such as Fascism or religion; or he may become interested in the law and feel that as long as he has the law on his side he is sufficiently in the right, unpopular though such a code of conduct may make him socially. In the second case, every wish, no matter how selfish or childish, is gratified, regardless of the consequences; then, after the individual has suffered the penalties of his selfishness for some years, he begins to feel that he has a good excuse for hating people. This makes him more selfish than ever and at the same time gives him the childish satisfaction of feeling that his impulsive conduct is justified.

Such individuals who do not have normal inner restraints on their conduct are called psychopaths. They used to be called "moral imbeciles" because they seemed to be unable to understand simple moral values. Sometimes they are called "constitutional psychopathic inferiors," with the idea that they are born that way, which may be partly true. It may be that their brains are deficient from birth in the ability to store energy and their minds constitutionally unable to go through the process of forming a Superego.

As far as personality make-up is concerned, then, there are two kinds of psychopath. The first type, the latent, or passive psychopath has a weak Superego but behaves fairly well most of the time because he accepts guidance from an outside source, such as religion or law, or at times by attaching himself to a stronger personality and accepting him as an ideal. (We do not speak here of those who use religion or law as an auxiliary to inner conscience but of those who use such doctrines *instead* of an inner conscience. Thus, they are not guided by any ordinary considerations of decency and humanity, but only by their interpretation of what "the book" says. "Christians" who discriminate against Jews and Negroes, and lawyers who are guided not by what it would be decent to do, but only by how much one can do and still keep out of jail, are outstanding examples of latent psychopaths.) The second type, the active psychopath, has neither inner nor outer restraints, but may curb himself temporarily and put on a good front for a short time in order to be sure of getting exactly what he wants in the end.

As far as behavior goes, there are as many different kinds of psychopath as there are kinds of behavior. There are sexual psychopaths, who attack little children, old women, or other unusual sexual objects; criminal psychopaths, who will commit cold-blooded murder or break into poor-boxes; seducing psychopaths, who will knowingly give a young man or woman a venereal disease; obstructive psychopaths, who will lie down on the job or deliberately gum things up, coldly selfish about how much danger or extra work this may mean for others, or how much past work their conduct may render useless; and exhibitionistic psychopaths, who will expose their bodies, or show off in an unreasonable way even at the risk of other people's lives, as by stunt driving a car in heavy traffic. One can, in fact, make up a name for any kind of psychopathic conduct. The important thing is that such conduct, in whatever field of activity, gratifies some wish of the psychopath in spite of or because of the trouble and unhappiness he causes others and often himself.

The range of a psychopath's activities depends upon his intelligence and his opportunities. If he is wealthy, he may cause trouble on a magnificent scale, something like the Roman Emperor Caligula, who sank festive barges full of people to amuse himself.* If he is powerful, he may gratify his whims in the most tragic way, like the commandants of concentration camps who spent time devising tortures for their victims. If he is poor but intelligent, he

* Although he stands as a memorable example of "conscienceless behavior" similar to that of a psychopath, actually Caligula is thought to have been a schizophrenic.

may specialize in swindling people; if he is poor and unintelligent, he will do things requiring little originality, such as turning in false fire alarms, playing practical jokes, or selling information to criminals, or, in time of war, to the enemy. Many gossips are of this type, gratifying their destructive impulses in a way which they enjoy by spreading scandal. A certain number of psychopaths find that morphine and other drugs make life pleasant for them and become drug addicts.

Let us follow the career of an intelligent psychopath, and see what havoc he leaves behind him.

Ludwig Farbanti, Olympia's undertaker, had once owned the Olympia Cannery, and it was largely because of the doings of his only child Loki that he had had to sell it to Midas King.

Loki was a problem from infancy. He bit his mother's breast when he was nursing, and his toilet training was almost impossible. When he started school all the little girls were terrified of him because of his cruelty. One day he found a penknife and jabbed it through the hand of Minerva Seifuss, who sat next to him. After that he had to be put into a private military school but they couldn't do much with him either. Punishments had no effect except to make him run away. He was above the average in intelligence, however, and managed to pass his examinations in spite of all this. At college he was always in debt, and began to forge his father's name to checks. Since Mr. Farbanti always made good in the end, out of respect to him none of the tradesmen of Arcadia complained to the police.

During his summer vacations, Loki spent his time traveling in idleness from one city to another, and he never managed to live within his generous allowance. He was always trying to impress someone and had to have a large wardrobe, stay at the best hotels, and entertain large numbers of people. He didn't choose his companions with very good judgment, however, and during these jaunts he caught gonorrhea twice and was in jail many times for drunkenness. Finally his father, unable to keep up with his lavish expenses, declared for the last time that he would no longer make good any bad checks that Loki passed. This time he meant it.

This did not deter Loki. If he saw something he wanted, he bought it. He was so well dressed and was such a good talker that he had no trouble in pushing checks. He never saved enough money to buy a car, but he always had one somehow or other, and being a free spender he was popular with the girls. He got several of them into trouble, but it was not until Ambrose Paterson, the electrician, came after him with a gun for trying to seduce his younger sister Daphne, that Loki left Olympia and Arcadia for good. It was on account of these girls that Mr. Farbanti had to draw on his capital, and that finally led to his selling the cannery. He was willing to let Loki suffer for his sins, but he felt that at any cost he had to keep the girl friends from unnecessary misery.

Loki went to Los Angeles, where he talked himself into a job as a radio announcer by claiming that he had had a lot of experience. Here he first learned how really effective his voice was, and he began to use it to impress people. One night for amusement he happened to go to a religious meeting with a rich middle-aged woman with whom he was living. The size of the collection was a revelation to him, so he studied the matter and decided to set himself up in business with the aid of his lady friend. He read a few books on Theosophy, Spiritualism, and Christian Science, and made up a cult called "You Are Glad." With his friend's financial and social backing, and his own eloquence and persuasive power, he soon became a popular preacher and evangelist, and after a while he was even able to start branches in several western cities. As time went on, he made a rule that his true followers must turn over all their money to his church. He bought some apartment houses and allowed his disciples to live in them—at a price. He organized a co-operative restaurant in each house and charged a liberal amount for meals. By this and other methods, most of his disciples' earnings as well as their capital ended up in the church fund, which was all in his name.

One day he decided that he was getting tired of putting up a preacher's front, and that for other reasons the time had come to leave. Without giving them any inkling that he was actually leaving, he subtly prepared his followers for his departure so that they would not become alarmed too quickly. He turned into cash as many of his church's assets as he could, decamped with the money and went to Germany, where he and an American bankrobber named Maxie lived high for a while. After Maxie died, Loki got interested in the National Socialist Party. When the war began, Loki was writing anti-American propaganda for the Nazis, under an assumed name.

Some of his followers saw the light when he disappeared, and went to the police. Many of them, however, still believe in him, because of the way he had prepared them for this event. To this day, some of them swear that it happened at one of his meetings, and that they saw the angels raise him up to Heaven with their own eyes. The mother of the sixteen-year-old girl he took to Germany with him and later introduced to a procurer for a Buenos Aires brothel, committed suicide when one of Maxie's friends tried to blackmail her and told her what had happened to her daughter.

Loki's story illustrates many of the things we have said about psychopaths. It is obvious that Loki's conscience did not deter him from doing what he wanted to do when he wanted to do it. It is also clear that his intelligence did not deter him either. When he wanted to drink or to have sexual intercourse, he did it, regardless of the consequences. If either his conscience or his intelligence had controlled his impulses, he would not have caught gonorrhea or gone to jail, or taken the risks he did in cashing bad checks. His behavior is a little different from those who form a conscience and then behave badly in order to defy it or to revenge themselves on their parents. Loki's behavior was bad from the beginning and never showed any signs of improvement. In many situations he injured himself more than he did other people.

Certain of the events in Loki's life are typical, and can nearly always be found in the life history of the average psychopath. They are nearly always badly behaved in infancy and at school. If they attend a well-run school, they are nearly always expelled. They run up bad debts, trade on their family's good name if it exists, wander around the country, show off as extravagantly as they can arrange for, catch gonorrhea, go to jail, get into trouble with women, fool people by glib talk, flee from discipline of every kind, and cause grief to almost everyone with whom they come in contact. So much are these things a matter of course in the lives of such people that if the haggard parents finally come to a psychiatrist for advice, the doctor, after listening to the beginning of their tale, can often guess the rest.

Why some individuals from their earliest days fail to acquire the usual conduct-controlling mechanisms is something which psychiatrists have been unable to explain quite satisfactorily as yet. It is interesting to think, in this connection, how much the attitude of "wild" animals, which seem to be unable to form anything resembling a Superego, and can be "tamed" only through fear, resembles the attitude of the psychopath; while the attitude of those animals of which we make house pets, which do seem to be able to form something resembling a Superego, is much closer to that of a socialized human being.

## 7

## What is sexual perversion?

In the normal course of growth Physis directs the individual toward the opposite sex of adult human beings as his true libido object. Only if something goes amiss will he select another object for his affections, such as members of the same sex, little children, old people, or animals. In the same way Physis directs him toward vaginal sexual intercourse as his preferred aim, so that libido may accomplish its biological end of uniting the sperm and the egg to create a new individual; but if something goes wrong he may adopt another method for the greatest satisfaction. Thus some people prefer unusual objects for gratifying their libido tensions, some prefer unusual methods and some are unusual in both respects. All these people find that either society, their own Superegos, or perhaps their thwarted Physis makes them unhappy. Such unusual preferences are called sexual perversions.

Perversions are usually the result of not growing away from some infantile or childish way of obtaining sexual pleasure. Children are often seen in sexual play with members of the same sex or animals, and we have noted that infants get libido relief from sucking, anal activity, or playing with their own sexual organs. An individual who does not grow away from these childish pleasures will try to get relief by similar methods in adult sexual life. Since human beings are experimenters at heart, it should be understood that mere experimenting with unusual sexual activities is not perversion. Only when an unusual activity is *consistently preferred* to the conventional ones should it be called a perversion.

8

## What is masturbation?

Masturbation is sexual satisfaction in which the individual has no partner at all, or only an imaginary one. Sometimes when two people of the same or opposite sexes cause each other to have an orgasm with their hands, this is called "mutual masturbation." Because Americans usually marry late, long after the sexual glands are fully developed and the libido, not satisfied with indirect relief, is clamoring for sexual orgasms, most boys and girls in this country go through a period of a few years during which they have to find sexual satisfaction outside of marriage. Usually they find it partly in masturbation which they accomplish by rubbing their sexual organs in various ways. Nearly all boys and at least half of all girls go through a period of such activities while they are growing up, in addition to the stimulation of their sexual organs during early childhood which serves a similar purpose.

Masturbation does *not* cause insanity, nervousness, weakness, impotence, frigidity, tuberculosis, pimples, slime under the heart, or any of the other things which young folks hear about from various people, young and old; and a drop of semen is *not* equal to a quart of blood, as some gentlemen have been known to tell their young charges it is. A normal person who masturbates unwisely may feel a little washed out for a day or two afterward, but that is all. It is true that nervous people and people on the verge of a breakdown sometimes masturbate more than usual, or more than other people, and are sometimes more sensitive about it, but this does not mean that masturbation causes their nervousness or their breakdown. In such cases excessive masturbation may be an attempt to diminish the nervousness or prevent the breakdown by relieving the Id tensions which are causing the trouble or are threatening to overwhelm the Ego. Such a method of treatment cannot be conscientiously recommended, however, as it may make matters worse by increasing the tension of the Superego, among other things.

The chief harm of masturbation, besides the self-reproaches and the washed-out feeling which follow it in many people, has to do with later love life. Masturbation is easy and doesn't require any courting. The masturbator can have anyone he or she desires for an imaginary partner without having to go to the trouble of winning trust and affection, and can do pretty much as he or she pleases with this partner without regard to the "partner's" feelings; and, above all, the masturbator doesn't have to wait for satisfaction. Later on, however, in normal courtship and marriage, the individual may have to do things he doesn't like to do and make sacrifices in order to win the one he loves. He will also have to consider his partner's feelings during their sexual activities. In addition, he will have to wait for his satisfaction until the partner feels that the time is ripe. The courting and waiting period may seem boring and difficult to the masturbator, instead of being a delightful time of anticipation. Like the infant, he wants what he wants when he wants it, without regard to anyone else's feelings. The result is that he may be unable to go through with a normal courtship, and when he is married and has to respect the desires and delicacy of his partner, he sometimes feels thwarted and does not enjoy the relationship.

In other words, he may get so he would rather do things *to* an imaginary partner than *with* a real one, and so he may remain a bachelor or become an unhappy married man or divorcé. Good sex is not doing things to somebody, but doing things with somebody. Doing things to somebody, even a real partner instead of an imaginary one, is merely a form of masturbation with another person present, and is different from the experience of mutual sexual pleasure that comes from an adult sexual emotion. The undesirable feature of masturbation, then, is not that it stunts physical growth, which it doesn't, but that it may help to stunt emotional growth, as it sometimes does.

The best "cure" for masturbation is to marry the person one loves—the *right* person. On the other hand, the worst remedy for any kind of unhappiness is to marry the wrong person.

# 9

## What is homosexuality?

Homosexuality is love of the same sex. Some people can get almost equal pleasure from making love to either sex. These people are called bisexuals.

Many beautiful things have come out of homosexual relationships, such as some of the philosophy of Socrates. Nevertheless, one rarely sees a happy homosexual. Homosexuality nearly always means a thwarted Physis and a troubled Superego. It is contrary to the customs of our society and so leads to poor social adjustment even under the best circumstances. Furthermore, it is against the law for men and can lead to real disasters because of this. Curiously enough, while nearly every state has laws against male homosexual activities, there is none* which has laws against homosexual activities in females.

Homosexuals obtain their sexual satisfaction in whatever ways their imaginations can devise and their consciences permit. Homosexuality occurs in both sexes, and may be overt, with actual love making, or latent and hidden. If it is latent but conscious, the individual has to restrain himself from trying to do what he would like to do because of the possible consequences in regard to society and his own conscience. If it is latent and unconscious, and the individual is not even aware that he has such desires, they then have to obtain their satisfaction in disguised form through displacements and sublimations. Nearly everybody has homosexual desires of which he or she is not aware. Usually they are well repressed and cause little trouble, but in some people they are so strong that it requires a continual struggle to keep them from coming to the surface, and this may keep the individual in a perpetual turmoil for no reason that he can determine. The last defense against such desires becoming conscious is usually a mental illness, and such illnesses of the type called "paranoid" are defenses against unconscious homosexuality.

* As far as the author and his friends in the legal profession can ascertain.

It is said that some homosexuals have more than the usual amount of sex chemical, or "hormone," of the opposite sex in their blood. All men may have both male and female sexual hormones in their blood, some experimenters believe, but in normal men the male hormone is in excess. In some men, however, the balance may be upset so that the female hormone gets the upper hand. One may suppose that the corresponding upset can occur in women. Some homosexuals, accordingly, are pretty resentful against nature, since they rightfully feel that their condition is an unjust affliction which is not their fault. (The above does *not* mean that we can cure homosexuality by injecting the appropriate hormones. There are many unknown factors which make such treatment ineffective.)

There are roughly four ways in which homosexuality may develop. The individual may show signs of it from early childhood, by dressing frequently in his sister's clothes, for example. When such boys grow up they may look quite feminine, which results in all sorts of humiliations, so that they may become bitter. Men hate them because they make them feel uneasy by stirring up latent homosexuality. Women hate them because they are rivals in love. This type of homosexual can generally sense just how close to the surface overt or latent homosexuality is in any other man. The corresponding development may take place in girls, with similar consequences.

There are some men (and all this applies correspondingly to women) who seem quite usual until they grow up, and then they find to their surprise and anxiety that men interest them more than women. A third kind of homosexual development occurs in prisons and other places where there are no women available. As libido piles up, people get less and less particular about their sexual objects, and if the preferred one is not available they will often take whatever they can get. A girl that a man would not walk down the street with in his home town may seem like a glamorous beauty if she is the only woman on an island in the Pacific, because the strong libido tensions mold her image into such a form. Experiments with marijuana show that a usually normal man may even make love to a bridge lamp if his libido becomes aroused sufficiently and there is no reasonable outlet available. It is not surprising, then, that where there are no women, men will sometimes turn to each other for sexual satisfaction, and similarly among women who are cut off from the opposite sex.

There is a fourth way in which a girl or boy may develop overt homosexuality, and this is by seduction. A good example of this is the "jocker." A jocker is a young, rather weak hobo who is protected by an older, tougher "wolf," who in return uses the boy for sexual satisfaction. Sometimes terrible fights ending in murder occur among tramps and hoboes when two "wolves" take a fancy to the same boy. Seductions are not too uncommon in boys' and girls' boarding schools, and the seducing teacher has been a theme for plays.

Among homosexuals of both sexes, there are four types of lovers. There is the man who acts as a man, the man who acts as a woman, the woman who acts as a man, and the woman who acts as a woman. There are also, of course, mixed types and alternating types, men who act as men sometimes and as women at other times with their male partners, and similarly among women. Thus there are male male homosexuals, and female male homosexuals; female females, and male females. Groups of homosexuals are found in certain night clubs in every large city. A group of men who dress and act like women will cluster around a manly looking fellow who is their male lover, fighting as jealously over him as a group of women would; or several manly looking men may court the same effeminate one. Plato in his dialogues describes some of these groups. In other places, one finds groups of women dressed in male fashion, with short-cropped hair and often with deep voices, gathered around a beautiful creature who acts as the female for all of them, and who queens it over them as any woman would who had a dozen lovers to choose from. On the other hand, there are the quieter relationships of homosexuals who find mates and pair off to form sexual friendships or "marriages," often blended with highly spiritual feelings which may result in beautiful works of art and literature.

From what we have said, the possibility of "curing" homosexuals is fairly apparent. The man or woman who has taken this direction since childhood is the most difficult to treat, while the man or woman who has turned to homosexuality because of lack of available heterosexual partners is the easiest. From some statistics, it seems that about half of those suffering from "sexual disorders" are cured if they go through with six months or more of psycho-analysis.

What is society to do with homosexuals? Their lives are difficult enough as it is, and punishment is not indicated. The best thing one can do is treat them as politely as one would anyone else. They on their part, of course, should be expected to abide by the ordinary rules of decency such as apply to relationships between men and women: namely, they should not seduce minors, nor force them-selves on people who are not interested in their company; they should not flaunt their desires in public by dressing in clothes of the opposite sex or otherwise; and they should not embarrass those around them by making love or talking about it in public. If they behave themselves and control themselves as discreetly as people with heterosexual desires are expected to do, their private lives should be no more concern of anyone else's than should a normal person's. Putting them in jail often (or even usually) results only in providing them and the other prisoners with added opportu-nities for sexual activity. Many psychiatrists feel that the laws con-cerning homosexual activities should be changed.

## Footnotes for Philosophers, Chapter Seven

1. *Alcoholism*

The well-known work of fiction, *The Lost Week-End,* can be read with benefit by everyone who has an alcohol problem with himself or in his family. For facts about alcoholism, con-sult:

*Alcohol Explored*, by H. W. Haggard & E. M. Jellinek. Doubleday, Doran & Company: New York, 1942.

2. *Drug Addiction*

A good beginning, with bibliographical references, for those who wish to read up on this subject is the article "Drug Addic-tion," by C. E. Terry, in *Encyclopedia of the Social Sciences*, Volume 5. This useful reference book can be found in most public libraries.

3. *Marijuana*

Historically, this is perhaps the most interesting drug known to man. For a full discussion, see:

*Marihuana*, by Robert Petrie Walton. J. B. Lippincott Company: Philadelphia, 1938.

4. *Alcoholics Anonymous*

The facts and implications set forth concerning this organization are based on observation of the natural history of one group in the vicinity of New York City. The best thing for alcoholics to do if they do not wish or are unable to go to a psychiatrist, is to write A.A., who will be glad to give them the benefit of their experience and every other assistance to help them overcome their habit.

> National Secretary,
> Alcoholics Anonymous,
> P.O. Box 459,
> Grand Central Annex,
> New York 17, N. Y.

5. *Delirium Tremens*

The relative merits of "cold turkey" and tapering off are still under discussion, but the well-known Bellevue and Boston Psychopathic studies are far more convincing than anything the proponents of tapering off have been able to bring forth. "Cold turkey" is almost universal in teaching hospitals, where the results are carefully controlled, while tapering off is usually practiced in smaller sanitaria. Fewer people die with "cold turkey."

6. *Psychopaths*

We refer here to the common usage of the word and not to the technical usage of Eugen Kahn as outlined in his *Psychopathic Personalities* (op. cit.). The distinction between "latent" and "active" psychopaths in the sense employed in the text is useful in clinical work. It assumes that the psychopath suffers primarily from a weak Superego and minimizes masochism and a desire for punishment as primary driving forces in "psychopathic" behavior. A short discussion of this controversial term, "psychopath," by Paul Preu, is to be found in Chapter 30 of *Personality and the Behavior Disorders* (op. cit.). For case histories and an understanding of their dynamic psychology, see:

*Wayward Youth*, by August Aichorn. The Viking Press: New York, 1935.

7. *Sexual Perversion*

The expression "get relief" is used here not because sex should be experienced as "getting relief," but because in terms of psychic economy that is what happens: a tension is relieved.

For an understanding of how sexual perversions come about, Freud's "Three Contributions to the Theory of Sex" can be read in *The Basic Writings*. Chapters 20 and 21 of his *General Introduction*, and Ives Hendrick, op. cit., are easier reading, however. For a description and discussion of various perversions, with many case histories, Havelock Ellis is the classic.

*Studies in the Psychology of Sex*, by Havelock Ellis. Random House: New York, 1940. (All the volumes compressed into two volumes on thin paper.)

8. *Masturbation*

The American Medical Association, 535 North Dearborn Street, Chicago, Ill., publishes a series of 25¢ pamphlets on sexual hygiene for various ages by Dr. Thurman B. Rice, and also one entitled "Sex Education for the Adolescent," by George W. Corner & Carney Landis.

For a short article designed to assist the general practitioner in dealing with this problem in his patients, in which some pertinent facts are summarized and some practical hints and interpretations are outlined, see:

"The Problem of Masturbation," by Eric Berne. In *Diseases of the Nervous System*, Volume V, No. 10, October, 1944.

9. *Homosexuality*

For further information, the works of Freud and Havelock Ellis may be consulted. Stekel gives very extensive case histories. Abraham Myerson did some of the work on sex hormone ratios in homosexuals. The bridge lamp incident was personally observed and is unpublished. For a study of homosexuals in the American setting, see:

*Sex Variants*. A Study of Homosexual Patterns, by George W. Henry. Paul B. Hoeber, Inc. (Harper & Brothers): New York, 1941. (2 volumes.)

# PART
# III

---

# Methods of Treatment

---

### CHAPTER EIGHT

# PSYCHIATRIC TREATMENT

---

## I

## What is "going to a psychiatrist"?

"GOING TO A PSYCHIATRIST" means going to a physician who specializes in the study of human emotions. Going to a psychiatrist can help people become happier and more efficient and better able to cope with themselves and with the people and things around them. A psychoanalyst is a psychiatrist who specializes in one form of psychiatric treatment, namely, psychoanalysis, which, as we shall see in the next chapter, is the study and readjustment of the patient's Id tensions. Other psychiatrists use various other methods of treatment: different forms of psychotherapy, drug therapy, hypnosis, and shock treatment. "Non-analytic" psychiatrists are generally referred to simply as "psychiatrists," to distinguish them from psychoanalysts, just as "non-operating" doctors are called "physicians" to distinguish them from surgeons, although actually every physician is something of a surgeon and every surgeon is something of a physician. The psychoanalyst is mainly concerned with the patient's unconscious wishes, while the psychiatrist is mostly interested in the patient's conscious reactions to his surroundings.

Whenever one person goes to another over a long period for advice or help, a powerful and complicated emotional relationship arises. This happens whether the adviser and the client are conscious of it or not. It may show itself in conscious feelings of like, dislike, gratitude, or resentment, but its power and energy are derived from the unconscious. One of the psychoanalyst's chief aims is to analyze and dissolve this relationship, while the psychiatrist's aim is to maintain it so that he can continue to use it as a weapon in treating the patient. Thus correct psychoanalysis should result in independence, while correct psychiatric treatment requires some degree of dependence on the psychiatrist.

Psychotherapy includes those methods of treatment which depend for their effect on the emotional relationship between the patient and the doctor. One of the great scientific problems of all doctors is to determine how much the result of their treatment depends upon this emotional factor, and how much is due to the actual physical or chemical methods employed. Even the most impersonal surgical procedures are affected by such emotional factors. The amount of anesthetic required and the rate of wound healing after an appendix operation may be influenced by the patient's attitude toward the doctor.

There are several kinds of psychotherapy: unconscious and conscious, informal and formal. Unconscious psychotherapy means that the doctor, and usually the patient also, are unaware that the treatment is influenced by emotional factors, as is often the case in surgical operations. Conscious psychotherapy means that the doctor, but not always the patient, is aware that he is using his emotional power in the treatment. Informal psychotherapy means that the doctor is conscious of what he is doing, but makes up his treatment as he goes along: this is the kind of treatment that is used by the family doctor in certain situations. Formal psychotherapy means a carefully thought out plan to use the emotional situation for the patient's benefit according to a definite method: this is the kind of treatment which is given by a psychiatrist or psychoanalyst. When we speak here of psychotherapy, it is the last kind we are referring to.

Each psychiatrist naturally chooses the kind of psychotherapy that will give the best results in the shortest time, and this depends on the doctor's personality as well as the patient's. Thus, some psychiatrists like to use hypnosis because they do their best work with it, but others can do better without it.

While an analyst usually likes to see his patients every day, a psychiatrist may be able to perform his task without such frequent visits. In treating Cary Fayton and Janus Gay after they recovered from their breakdowns, Dr. Treece saw them only once a month.

He did not think it wise to probe too deeply into their unconscious minds, which had already been too active; his only aim was to see that they were getting along all right with themselves and with the world from month to month, at least sufficiently to carry on their occupations.

There are many methods of psychotherapy. Re-education and persuasion attempt to teach the patient to handle his emotional reactions better, without trying to readjust his Id tensions. Suggestion, which includes hypnosis, is an attempt to use the doctor's authority to change the patient's images without seeking their origins in the Id. Distributive analysis and synthesis is similar to re-education except that it involves a long and detailed study of the patient's life, tracing back the conscious developments and changes in his drives and reactions; next to psychoanalysis, it is probably the most effective method of treatment for a long-term result. Total push tries to get the indifferent patient interested in as many things as possible in order to re-establish his contact with reality. Occupational therapy attempts, among other things, to get him away from his own troubles by giving him something concrete to accomplish. Musical therapy attempts to influence the disturbed patient's way of feeling and thinking by programs carefully selected for his special needs and those of the group he is with.

Most psychiatrists use a mixture of these methods according to the individual patient's needs. This is especially true of sanitarium treatment, where facilities are at hand for all forms of activity. It should always be remembered, however, that the skill of the psychiatrist is far more important than any amount of fresh air, sunshine, and golf. Very few psychoses or neuroses are due to lack of golf. A well-mowed lawn makes the patient's family feel comfortable and impresses his banker, but it is not a substitute for psychiatric skill. A sanitarium should be chosen with only one thing in mind: that the doctor in charge shall be good at being a psychiatrist. Whatever his other qualifications, they are less important for the future of the sick patient.

## 2

# What is hypnotism?

An Indian Yogi once demonstrated before the Calcutta Medical Society that he could stop his pulse beat. The doctors suspected some trickery, so they placed the man before an X-ray machine and looked at his heart through a fluoroscope. They found to their astonishment that his heart had indeed stopped beating and that he was able to stop it for as long as sixty seconds at a time while they looked at it through the X-ray screen. Many Yogis after years of training are said to be able to do things which are almost as remarkable, such as sticking needles through their cheeks, pulling out their colons to wash them in the Ganges, and developing their tongues to such a length that they can touch their foreheads with them.

In the Middle Ages, and even now, hysterical young girls have been able to show stigmata: that is, designs written on their skins in raised wheals. There are many reports of girls having cross-shaped blotches appear on the palms of their hands.

In some freak shows there are men who can be stuck with hat-pins without apparently feeling any pain. Many people remember seeing Houdini stick pins through his cheeks without bleeding or showing signs of pain.

People who are hypnotized can often be made to do some of these things. They can be made not to feel pain and not to bleed when pins are stuck into them or through their cheeks. They can be made to have wheals appear beneath strips of court plaster pasted on their arms.

The action of the heart, bleeding, the appearance of wheals, and probably to some degree the feeling of pain, can all be controlled by the same P and S nerves we became familiar with in discussing the relationship of emotions to disease. These nerves belong to a part of the nervous system called "autonomic"—which means much the same as automatic—because it cannot ordinarily be controlled by will power; it takes care of the automatic responses to emotions without the individual's thinking about them. Thus, when we are angry our hearts automatically beat quickly, our skins flush, and we feel pain less than usual. When we are afraid, our hearts may skip a beat, our skins turn pale, and we become sensitive to the slightest pain.

This gives us a definition of hynotism: hypnosis is a state wherein the autonomic nervous system is brought under control so that its reactions can be willed. It may be under the control of the individual himself as in the case of the Yogis, or under the control of another person, as in the case of a hypnotized subject. In the latter case, the subject falls more or less asleep before unusual things can be made to happen at the suggestion of the hypnotist. Since the autonomic system is related to the unconscious, we may say that hypnotism is a way of temporarily affecting the unconscious through conscious suggestion and willing.

This enables us to understand how neurotic symptoms can often be influenced under hypnosis. Since such symptoms come from unconscious Id wishes, they can be affected by anything which penetrates the barrier between the Ego and the Id to change the unconscious images concerned. For example, the neurosis of Si Seifuss was based on an unconscious image of himself as "a wicked man who was responsible for the deaths of ten others." When this image discharged its energy under hypnosis, he got better. Symptoms can be produced under hypnosis by the same method of image changing which cures them. In the case of a hypnotized subject who forms a wheal under a piece of court plaster, the hypnotist describes to the subject a new image of himself in which he has a wheal on his arm, and his body changes to correspond to this new image.

During hypnosis the Superego probably remains independent of the hypnotist, so that a person under hypnosis will not do anything which his Superego would not normally allow him to do. One of the famous examples of this is the case where the hypnotist gave the subject a rolled newspaper and told him it was a sword with which he was to stab his best friend. The subject behaved exactly as though the newspaper really were a sword, and after he had "stabbed" his friend, he showed signs of deep guilt and grief. The next time he was given a real sword and was told to do the same thing, whereupon he woke up. There is thus no danger of the subject doing anything without inner motives under hypnosis. His Superego will protect him as it does when he is awake.

In a way, hypnotic cures are really faith cures. The subject has to begin with a deep faith in the hypnotist in order to be hypnotized. He may pretend to others and himself that he doesn't have such faith, but deep down he must have it, or he wouldn't go under. Whatever his conscious ideas may be, his unconscious resistances must be removed in order for him to fall asleep. We already know that in a conflict between the unconscious and the conscious the former usually wins, especially in a situation involving human relationships.

With a suggestible patient, whose images are easily molded by an outsider, the cure of the symptom may be permanent. More often it is only temporary. If the unrealistic image has been warped through long years of *inside* stress, the effect of the treatment will soon wear off, since the twig was early bent and so the late tree cannot easily be straightened, but only twisted into a shape that may look straight for a while. If the symptoms are brought on by a sudden *outside* stress, such as starvation, infection, combat, fear, injury, or uncertainty, the relief obtained by hypnosis may be more permanent. In other words, if the symptoms are based mainly on the unfinished business of childhood, they will be more difficult to cure by hypnosis than if they develop principally from the unfinished business of recent times. The more recent the tensions, the more lasting the cure. That is why the results with hypnosis during the war were better near the battlefield than after the patient got back to this country.

Is hypnosis the best way to remove neurotic symptoms in a hurry? Much depends upon the personality of the psychiatrist. Some do better with ordinary psychotherapy because their unconscious curative powers come out to best advantage in a psychiatric interview rather than in a hypnotic séance. The success of any psychiatric treatment probably depends upon the relationship of the patient's Id to the psychiatrist's, whether the doctor realizes it or not, and it happens that some psychiatrists reach the patient's unconscious most easily through hypnotism, and others by talking or listening. Whichever method brings out the most powerful response when used by any particular psychiatrist, will be that doctor's most effective way of treating people.

There is more to hypnotic therapy than just hypnotizing the patient and changing his images. The changed images must be fitted into his waking personality. This usually means sessions of discussion after the hypnosis is over. Many psychiatrists feel that they can cure the same symptoms in the same length of time without hypnosis and get a better result, since from the beginning the changed images become a part of the patient's normal personality; and, in addition, which is not often the case while the patient is under hypnosis, the cure of the underlying neurosis, as well as of the symptoms, can be begun. They think they can do the patient more permanent good while they are removing hysterical hoarseness in a forty-five minute interview than while they are removing it in a forty-five minute hypnotic session.

There is a danger in hypnotism that the therapist may remove the symptoms without offering anything in return. Since neurotic symptoms are defenses against Id wishes which cannot be gratified, removing the symptoms sometimes weakens the individual rather than strengthens him, though he appears better off to the inexperienced eye. We remember that when Dr. Treece was able to restore Horace Volk's voice, Horace became very anxious and depressed. An affliction which affected only his talking was replaced by one which affected his whole personality and made him less able to carry on than he was before. Dr. Treece, being an experienced psychiatrist, was not proud of his "cure" when he made Horace talk, since he realized that the most important part of the treatment was still to come: he had yet to find a way of relieving the tensions which caused the symptom.

Nature's defense is usually the best, and if we take this away from the patient without offering anything in return, a new symptom is apt to appear which may make him worse off than he was before. Thus, a hypnotist may "cure" a hysterical stomach-ache, only to have the patient go "blind" a few weeks later. This can sometimes be prevented by using the information gained under hypnosis or in subsequent interviews to find a less damaging way for the patient to relieve his tensions. In some cases the support given by the image of the psychiatrist may make him feel more secure than his symptom previously did, and then he will remain free of obvious symptoms as long as he knows that the psychiatrist is there to help him if he needs it.

Besides the recent increase in its use as a method of psychiatric treatment, hypnotism has caught the public eye as a method of anesthesia. Hypnosis has been successfully used as a pain killer in childbirth, dentistry, and in surgery for minor operations. Since the usual dangers and discomforts of an anesthetic are absent, it is a valuable tool in the hands of those who can use it effectively, and their number is increasing. Its use in major operations and even in childbirth is risky, however; it is likely to be uncertain, and it cannot be used on everyone since the depth of sleep necessary for success cannot always be induced.

Hypnotism has always taken the public fancy because it is dramatic. That is why many patients are more impressed by it than by more thorough but less theatrical treatment. It can be used as a stage and parlor trick by those whose minds work that way. It is said that some Indian fakirs can hypnotize groups of people all at the same time, and recently an American gentleman has tried to do this over the radio. Conservative psychiatrists regard such attempts as a form of showing off.

## 3

## What about "truth serum"?

Various drugs have been used at different times for the purpose of loosening people's emotional blocks and making them feel and talk more freely. Nowadays, as a result of war experience, two drugs are popular: in America, sodium amytal is usually employed, a drug often used as a sleeping powder when taken by mouth; in England many psychiatrists prefer sodium pentothal. This latter drug is used in both countries as an anesthetic for short operations. In the treatment of neuroses, these drugs are injected into the blood until a state of drowsiness results and the patient is then questioned in his drowsy state. Since his repressions are weakened by the drug, he is supposed to be likely to say things under these conditions that he could not talk about or feel about without the injection.

Almost everything which has been said about hypnosis applies to the use of these drugs. The drugged condition is an "artificial" state like hypnosis and so it is difficult for the patient to bring the things that happen into relationship with his waking personality. And again it has to be remembered that removing a symptom weakens the patient's defenses against inner turmoil, and while it may be temporarily satisfying to the patient and his family to have a symptom "cured" quickly and dramatically, in the long run it may do the patient more harm than good. Unless the doctor takes the time to give him some source of security to replace the symptom, he may substitute general unhappiness, sluggishness, and depression for inability to talk, or a psychosis for severe headaches.

The case of Moses Tock illustrates one of the dangers of drug treatment. Mr. Tock, the junior partner in the law firm of Savitar, Teazle, & Tock, began to suffer from blinding headaches. Dr. Treece, who knew Mr. Tock well, had been worried about him for some time. He suspected him of being paranoid. All medical tests were negative, so Dr. Treece allowed one of the internes at the hospital to give Mr. Tock sodium amytal in an attempt to cure his headaches. The treatment worked. For three days, Mr. Tock was in fine shape. Then he began to complain of pains in his lower abdomen. After a while, he began to hint that he had been poisoned. Two days later, he said flatly that the pain was being caused by mental radio, and that he knew just who was behind it all, namely, Mr. Savitar. A week later, he had a paranoid psychosis in full flower. His headaches had been his last defense against a slowly developing and carefully hidden psychosis of two or three years' duration. Dr. Treece never forgot the lesson about sodium amytal he and the interne learned from this. After that he always made absolutely sure that he was not dealing with a psychotic before he allowed the drug to be given.

Just as in the case of hypnosis, many experienced psychiatrists feel that except in the most acutely anxious cases, nothing can be accomplished with drugs that cannot be accomplished better in the same length of time by psychotherapy alone. They maintain that the patient will rarely give any information about himself or show any feelings under either drugs or hypnosis that he will not reveal in the waking state with proper handling. They also feel that when the patient is not "ready" to get better he will not get better with any method of treatment, and when he is "ready" he may get better by any of the three methods, hypnosis, drugs, or simple psychotherapy, and that the result will usually be more lasting if "artificial" aids are not used. In the days before psychoanalysis, for example, hypnosis was widely used in treating hysteria; in fact Freud himself used it for this purpose for many years. But it was soon found that better, deeper, and more lasting results were obtained without it, and its use was abandoned by the early analysts.

It would seem that the only unquestioned usefulness of such drugs is in cases where the patient is so anxious and jumpy that it is impossible for the psychotherapist to get him to sit still long enough to talk over his troubles. This, of course, was the situation in many neuroses of the battlefield.

## 4

## What about shock treatment?

Shock treatment is generally given in one of three forms. Some psychiatrists have experimented with other methods, but the three recognized ones are metrazol shock, electric shock, and insulin shock.

Metrazol is an artificial chemical made in the laboratory. In small doses it is an excellent heart stimulant and is often used as such in cases of drowning, shock following operations, and poisoning from sleeping pills. In large doses, injected into a vein, it produces a convulsion similar to an epileptic fit. In the treatment of psychoses, such injections are given about three times a week for two to seven weeks. Patients are often frightened by metrazol, and it is gradually being replaced by electric shock in most cases.

Electric shock produces the same effect as metrazol, but it is easier to administer, many patients are less afraid of it, and the convulsions are usually less violent. Both these remedies are properly applied only in cases of severe psychoses, as an alternative to months or years in a mental hospital.

Electric shock is given by means of a special medical machine which can be set for the proper dose. When the switch is pulled the machine delivers the amount of current it was set for, which might be, for example, 200 milliamperes at 110 volts flowing for half a second. The results claimed for this treatment in various psychoses differ in different clinics. Most authorities feel that it yields the best results in the long-lasting depressions of the change of life, the so-called "involutional melancholias," which before this form of treatment was introduced often required years of hospitalization.

No one knows how these treatments work. Many psychiatrists feel that it is advisable in each case to consider very carefully whether other methods such as psychotherapy cannot be used instead of shock treatment. Most of these doctors agree that there are certain cases where metrazol and electric shock should *not* be used.

1. Very few doctors favor its use for neuroses, and fewer and fewer are using it for schizophrenia.

2. Few psychiatrists are daring enough to use it in their offices, as the patient may be temporarily confused after a certain number of shocks, making it inadvisable for him to be at liberty to wander around outside of a hospital or sanitarium.

3. Conservative psychiatrists refuse to use it if there is any chance that the patient will get better without it. This applies especially if the patient has had a previous psychosis and has recovered by himself. It is a good policy to call in two outside psychiatrists before shock is given, to confirm the opinion that the patient will not get better without it, and it is best to include one psychoanalyst in the consultation.

4. Shock should never be used merely for the purpose of quieting the patient unless he is suicidal, homicidal, or is wearing himself out to a dangerous extent by overactivity; and even then it should only be given as a last resort after everything else has been tried, and in such cases a consultation with a psychoanalyst is also advisable.

While electric shock is most commonly used for cases of prolonged melancholia, insulin is chiefly used in schizophrenia, particularly in younger people. The same insulin is used which is used to treat diabetes. With diabetics, one of the doctor's main concerns is to avoid giving too much insulin, as an overdose will cause weakness, shakiness, and finally unconsciousness. With schizophrenics, such a state of insulin shock with unconsciousness is deliberately produced under the constant eye of doctors and nurses who do not leave the patient alone even for a moment. As the large dose of insulin (twenty to fifty times as much as a mild diabetic uses) begins to take effect, the patient gradually grows more and more drowsy, until he goes into a state from which he cannot be roused by ordinary methods.

After he has been in this state for an hour or two, he is given a large quantity of sugar by injection or otherwise, and then occurs an astonishing event: in a mere matter of seconds, the previously psychotic patient comes out of his profound coma to sit up and talk normally. The long-term effectiveness of the treatment, many psychiatrists think, depends mainly upon the use made of this period just after waking up, when even very sick schizophrenics may be able to respond normally for an hour or two. This gives the doctor a chance to carry on psychotherapy which he could not do otherwise because the patient would not co-operate sufficiently. Insulin is thus properly used, conservative psychiatrists say, in the same way as hypnosis and sodium amytal, as a method of getting the patient into such a state that the doctor can apply psychotherapy. (Hypnotism and sodium amytal, however, are not very effective with schizophrenics.) Many psychiatrists, on the other hand, feel that the curative properties of insulin are due almost entirely to its chemical effect on the patient's brain, regardless of psychotherapy. It requires from thirty to fifty daily shocks to "cure" a schizophrenic in favorable cases.

Since the three types of shock treatment we have described are regarded by some merely as methods for making psychotherapy easier, the question comes up as to whether psychotherapy alone could not be used in psychoses, without first exposing the patient to shock therapy. The answer is that we are learning more and more about how to do this, but there are many psychotics whom the doctor cannot "reach" without artificial assistance. One reason for this of course is that there are not enough doctors who specialize in psychiatry and psychoanalysis to put in the enormous amount of time which would be required. There are about 500,000 people in mental hospitals in this country, and only about 4,000 psychiatrists to take care of them, aside from the millions of neurotics who could benefit by psychiatric treatment. Since a doctor can make four or five times as much money in other specialties with the same amount of training and skill, it is not surprising that the psychiatric profession is not overcrowded.

There are two other items which should be mentioned in connection with shock therapy. The first is the use of curare, a poison known to every reader of mystery stories. This drug, which paralyzes the muscles, was originally brewed from various herbs by South American Indians for the purpose of poisoning their arrows. It is now used in some clinics to prevent the violent muscular contractions of the usual convulsion, without interfering with the curative effect of the shock. Its use is questioned by some psychiatrists, however, on the grounds that it does diminish the effectiveness of the treatment, and that it is too difficult to estimate accurately the proper dose. The only way to settle this disagreement is to observe over a period of years a large number of patients treated with and without curare. Such observations are now being made.

It has been found that cutting the bundles of nerves in the front part of the brain seems to benefit many patients who have suffered from incurable agitation and melancholia for long periods. After this operation they are able to leave the hospital, perhaps for the first time in years, and start again to live more or less normal lives. Sometimes, however, they are *too* irresponsible and carefree after the operation and have to be watched constantly to keep them from getting into mischief, so that in some cases the cure seems to the relatives to be as bad as the disease. Fortunately this does not always occur. While the operation itself is not serious, its effects are permanent, since the nerves never grow together again, so that it is usually done only in the most serious and prolonged cases of melancholia. Some experiments in this direction are being tried in other forms of psychosis, but so far the results are uncertain. This operation should not be undertaken unless at least two well-qualified psychiatrists have agreed that it is the best possible treatment.

## 5

# What are brain waves?

We have already discussed the fact that there are electric currents going up and down the nerve cords, and that these can be measured by a galvanometer. The brain itself also gives off pulses of electricity. These are so small that they are quite impossible to measure by ordinary methods; they have a power of about 20 millionths of a volt (ordinary house electricity is 110 volts). They can be detected, however, by carefully built amplifiers, and the waves can be recorded by means of special magnetic pens or thrown on the screen of a television tube. The shape and size of the waves give much information about the state of the brain or encephalon, and these electric telegrams from the encephalon, or electroencephalograms, are of great value in detecting certain diseases of the nervous system.

The waves which come from different parts of the brain have different shapes. Usually eight small discs of metal, about the size of a split aspirin tablet, are glued to the scalp in various places and connected to the amplifiers by thin wires. Then the receiver is turned on and the "broadcast" is recorded.

As a fascinating experiment, instead of making the magnets control a pen they can be connected to a loudspeaker so that the pulses make noises instead of ink lines. In this way the electric throbbing of the brain as it works can actually be heard.

The German, Italian, American, Russian, and English doctors who first discovered these brain waves found that they were changed by many things. They changed with age, and whenever the subject opened or closed his eyes. They changed when he tried to work arithmetic problems, or when he became excited or anxious. They changed when he fell asleep, but not when he was hynotized (showing that this state is different from sleep).

The chief medical use of the "electroencephalograph" is in detecting epilepsy and brain tumors. Epileptic records show runs of smooth waves suddenly interrupted by bursts of powerful electrical discharges. Similar bursts occur in the families of epileptics in many cases, even in relatives who never had and may never have epilepsy, showing that the tendency to have fits is sometimes inherited, but that the emotions and other strains which actually cause fits may not affect everybody who has the tendency. This helps us to understand why epileptic fits may begin after a severe emotional shock or an auto accident in people who have not had them before but do have epileptic relatives.

Naturally it is necessary to know which part of the brain a tumor is growing in before an operation can be undertaken, and sometimes the electroencephalogram supplies the best clue. Since the tissue in the tumor is different from the tissue in the rest of the brain, it gives off a different kind of electric wave. By glueing electrodes to different parts of the scalp and "triangulating" like a surveyor, the exact point of origin of the abnormal impulses can often be located, and this tells the surgeon just where to go in.

No one knows exactly which part of the brain the normal waves come from, except that they probably arise in the same parts that handle conscious, "thinking," or Ego, activity, since if these parts are removed from an animal a different kind of wave appears that seems to come from the "unconscious" or "feeling" parts of the brain. The fact that the usual waves come from the "conscious" parts of the brain enables us to understand why the former change when the person is asleep or in an epileptic fit, since in such cases the "conscious" is no longer in its usual state.

6

What is an air encephalogram?

X-ray pictures are shadow pictures. X-rays do not pass easily through bones, but they do pass easily through flesh. In an X-ray picture of an arm, the bones cast more of a shadow than the flesh and therefore show up more whitely. If a bone is broken, the X-rays pass through the gap where the fracture is and make a flesh shadow where a bone shadow should be, so that the doctor knows that the bone is interrupted at that spot.

The brain is something like a coconut. It is a thick shell with watery fluid in the middle of it. Since X-rays go through the fluid and the brain equally well, an X-ray of the head does not tell much about the shape and size of the inside of the brain, nor how much space inside the skull is taken up by fluid and how much by brain tissue. If the brain shrinks, it leaves a fluid-filled space between the brain and the bone; if a tumor grows out of the brain into the fluid space, naturally some of the fluid has to be pushed out to make room for the tumor. None of this can be seen in an ordinary X-ray picture because the brain and the fluid cast the same amount of shadow.

Air, however, does not cast any shadow in an X-ray picture, and therefore can be used to show the outline of the brain.

The fluid is drained out from the skull and replaced by air. The shape and size of the brain can then be seen, because where the brain isn't the air is, and the X-rays will pass through and make no shadow; where the brain is and the air isn't, the X-rays will be stopped and make a shadow on the film. If the brain is shrinking, it will make a smaller shadow than usual, surrounded by a lot of air. If a tumor is growing into the hollow in the center of the brain, it will make a shadow corresponding to its own shape, because where the tumor is the air isn't. Abnormal cavities in the brain will show up similarly, as in the case of Philly Porenza mentioned in the first chapter. Such "diagrams" of the brain made by means of air are called air encephalograms.

The fluid is drained out by performing a spinal tap, such as we have previously described, except that instead of taking away only a few drops of the fluid that drips out, it is all taken away. The more fluid that is removed and replaced by air, the better the X-ray pictures will be. The procedure is likely to cause a headache, so some doctors inject pure oxygen instead of air, since this may be absorbed more rapidly by the blood and allow the cavities to refill with fluid more quickly.

Sometimes the procedure does more than just make it possible to take good X-rays. In certain cases of epilepsy which are due to scars and bands going between the brain and the skull, taking the fluid out and putting air in may loosen or detach the scars so that they no longer pull on the brain and irritate it, and then the fits may stop.

# 7
# Can mental illnesses be cured?

The simplest way to answer this question is to quote figures which show how much better psychiatrists can do now than they used to do. It should be borne in mind that most of the patients who received shock treatment also received the benefits of the latest developments in psychotherapy, and that this undoubtedly played a large part in obtaining the results.

The first set of figures shows what used to happen just before modern methods were introduced in the late 1930's. These patients were observed by the doctors for five years after they first came to the hospital.

| Psychosis | % cases recovered | % cases improved | Total % good results |
|---|---|---|---|
| Schizophrenia | 10% | 22% | 32% |
| Manic-depressive | 50% | 11% | 61% |
| Involutional Melancholia | 26% | 21% | 47% |
| Total | 33% | 16% | 49% |

The second table shows what happened with electric shock treatment.

| Psychosis | % recovered | % improved | Total % good results |
|---|---|---|---|
| Schizophrenia | 0% | 7% | 7% |
| Manic-depressive | 71% | 8% | 79% |
| Involutional Melancholia | 85% | 15% | 100% |

The third table shows what happened with insulin treatment in schizophrenia. Insulin shock treatment is seldom used for other types of psychosis because the results do not warrant it.

| | % recovered | % improved | Total % good results |
|---|---|---|---|
| Without insulin | 4% | 19% | 23% |
| With insulin | 13% | 52% | 65% |

About twenty-five per cent of the cases who "recovered" or improved with insulin therapy got sick again, however.

The fourth table shows the combined results of psychoanalytic treatment in several cities in Europe and America over a period of years up to 1941, in those cases where the patient continued treatment for six months or longer. It should be borne in mind that psychoanalysis requires one to two years, or even longer in some cases, to produce the best results.

| Condition | % recovered | % much improved | % improved | Total % good results |
|---|---|---|---|---|
| Psychoneurosis | 32 | 31 | 30 | 93 |
| Sexual disorders | 36 | 12 | 40 | 88 |
| Stammering | 25 | 25 | 25 | 75 |
| Alcoholism | 16 | 21 | 37 | 74 |
| Psychosis | 11 | 14 | 40 | 65 |
| Total | 28 | 28 | 30 | 86 |

The studies upon which these figures are based were all made by highly qualified and experienced psychiatrists, who had the best modern facilities and well-trained staffs available to assist them in their observations of the various groups of patients.* We may therefore consider them to be carefully planned and as reliable as it is possible to be in such matters. By and large, the figures agree with other similar studies. Because it is so difficult to continue to observe patients to see how long their improvement lasts after they leave the doctor or the hospital, and to make reliable estimates of the subtle qualities of human happiness and efficiency, it is not possible to supply tables which cover the subject sufficiently to satisfy rigid scientific requirements. We can consider the above figures, however, sufficient to give us a general idea of the possibilities of modern psychiatry.

The figures at hand demonstrate the following in regard to psychoses: first, about one third of all schizophrenics, nearly two thirds of all manic-depressives, almost half of all the so-called "involutional melancholics," and as a group, about half of all psychotics, improved without any shock treatment at all. Secondly,

* The actual sources are given in the footnotes at the end of the chapter.

electric shock apparently did more harm than good in schizo-phrenia, considerably improved the results in manic-depressives, and appeared to be almost miraculous in involutional melancholia. Thirdly, insulin shock treatment improved the results in schizo-phrenia, but in many cases the improvement was only temporary.

There is no reliable standard of comparison for the figures on the psychoanalytic treatment of the neuroses, but the last table serves to show that for the vast majority of neurotics there is no need to continue to suffer if psychoanalytic treatment is available to the individual, since twenty-eight per cent of all patients who took psychoanalytic treatment for six months or longer recovered, while eighty-six per cent derived considerable benefit. The tables also show that the results of psychoanalytic treatment of psychoses (as a group) compare favorably with the results obtained through shock treatment, and are better than the results obtained with other forms of treatment.

Too many people are apt to regard neuroses, and even more so, psychoses, as incurable, and these figures should do much to hearten such pessimists.

## Footnotes for Philosophers, Chapter Eight

1. *Psychotherapy*

The principal methods have been mentioned. For more de-tailed discussion, see:

"Psychiatric Therapy," by Kenneth E. Appel. Chapter 34 in *Personality and the Behavior Disorders*, op. cit.

2. *Hypnosis*

The powers of the Yogis, as confirmed by the Calcutta Medi-cal Society, are recounted in:

*The Mysterious Kundalini*, by Vasant Gangaram Rele. D. B. Taraporevala Sons & Company: Bombay, 1929, 2nd ed.

The discussion of the relative value of hypnosis and of psy-chotherapy in the waking state *in the same amount of elapsed time* is based on personal experience in conjunction with other therapists.

Most popular books on hypnotism are highly misleading. The

following are two of the more serious articles on the subject outside of the periodical literature:

*Hypnotherapy*, by Margaret Brenman & Merton M. Gill. Josiah Macy, Jr. Foundation: New York, 1944.

"Hypnotism," by Arthur Jenness. In *Personality and the Behavior Disorders*, op. cit., Chapter 15.

3. *Narcotherapy*

See *Men Under Stress*, by Grinker & Spiegel. Op. cit.

4. & 5.

The subjects covered in these sections are discussed in detail in *Personality and the Behavior Disorders*, Chapters 34 & 33, by Kenneth E. Appel and Donald B. Lindsley, respectively.

7. *The Results of Therapy*

The figures cited in this section are chosen because they are easily available to the layman, since they are also quoted by Appel, op. cit. They are modified here from the following original sources: Table 1 from Bond and Braceland, 1937; Table 2 from Smith et al., 1942; Table 3 from Malzberg, 1938; Table 4 from Knight, 1941.

### CHAPTER NINE

# PSYCHOANALYTIC TREATMENT

---

## I

## What is psychoanalysis?

FIRST OF ALL, psychoanalysis is a method of treatment, and every analyst is first a physician. He tries to relieve his patients of their complaints, and also to send them forth free of unnecessary doubts, unreasonable guilts, distressing self-reproaches, faulty judgments, and unwise impulses. Psychoanalysis tries to remold the personality, and not merely to comfort the patient. But the analyst is only a guide and adviser, and the patient or "analysand" has the responsibility in the end for the finished product.

Secondly, analysis is a method for the scientific observation and study of the personality, especially in regard to wishes, impulses, and motives.

Thirdly, analysis is a system of scientific psychology. This means that the observations and ideas of psychoanalysis can be used in an attempt to predict human behavior and the outcomes of human relationships, such as marriage and parenthood.

The system of ideas we have set forth up to this point are mostly the results of psychoanalytic observation. We shall now deal with psychoanalysis as a method of treatment.

## 2

## How psychoanalysis is carried on

The process of psychoanalysis consists in the study and reorganization of the personality in order to enable the individual to store tensions with more wisdom and less discomfort until the appropriate time for relief, and also to express freely without doubts or guilts, in accordance with the Reality Principle, tensions whose relief is permitted or demanded by a situation. For example, it tries to enable him to conceal irritation when it is wise to do so, and express anger when it is worthy to do so.

Psychoanalysis attempts to do this by studying the Id tensions of the individual, opening avenues for relief when it is practical, and bringing them as much as possible under conscious control. To complete the process requires sessions lasting about an hour, three to six times a week, for at least a year. If the study lasts less than a year, or there are fewer than three sessions a week, it is almost impossible to carry it through to completion. If the extent of the treatment is cut in either of these two ways, the psychoanalytic method may be used, but the individual will not have been psychoanalyzed. A complete psychoanalysis is always a long and tedious process. Nothing short of this constitutes "a psychoanalysis."

In order to make the unconscious conscious, and to bring under observation the unsatisfied tensions which have collected in the Id since earliest childhood, the patient usually lies on a couch, at the head of which sits the analyst out of the patient's sight. Thus the patient's mind is free to work without distractions. He cannot see the doctor's face and so is not disturbed by the latter's facial reaction, if any, to what he says. This avoids some interference with the free flow of thoughts, since the likelihood that in most cases if he had an idea as to what made the analyst look pleased or displeased, he might tend to regulate what he said accordingly, and might be influenced more than was desirable by observing the doctor's behavior. The doctor can also relax better and concentrate harder on what the patient says, since he is not under the continual scrutiny of the latter.

The method used is called "free association." By this is meant the free expression of a free flow of ideas not hindered or changed by the usual conscious censoring forces: the conscious Ego Ideal (politeness, shame, self-respect), the conscious conscience (religion, education, and other principles), and the conscious Ego (orderliness, reality-testing, conscious desire for gain). Indeed, the very things the patient would usually not say are often the most important ones for the analysis. Thus, he will sometimes underline the significant things by his very hesitancy. It is the things the patient feels are obscene, wicked, rude, irrelevant, boring, trivial, or absurd, which the analyst frequently pays special attention to.

In the freely associating state, the patient's mind often becomes crowded with desires, feelings, reproaches, memories, fancies, judgments, and new viewpoints, often in an apparently disordered jumble. And yet in spite of the seeming confusion and lack of connection, every utterance and gesture has its bearing on some ungratified Id tension. As the hours go by, day after day, meanings and connections begin to appear out of the disordered skein of thoughts. Gradually there may develop over a long period some central themes referring to a series of ungratified infantile tensions long buried from conscious recognition which are at the bottom of the patient's personality structure and from which his symptoms and associations arise. The patient's experience during the analysis may be a feeling of jumping from one thing to another without rhyme or reason, and often it is difficult or impossible for him to see the common threads running through them all. This is where the skill of the analyst performs its function, by detecting and pointing out the underlying tensions which bring forth and hold together the seemingly disconnected associations.

The analyst keeps a strictly neutral attitude toward his patients, even though his life is bound up with theirs daily for one or more years, and he relives with them in minute detail their current and past experiences.

Since the analyst's job, in a way, is mostly to point out to the patient when he is fooling himself, the doctor must maintain a continual attitude of self-criticism to make sure that he is not, out of sympathy or irritation, allowing the patient to fool the doctor as well as himself. An emotional attitude on the part of the analyst toward the patient is called *counter-transference*. The analyst must be just as skillful in detecting and handling such feelings in himself as he is in detecting and handling the patient's attitude toward him, which takes the form of *transference*.

This is one of the chief reasons why it is necessary for an orthodox psychoanalyst (that is, a member of the International Psycho-Analytical Association or one of its recognized institutes) to be analyzed himself before he starts to practice, for if he did not understand his own unconscious tensions thoroughly, he might unwittingly allow his judgment to be influenced by some countertransference or his own mood or sympathies of the moment, and he might lose sight of or damage the long-term effect of the treatment. The purpose of analysis is not to make the patient feel comfortable while he is with the doctor, but to enable him to handle his own problems independently of the doctor in the long years to come. A misplaced word might encourage a harmful self-pitying attitude or seem to justify the patient's errors in judgment, which it is the purpose of the treatment to teach him to avoid; or on the other hand, it might increase the patient's already neurotic guilt feelings. This does not mean that the analyst lacks human feelings or sympathies. It only means that he has to be able to recognize his own feelings clearly, so that he will not regard in a prejudiced way what the patient says. The patient comes to the analyst for understanding, not for moral verdicts. The doctor remains neutral only for the patient's good, and not because he is cold.

Analysis does *not* make the patient dependent upon the doctor. In fact, it deliberately takes pains to avoid this, by analyzing and carefully dissolving this very bond (the relationship between the doctor and the patient) so that the patient will be a free individual, independent and able to stand on his own feet. This is the very purpose of analysis.

The reader will now understand that contrary to popular belief, when a parlor psychologist, or even a professional psychiatrist, fixes someone with a gimlet eye and says: "My, but you are an introvert!" this is *not* psychoanalysis. Psychoanalysis is a very special and definite method of observation and psychotherapy which takes a long, long time.

### 3

### What happens during an analysis?

During analysis, the image of the analyst tends gradually to become charged with all the piled-up energy of ungratified Id wishes which has collected since the patient's earliest infancy. Once this energy has been corralled in one image, it can be studied and redistributed, and the tensions partly relieved by analyzing the patient's image of the analyst. In ordinary language, this means that after a while the patient may become very emotional about the analyst. Since in reality he knows very little about the doctor, he must be acting and feeling in accordance with an image he made up himself. The analyst remains neutral throughout the treatment, and actually presents himself to the patient as not much more than a guiding voice. As there is no reasonable basis for loving or hating a neutral person, the feelings which swirl around the image of the analyst must not have been aroused by him, but by other people, and the patient with his permission and sometimes encouragement, uses the analyst as a scapegoat for tensions he could not relieve on their proper objects. He transfers his libido and mortido from these objects to his image of the analyst. That is why the attitude of the patient toward the analyst is called transference.

We may say this in still another way: during the analysis, in a manner of speaking, the patient may attempt to finish the unfinished business of his childhood, using the analyst as a substitute for his parents, so that afterward he can devote all his energies to the business of being an adult.

Of course this is an attempt which is never completely successful. The patient has to give up his defenses, painfully erected over a period of years, and meet his disagreeable and unacceptable Id impulses in the open and wrestle with them. He is willing to do this for the sake of getting better, for the sake of the money he is paying, and for the sake of the analyst's approval. It is sometimes an uncomfortable, distressing, and painful experience, and the analyst uses every method he can to make the patient anxious to fight hard to get well. Otherwise he may try to prolong his nice cosy protected relationship with the doctor. This cosy feeling, combined with his unconscious reluctance to part with his symptom defenses and the attention and self-pitying satisfaction he may get through them, might drag the treatment out indefinitely.

Analysis attempts to change emotions, not merely to call them names. It is a talking treatment only because words are the best way the patient has of expressing his emotions to himself and to the doctor. The important things are the feelings and what happens to them, and not the scientific words used to describe them.

The idea that analysis consists of deciding which adjectives to apply to a patient is entirely wrong. Adjectives cure no neuroses. It may be interesting, and perhaps reassuring, to be told that one is a thymergasic extroverted pyknophilic endomorph with an inferiority complex and disharmonious vagotonic borborygmi, but it is not curative.

Lavinia Eris, at the beginning of her analysis with Dr. Treece, asked:

"Doctor, at the end of this treatment, will you give me a sort of diagram of myself with a description of my personality?"

To which Dr. Treece replied:

"Madam, if at the end of the treatment you still wish to have a written description of your personality, then the treatment will have been a failure!"

There is one thing above all that we must learn: namely, that happiness depends upon the fluid and dynamic urges and feelings of the human spirit, and not upon a group of neatly labeled and classified gadgets which have only to be plugged in at the right time for the toast of life to emerge neatly browned and buttered. Unfortunately, the popular magazines, and many legitimate psychologists as well, only too freely encourage and elaborate the "dashboard" theory of the personality at the expense of the individual dynamic approach. Psychoanalysis leaves to others the answers to such questions as: "Are you intelligent?" "What is your charm quotient?" and "Are you a typical wife?"

Psychoanalysts are concerned with the problem, not of which statistic fits, but of Who is You? Or perhaps it was even better put by a long-forgotten movie comedian many years ago, when he kept asking people: "You are who?" Intelligence, for example, is a tool, and not really a part of You, and the important thing is whether the unconscious allows the individual to use this tool properly.

We often hear people say: "I could do it if I wanted to!" The answer to this is, "Of course you could!" Anybody can do almost anything if he wants to badly enough. There is a one-legged man who has become a great jitterbug. The important question is not,

"Could you?" but, "Do you want to as much as you think you do, and if not, why not?" Analysis is concerned mainly with desires and only incidentally with capabilities. Perhaps the question the analyst silently asks the patient can best be written thus: "How much are you willing to give up in order to be happy?" It will be seen that this has little to do with intelligence, charm, or statistics.

# 4

# Who should be psychoanalyzed?

Psychoanalysis was originally devised mainly for the treatment of neuroses. As time went on, it was found that many other people besides frank neurotics benefited from it. Among the most common types of neurosis, which we have previously discussed, psychoanalysis is most useful in hysteria and the anxiety neuroses. It is often efficient in the character neuroses, and can do a great deal for compulsion neuroses depending partly on how interested the patient is in getting the most out of the treatment. For hypochondriasis it is the best treatment we have, but this condition requires long analysis for reasons already noted.

Psychoanalytic methods are being used more and more in the treatment of psychoses and especially in the prevention of recurrences. It requires special training, talent, and effort to use them in these conditions, and doctors who are fully competent to treat psychoses by psychoanalytic methods are very uncommon.

As for "normal" people being analyzed, this is happening all the time. Many well-adjusted psychiatrists are being and have been analyzed for training purposes. Many social workers and psychologists also go through an analysis so that they will be able to understand people better and co-operate with psychoanalysts in treating others. In spite of the expense and hardship which younger people with limited incomes must go through to accomplish the task, most of these "normals" consider analysis the best investment they ever made or are ever likely to make, because they are happier, wiser, and more efficient human beings as a result. Everyone has ungratified tensions stored up from infancy, whether these tensions express themselves in openly neurotic ways or not, and it is always a help to have one's unsatisfied Id energies reorganized and partly relieved through analysis.

The question often arises, is psychoanalysis harmful to some people? The writer personally knows of no cases where the analysis of a neurotic or a so-called "normal" person in the hands of a well-trained and recognized Freudian analyst, carried through to the satisfaction of the doctor, has done anything but good to the individual. The greatest danger lies in treating a patient who is on the verge of a psychosis when the analyst does not realize that the patient is ready for a psychosis. This is one reason why analysts nowadays are required to have a thorough training in medical psychiatry before they are accepted by the American Psychoanalytic Association. Fully qualified lay analysts are also well equipped to detect this possibility, however.

Another kind of danger comes from people who break off an analysis in the middle, against the advice of the doctor, and then advertise the fact that they were psychoanalyzed by so-and-so (which is untrue since they did not go through with the treatment) and that it made them worse. This is much like a patient getting off the operating table before he is sewed up and then claiming that the surgeon made his wound bigger. Psychoanalysts hesitate to start treatment when they suspect that an individual is more interested in this kind of showing-off than in getting better.

## 5

## Who was Freud?

Like all great doctors, Sigmund Freud, the discoverer of psycho-analysis, was interested first in curing sick people, and secondly in finding out what made them sick so that similar sicknesses could be prevented from occurring in other people. To these purposes he devoted his life, trying to help people just as William Osler, the great physician, and Harvey Cushing, the great brain surgeon did, and trying to find something which would enable others to help them, just as Andrew Fleming, the discoverer of penicillin, and

William Ehrlich, the discoverer of salvarsan, "the magic bullet," did. Like nearly all great doctors, he was a dignified gentleman who was not interested in publicity, riches, or pornography. Since one of his most important discoveries was the significance of sexual tensions in causing neurosis, however, and since he made so bold as to publish his observations, publicity came to him in spite of all his efforts to live the quiet studious life which is so beloved of those who wish to devote themselves to science.

He is usually talked about as though he personally had discovered sex, and his name has even become a synonym for second-rate writers to use when they mean "sexual." It should therefore be said that sexual ideas are not "Freudian," but exist in the minds of those who call them so in an attempt to make Freud accountable for their own thoughts, of which for no worthy reason, they seem to be ashamed.

Even if he had not discovered psychoanalysis, Freud would have been a great man because of his other discoveries. He was the first to make a sensible and clear scheme of classification of the neuroses, doing for them what the great and respected Dr. Kraepelin did in classifying the psychoses. Thus, any doctor who makes a diagnosis of anxiety neurosis is practicing Freudian psychiatry, however much he might be horrified at the idea (as some doctors still are).

Another discovery of Freud's concerned a form of "spastic paralysis" in children called "Little's disease." Freud discovered the probable way in which this disease comes about.

Perhaps his greatest contribution to medical science, aside from psychoanalysis, was his connection with the discovery of local anesthesia. The development of local anesthetics, upon which a good deal of modern surgery is based, may be said to have started in large part from Freud's experiments with cocaine. An eye doctor named Koller is generally given credit for the discovery of local anesthesia, and in his first painless operation he used a cocaine solution which his friend Freud had prepared and given him in a little bottle. People who go to dentists as well as people who go to psychiatrists therefore owe Freud a debt of gratitude.

Thus, even before he had fully developed psychoanalysis, which is one of the great discoveries of our civilization, Freud had elevated himself to a position of eminence in medicine and psychiatry

Some of the doctors who criticize him are not aware of the other things he did, and have not themselves had a thorough psychoanalysis, nor thoroughly analyzed many patients according to his method. Many of these people say that they have analyzed patients but admit that they have not quite followed his method; yet they blame him because their treatment did not work. This is like a critic of Thomas Edison building a model of one of Edison's machines, but leaving out some of Edison's ideas and putting in a few of his own, and then criticizing Edison because the machine didn't work!

Freud's discoveries in psychology rank with Darwin's discoveries in biology, and have done perhaps more to change the thinking and viewpoint of people all over the world. The quality of the men who follow Freud's ideas, and apply them carefully, methodically, and sincerely, is a good testimonial to their value. The group of his older and respected followers contains men of culture, intelligence, and wisdom. Among younger men who enter the study of medicine, Freud's ideas have an almost irresistible attraction for many of those with the greatest intelligence and human understanding.

# 6

# Freud and his followers

Sigmund Freud was born in 1856 in what is now part of Czechoslovakia, and he died in England in 1939. He spent most of his life in Vienna, where he acquired a brilliant group of followers, who felt that by using his ideas they could do more to help neurotic patients than by any other methods. These men spread his ideas throughout Europe and America. After a while, some of them broke away from the original Psychoanalytic Society, and founded schools of their own. The best known of these dissenters are Alfred Adler and Carl Jung.

About 1910, Alfred Adler began to turn his attention to certain conscious factors in the personality, and gradually veered away from Freud's basic ideas, namely, the importance of the infantile libido and the driving force of the unconscious Id. After a while Adler himself realized that his ideas were getting farther and farther away from those of Freudian psychoanalysis, so he dropped this word and called his system "Individual Psychology."

His best known idea is the "inferiority complex." By this he means the feelings which center around an evident physical or mental handicap. Lameness, short stature, and stuttering are examples of such handicaps. "Inferiorities" arouse an intense desire to make up for them and gain power and prestige in some other way. At times this is done by developing some other organ than the one affected, but often it is accomplished by giving the inferior function special attention until it is developed beyond the average and can be used to raise the individual to a superior position in society. Thus we have the lame Byron becoming a famous swimmer, and the stuttering Demosthenes becoming a celebrated orator; while the undersized Napoleon got his compensation by becoming a powerful leader of fighting men.

The reactions started by the inferiority complex strengthen the "will to power," resulting in a forceful "masculine protest"; that is, an attempt to prove superior manliness. This striving for power, according to Adler, causes the symptoms of neurosis. Sometimes the masculine protest produces exceptional ability, as in the cases of Byron and Napoleon, but too often there is no way for the individual to prove his superiority in the world of competition, so he expresses his protest in a way which wastes the time and energy of himself and those around him. According to Adler, since women have a harder time asserting their masculine will to power, they have more neuroses.

Psychoanalysts feel that the methods of treatment advocated by Adler, which are based largely on reasoning with the patient, do not go deep enough to affect permanent changes in the individual's way of handling his energy, and that they are therefore more useful for guidance than for actual treatment.

Carl Jung's earlier books, especially those dealing with the psychology of schizophrenia, and with word-association tests, are highly regarded by psychiatrists. In 1912, however, he published a book on the psychology of the unconscious in which it appeared that his ideas were taking quite a different track from those of psychoanalysis. He began to call his system "analytic psychology," to distinguish it from psychoanalysis. Jung traveled in India and Africa, and after these journeys became especially interested in the mystical aspects of the mind. As time went on, his ideas became more and more different from his teacher's, and he began to stress heavily some teachings which he imported from the Orient and which have little relation to psychology as we know it in the western world. In addition, he gives less attention than the psychoanalysts to the relationships between the mind and body, so that it is more difficult to fit his ideas into the framework of modern medicine.

Many of Jung's ideas are striking and thought provoking, particularly his approach to the question of images, but the way he uses them appears questionable to many people.

Another discontented member of the Freudian family is Karen Horney. Adler, Jung, and Horney (as well as Rank and Stekel) are or were thoughtful psychiatrists with considerable experience, and what they have to say must be taken seriously and carefully considered before any opinion can be expressed as to the value of their ideas. No one can deny their observations, and they are entitled to their own interpretations of what went on with their patients. The only problem at issue is whether they were each justified in shifting the emphasis from the ungratified, unconscious Id tensions of early infancy to the various other factors which these authors are interested in. The orthodox Freudian psychoanalysts say that they were not, and point to their own observations and the practical results of their treatment as evidence to support their judgment.

Horney tends to emphasize the conflicts of the individual with his surroundings of the moment, rather than the residues left over from infancy. Orthodox analysts feel that she makes an error here, and that treatment directed mostly towards solving current conflicts will not have the lasting results which come from relaxing earlier tensions. Nevertheless, they appreciate the fact that, like Adler, she has made a useful contribution in giving special study to certain aspects of the personality.

One of Horney's chief attempts to introduce new ways into psychoanalysis is concerned with self-analysis. Psychoanalysis is a long and expensive procedure, out of reach of many people, and any valuable method of shortening the time required and reducing the expense would be a great contribution to the field of psychiatry. Dr. Horney feels that in some cases the patient may be able to continue analysis without the close guidance of the doctor, once he or she has learned the method. She claims that some people may gain a clear understanding of their unconscious tensions without the supervision of a professional analyst. She presents evidence to support this view. Dr. Horney herself, however, has expressed some misgivings about advising the widespread use of such a method. It seems proper to compare self-analysis as she describes it, to giving oneself a haircut rather than having a barber do it. Judging from what she writes, the qualifications that a patient must have to carry on self-analysis successfully include: a college education, a complete freedom from all the usual moral prejudices, and an extremely high degree of "psychological intuition."

The psychoanalysts of the Chicago Institute for Psychoanalysis, under the leadership of Dr. Franz Alexander, have been conducting experiments during the past few years in an attempt to cut down the time required for "psychoanalysis," sometimes to only a few visits in the course of a week or two. By using psychoanalytic principles in their psychotherapy, they have sometimes succeeded in relieving patients of one or more symptoms in a remarkably short time. Most orthodox psychoanalysts in other parts of the country, however, after studying the results of the Chicago group, feel that the latter are practicing a modified form of "going to a psychiatrist" (as described in the previous chapter), rather than practicing psychoanalysis. They feel that the Chicago analysts do effect some changes in the personalities of their patients, but that they are not the deep and lasting changes that orthodox analysts feel give the best results in happiness and efficiency.

Modified analysis of any kind is still in the experimental stage and is bound to be so for another twenty years until a goodly number of patients can be followed through various critical periods in their lives, such as the menopause, to see how they hold up after such treatment. For those who wish to or are forced to have a modified form of treatment, there is no reason why hope should not be held out, but most psychiatrists are inclined to make reservations for the present as to how far the good effects will go and how permanent they will be.

## 7

## Group treatment

While it is usually, though not always, preferable to have individual treatment in psychiatry, this may not be available to people of limited means. A complete psychoanalysis may cost as much as a new car (but less than a college education, though it is at least as valuable as the latter). It may run anywhere from $1500 up, spread over a period of a year or two. Single visits to a psychiatrist cost from $5 to $50. This is not excessive from the psychiatrist's point of view when compared on an hourly basis with what a surgeon of equal training earns, and considering that he may earn almost nothing from his profession until he is well beyond thirty; but it still puts paid individual psychiatric treatment out of reach of many people, since each case may require many hours of the doctor's time. Psychiatrists are well aware of the possible financial hardships which may add to the patients' problems. Much of the future of practical psychiatry, therefore, lies in group treatment, where the fees may be only a dollar or two per session for each patient.

There are different kinds of group treatment, each with its own value for the patient. The simplest kind consists of lectures and *pep talks*. Next in order of complexity and value comes "permissive" treatment, where the individual learns to give free expression to his thoughts and feelings, so that he no longer fights and fears them, and in addition relieves himself of a burden of pent-up conscious tensions. *Psychodrama*, which is more complicated still, consists of having the individual act out his conflicts on a stage, with the aid of a cast composed of other patients or trained assistants, before an audience of the remaining patients and the staff. The casting is carefully done so as to accomplish the maximum amount of good for the greatest number of patients. In a simple case, a man who resents his father may be cast as the father of a resentful boy, so that he will be able to feel his father's point of view. A young man who represses all his mortido in real life may be cast as the rebellious son, so that he will learn how to express himself, and find out how much aggression he has piled up inside him which he is unaware of. Severe emotional stresses may be re-enacted so that the subject can express himself fully and completely, and get rid of his pent-up fears and guilts, much as Si Seifuss did on an individual scale. Psychiatrists with a certain type of personality can obtain excellent results with some kinds of patients in this way. Other psychiatrists, who try psychodrama "out of the book," and are not really built to be casting directors, fail.

The most complicated, and in the opinion of psychiatrists who have used it along with other methods, the most useful form of group therapy is a modified form of *group psychoanalysis*. This is best employed with individuals of average or above average intelligence with long-standing neuroses of moderate severity. It employs free association, dream interpretation, and free expression of thoughts and feelings; and it attempts to study unconscious as well as conscious images and feelings, and to effect a deep reorganization of the emotional drives of the individual. At the present time, it is only employed in a few rare cases in this country, and is being most thoroughly studied in England. It is a new form of treatment which is still very much in the experimental stage, but the results are gratifying and sometimes startlingly effective.

In this form of treatment, in the author's experience, the groups consist of from six to fifteen patients. Usually the first two weeks are spent in getting acquainted and in learning something about how human beings work and what the object of the treatment is. Before entering the group, the patient has a thorough physical examination and a private interview with the psychiatrist. If a psychologist and a social worker, or other trained people, sit in with the group, each patient has a private interview with them also. Preferably the group meets every day at the same hour, but sometimes it is only possible to meet once a week. Naturally, the oftener the meetings take place, the more can be accomplished over a given period. Once in a while the groups switch times, since the material the patients bring up at different times of the day may help the psychiatrist understand them better. It is important for the psychiatrist to know as soon as possible what kind of personalities he is dealing with, and since he cannot spend much time with each patient, he may give them certain tests in order to have something to go on until he finds out in the group what each patient's problems are.

The members of each group are carefully selected so that they will have the best effect on each other, both in helping each other's personality development and in encouraging each other to talk freely and think clearly about what they have said.

There are various stages in group treatment: the stage of getting acquainted (forming transferences to the psychiatrist and to each other); the stage of "group feeling," when the members begin to feel that they have something in common; the stage of "real work," when they begin to see more clearly their difficulties in getting along with others and themselves; the stage of group adjustment, when they begin to understand how to get along better with people; and the stage of individual dynamics, when they begin to grasp their own Id drives and those of the others in the group.

The psychiatrist takes all precautions to see that the members will feel comfortable in the group, especially in making it clear that what is said in the meetings must be respected by those in the group and not treated lightly or discussed with anyone else on the outside. It is most important that the members of the group feel confidence in one another so that they will not be afraid to say what they want to.

The important thing about group therapy is that with a group of ten, for example, the psychiatrist can do for each individual far more than one-tenth of what he would accomplish in the same number of individual interviews. If this were not so, group therapy would have little reason to exist. As is often the case in individual therapy, between meetings and after the treatment is terminated the process of improvement seems to continue.

Under the best conditions, two people besides the psychiatrist, such as a female social worker and a male social worker or psychologist, are engaged in the treatment, and they and the doctor are available for individual interviews up to a certain point as their time permits. The members of the group are free to choose which of the three they want to see in such cases. If all three have been psychoanalyzed, conditions may be said to be ideal, but this is not absolutely necessary. It is possible, however, to carry on successful group therapy without the privilege of individual interviews and with only the psychiatrist attending.

By this method, distressing symptoms can be cleared up temporarily or permanently, and in some cases a real change in the individual's emotional make-up takes place; while what he learns about himself and how to get along with other people stays with him and is useful for the rest of his life.

Everyone will understand that each case is different, but just to have something to go on, one might say that in general the patient receives three times as much for his money in group therapy as he would receive in individual sessions, if he can spend only a definite small sum. In some cases this benefit is more, in some less.

Group therapy is even more desirable from society's point of view than from that of the financially limited individual. There are millions of neurotics in this country who are prospective or actual parents. Every neurotic individual who has children is likely to bring them up to be neurotic, so that for this reason alone, disregarding the other factors which encourage neurosis in the world today, the number of neurotics is continually increasing by geometric leaps. Every time a neurotic is cured, or at least given knowledge of his or her condition, the next generation benefits.

It would be impossible for the limited number of well-trained psychiatrists in this country, and the still more limited number of psychoanalysts, to make a significant reduction in the total number of neurotics in the population by individual treatment. Group therapy enables each psychiatrist to treat five or ten times as many patients as he could individually. Even if he cannot give each member of a group as much personal benefit, he can at least make each member a better parent by what he teaches him about human beings and about himself. From the point of view of the nation's future and the world's future, it is more important to go to a psychiatrist in order to become a better parent than it is in order to be cured oneself. This is where group therapy has its greatest value.

## 8

# Psychoanalysis at work

We shall not try to describe here an orthodox psychoanalysis, since that would be too complicated. We shall only try to show how a psychoanalytically minded psychiatrist thinks of his patients' problems. Dr. Treece did more talking and suggesting with Rex Bigfoot than he did with his regular analysands, which is why this case is chosen to present here, since the doctor's comments make it easier to follow his train of thought. The asterisks refer to the footnotes, which indicate the points illustrated as the case proceeds.

Life was a puzzle to Rex Bigfoot. In spite of his unusual name, Rex did not have Indian blood. His ancestors came from everywhere west of Omsk and east of San Francisco, and some of them had been great men. As a child, Rex had lived the normal life of a valley boy, joining the other boys in hoisting the neighbors' threshing-machines up on the roof of the barn, and dynamiting their privies.

For a while after he had married Gala Eris, the girl he had seen in his wonderful dream, he thought he had found the answer to his loneliness. Now his troubles had begun all over again, and he was even worse off than he had been after his father died. That is, it actually wasn't his father, but he always thought of him as his father. That had been one of the first things to puzzle him.*

Dr. Pell, the skin specialist, told Dr. Treece about Rex one day in January in the hospital dining room. Dr. Pell thought that psychiatry could help Rex, although some of the other doctors disagreed.† Dr. Treece said he would take the case, even though he wondered whether he would be able to accomplish very much.

---

\* Unless the affair is managed with the utmost care, children whose parents were divorced when they were very young often find life confusing even after they grow up.

† Skin specialists are one group of doctors who are especially interested in the possibilities of psychiatric treatment. They know from experience how powerfully the emotions can affect the physical manifestations of disease.

The next day, Dr. Pell sent Rex up to see Dr. Treece. Rex came into the office timidly. He was a large, heavy-set man, much too meek for his size, and was scared of nearly everybody. He managed to get along, however, by being very quiet and keeping out of people's way.* It was difficult now because people made fun of him if he took his hat off and they made fun of him if he kept it on. Dr. Treece didn't ask him to take his hat off,† and pretty soon Rex was telling him the whole story of his life, including all the secrets he hadn't ever told anybody before.

One thing Rex liked about Dr. Treece was that he didn't interrupt him much. Rex had a lot of things on his mind that he wanted to talk over with somebody smarter than he was, but all the doctors he had met so far had kept interrupting him with questions. This confused him and made him feel that he wasn't telling them the kind of things that they thought were important, and that maybe he was wasting their time. Dr. Treece let him talk about whatever he wished.‡

"My father died when I was fifteen. I always had trouble with him. He used to drive me out of the house even when I was only ten or eleven years old; then I would have to go and stay with my uncle, the Reverend Volk, who I didn't like. I was away from home when my father died, and felt very sad about it. I guess I had a nervous breakdown.§ My mother remarried seven years ago, when I was twenty, to an old man about seventy. I never liked him, either. He's ugly and bald-headed.

* Rex was a strong man physically, and had no need to fear anyone. What he was really afraid of was his own libido and mortido in his relationships with other people. He handled this problem by repressing his Id instincts and avoiding contacts with people which might activate his repressed urges.

† Psychiatrists usually let patients do as they please, especially at the beginning of the treatment. The psychiatrist's job is to observe what the patient does and help him understand why he does it, not to teach him manners.

‡ The psychiatrist wants to know what *is* troubling the patient. Some people like to tell the individual what *they* think *should* be troubling him.

§ This illustrates the ambivalent feelings which a neurotic father arouses in the child. Rex wanted only to love his father, but his father wouldn't let him. He made Rex hate him as well. Rex's breakdown had two main sources: first, the loss of a loved one; secondly, guilt resulting from unconscious death wishes due to his father's hateful behavior. The latter is exactly the same mechanism we saw in the case of Wendell Meleager following his uncle's death.

"I feel awfully tired. I cry sometimes, I am so tired. I don't feel rested when I wake up in the morning. * My appetite is poor and I don't have much desire for sex. That worries me. This all began in September, when I lost my old job.

"I'm going to tell you the real trouble, which I have never told anybody before. My mother was only sixteen when I was born. She divorced my real father right after I was born, and I never saw him. I might as well have been born out of wedlock. I guess she was pregnant when she married him. The man I called father all my life used to say when I was a kid: 'You are no child of mine!' I didn't know what he meant then. The boys on the street used to call me names, and I didn't know what they meant either. Right after my father died, my cousin Horace Volk told me he wasn't really my father. He heard it from his father. I didn't believe him. When my mother told me, I knew it was true, but somehow I still didn't believe it. I was so mixed up I ran away from home for a few days. She told me she was about six weeks pregnant when she married my real father.† I guess I never forgave her for having me that way. In the first place, she shouldn't have got into that fix, and in the second place, she should have left Olympia where everybody knew about it and made fun of me. Excuse me for crying a little when I tell you this.‡ As I said, I never told anybody about it before.

"I began to lose my hair last August. Up to then I had a lot of bushy black hair. It began to fall out. I guess I was worried. I had a fight with my boss, and he told me I would be through at the end of the month. I never did get along with him, and I was worried about it for quite a while, as I knew I would lose that job sooner or later. It was the kind of job I like, working on the roads outdoors with only a few other men. I knew if I lost it I'd have to go into a factory where I'd be working indoors with a crowd of men,§ and

* Rex didn't feel rested in the morning because he had done a hard night's work keeping his Id tensions under control.

† Some things are better left unsaid.

‡ This kind of crying, which is an outlet for long pent-up grief and anger, is beneficial and healing. It helps to relieve Id tensions and readjust them in a more healthy way.

§ Thus subjecting his already disturbed Id tensions to further turmoil.

all kinds of inspectors and supervisors coming around.* That kind of job where they watch you close always did beat me.

"Well, it happened just that way. I had to go to work for Mr. King in the cannery. Four days after I started there, I was taking a shower, and all of a sudden I noticed my hair was coming out in handfuls. It has been coming out ever since, all over my body. I don't even have to shave any more, and I'm ashamed to take my hat off because I'm as bald as a cantaloupe, and my skin is so smooth, like a woman's, I'm afraid to get undressed in the showers in front of the other men." †

After Rex had talked for about an hour, the visit ended, and Dr. Treece looked over the reports that Dr. Pell had sent him. Rex had had all the tests in the book, and there was nothing in his medical history to account for his condition. There was hardly a hair left on his body. His head, face, armpits, pubis, arms, and legs were almost completely bald. He had gone to various doctors and tried lotions, ointments, massage, vitamins, hormones, sun lamps, infrared lamps, and every other physical treatment that they could think up, but the remaining hair continued to fall out. At the time he came to Dr. Treece, all other treatments had been given up.

Rex came to the office the next afternoon and told about a dream he had had.

"I had a dream I want to tell you about. I never had a dream like that before," he said. "I never did dream much anyway. I haven't had one for over four months. This was different from any dream I ever had. It was about you.‡

"I was in an enclosure like a garden, with a fence around it. You were there with me.§ Then I saw six things shaped like funnels,

* After what his experiences with his father did to his Id tensions, it is no wonder that Rex had difficulty getting along with those in authority.

† This affliction is not as rare as one might think. It is called "alopecia totalis."

‡ This meant that Rex's unconscious was beginning to form an image of the doctor. This was a good sign, since this was the image which would play the greatest part in curing Rex, and the quicker it was formed the better. See the discussion of the case of Horace Volk, Rex's cousin. In difficult cases it may take months for such an image to show itself.

§ This was an especially good sign. It meant that Rex was ready to admit the doctor into the fenced-off garden of his innermost emotional life.

cyclones they must have been, coming toward us, and I said to you: 'This is the end of the world, this is the end of time.' * Then I woke up. The dream made me afraid."

As Rex had no experience in interpreting dreams, Dr. Treece tried to help him. He suggested that Rex tell him what the dream reminded him of.

"Suppose we start with the fence," he said. "What does it remind you of?"

"Nothing," said Rex, thinking for a minute. "I never saw a fence like that before."

"Well, what about the six cyclones?"

"They don't remind me of anything. I have six brothers, if that means anything."

"Well!" said Dr. Treece, and went on to discuss his brothers with Rex. Rex said he had always felt that they were closer to his father and mother than he was, because he was a stepchild. From there they went on to discuss how a child needs to feel loved and to be allowed to love in order to grow up to be happy. Rex said suddenly:

"I guess the fence separated me from the people outside and kept them off my private property. But you were on the inside."

"Well," said the doctor. "There were your six brothers threatening your safety like six cyclones, just when I was beginning to make you feel safer. You have to fence off your private feelings and keep the world away from them because you are worried about your origin. People might find out too much if you didn't fence them out of your mind. But you're willing to admit me as a friend, someone who will try to help you instead of harm you if you let me inside the garden of your feelings, do you see what I mean?"

"It's true," said Rex. "I don't like to let people get too friendly with me, not even my wife. I feel kind of ashamed of myself."

"The dream means: 'I feel safe with you inside the enclosure, but it can't last, there are too many threats.'"

"I have a hunch your feelings toward your mother trouble you

* Even a simple man like Rex, with little education, can be a poet in his dreams. There is a hint of similarity between Rex's dream and that of Pharaoh described in Genesis, Chapter 4.

more than you think.* You must love her, but you also told me you resented the way she got pregnant with you. That's one reason you feel mixed up. I think there are other things about her that you have forgotten, but which still rankle in your mind even if you don't know it."

"I guess I feel pretty ashamed of her."

"One thing we find is that these things that happen to the body from anxiety are often useful to the person in some way.† For example, it seems to me the chief effect of your baldness, besides worrying you, is to keep you from going places. Could it be that you are so ashamed of yourself and your mother that you like to avoid going out places?"

"That's true. I like to be alone. I'm always making excuses to my wife not to go places she wants me to take her, such as church. I get all worked up to it and then at the last minute I beg off. I feel awful bad about it sometimes, but it just beats me to go out where there are a lot of people."

"Well, you see, now that you are bald, you have an excuse not to go places, without having to feel guilty about it. So your baldness is not all to the bad, is it?"

"I guess you're right in a way. I see what you mean, anyway."

When Rex had gone, Dr. Treece felt quite encouraged. He made his usual notes about what Rex had said, for use both in talking to Rex and for the future, in case he ever had a similar case and wanted to check what was behind such a symptom. He added:

"I don't think this man's hair will begin to grow yet, in spite of his good relationship with the doctor, which in some cases would be enough to start the cure of the symptom. He still has a fear of being overwhelmed by 'cyclonic events' if he gives up his baldness

---

* Most psychiatrists, especially psychoanalysts, use intuition in their work, and if they are careful and experienced, it rarely lets them down. Dr. Treece didn't explain to himself why he felt this way, it was just a "hunch," and later turned out to be correct. Similarly, after hearing Rex's dream, he had a hunch the cyclones represented his brothers, and was sure in his own mind, even before Rex told him, that Rex must have six brothers.

† This is known as the "secondary gain" of illness. An illness nearly always helps the individual to gratify some of his infantile Id tensions, such as the desire for attention, the desire to dominate the household, the desire to punish oneself and others, and so on. The unconscious, unless it is kept under control, uses illness the way it uses anything else, for its own selfish purposes.

now. When his dreams show complete confidence in me, I think his hair will begin to come back." *

At the third interview, Dr. Treece explained to Rex about "free association." He had Rex lie down, while he sat in a comfortable chair at the head of the couch, out of Rex's sight; but Rex didn't do very well in the reclining position. He lay for a long time without saying anything at all. After many minutes had passed in silence, Dr. Treece decided to give him some further idea of what he wanted.

"Everyone's thoughts come to him in a different way," he explained. "I don't expect your thoughts to come just the way mine do, but at least you will get an idea of what I mean by 'free association.' You can start from practically nothing, even the color that you see when you close your eyes. I'll start from that.

"When I close my eyes, I see a red color. This reminds me of the red flag, which reminds me of Russia, which reminds me of Communists, which reminds me of a girl I once knew who was a Communist. She later became very religious, which reminds me of a religious girl I knew as a child, which reminds me of how her big brother scared us one time when he caught us kissing. At that time we were about five years old. I was so scared that I never played with her again. I haven't seen her since, but I heard later that when she grew up she became very fat. That reminds me that I never liked to eat fat unless it was crisp and brown, almost burned."

At this point, the doctor opened his eyes and said:

"You see, I started out with a red color and got from that to religion, and then to my childhood friend and then to burned fat. From there I could go in several directions. I would like to say that I held back a few things because it is not desirable for you to know much about my private life,† but in your case you should hold back nothing."

* Conscious confidence is not enough. The "confidence" must penetrate to the unconscious to effect an alteration in neurotic symptoms, since these are not under conscious control. Dreams reveal the true attitude of the unconscious, which may be quite different from the patient's conscious attitude.

† As we have learned, the image which the patient forms of the doctor plays a very important part in the treatment. The more nearly this image is formed spontaneously from the patient's own unconscious, and the less reality he has to base it on, the better the treatment will progress. The cure really

Rex tried again, but was still unable to think of anything to say. Dr. Treece didn't seem to mind.* He shook hands with Rex at the end of the hour and said: "Don't feel hurried. I know it is difficult for you to do something new. We shall have plenty of time."

The following day, as soon as Rex came into the office, the doctor had him lie down and repeated the instructions about free association. Rex still had a hard time. There would be a long silence, and then the doctor would ask: "Well, what have you been thinking?" And Rex would answer, "Nothing, nothing seems to come into my head. It beats me." Finally, however, Rex thought of a girl friend who had jilted his oldest brother after he made her pregnant, and told the doctor about this thought. With some persuasion, he told more details of this affair, and gradually he began to talk freely. Once he got started, he found to his surprise that the thoughts came easily. After a while, however, there was another long silence, until the doctor again asked Rex what he was thinking. Rex said slowly:

"I'm going to tell you something I never told anybody before. I don't remember much about it, and sometimes I wonder if it actually happened. Other times I'm sure it happened.† I think it really did. It's kind of mixed up and vague though.

"I remember going for a walk with my mother and she met some man, and he made love to her right there in a wheat field right

---

proceeds from the patient's own unconscious feelings, and in some ways, the less interference there is from reality, the better. Hence the less the patient knows about the doctor's private life, the better. Some people realize this instinctively and this is one reason why sick people in San Francisco sometimes summon a specialist from New York, while sick people in New York sometimes call in a specialist from San Francisco. The image of the doctor plays an important part in curing any kind of illness, "physical" or "mental." This accounts for some of the cures effected by quacks, and also throws light on the old saying that "a prophet is not without honor save in his own country."

* Such silence is eloquent and meaningful to a psychiatrist. In this case it was a reflection of Rex's fear of expressing his Id instincts in any sort of definite action.

† Later events showed that it really had happened. In any event, in such cases one can usually be sure that something *like* it has happened. But in many ways it doesn't matter whether it happened or not. The important thing is that the patient had such an image in his mind, and that this image played an important part in the formation of his neurosis. Whether or not the image was based on reality is another question. It is images which cause neuroses, and not realities.

in front of me. I guess I was about three years old at the time. I thought there was something wrong about it, but I didn't know just what. I had a feeling that I shouldn't be there. It seemed like kind of a dirty trick to do it in front of me. I think the feeling I mostly had though was that it was wrong against my father.

"I don't know who the man was. I don't think I ever saw him again. I can't figure out anybody it might have been. He was a heavy-set man. I don't remember anything else about how he looked, except that he was bald.

"I never told anybody about this before. My mother was about nineteen at the time, near as I can figure. I was pretty mad about it then, but I think I have forgiven her for it now.

"Now I'm thinking about different things the boys used to do back home. Well, the particular thing that comes to me is one time when we all crawled a mile through a field in the moonlight to steal some cantaloupes, and after we got them we found they were green. I am wondering if this treatment will take too long. It makes me nervous. I think you are a nice fellow, but I always feel as though you was mad at me and was going to call me a bastard." *

Rex brought up several other memories. The doctor listened carefully and when nearly an hour had passed he stopped Rex and began to talk about the things he had said. He pointed out that nearly all the memories had to do with "forbidden fruit." Rex did not understand this expression, and Dr. Treece explained that it referred to things people were not supposed to do but found pleasure in doing. Besides that, all the memories were connected with disappointments. His brother was disappointed by his girl friend, Rex was disappointed by his mother, and the boys were disappointed in their melons. All the people in Rex's mind who did things they were not supposed to never seemed to get any good out of them. This feeling kept Rex from doing many things that other people would not hesitate to do, which partly accounted for his extreme caution and meekness.

Rex hadn't realized that all the things he had said had something

---

* Rex did not realize what he was actually saying here, part of which might be phrased as follows: "Whenever I express myself in any way it makes me nervous. This is because I am afraid that if I attract attention people will learn the secret of my birth, and then even the nicest ones will not hesitate to call me a bastard, even though I am really a legitimate child."

in common. He thought they were just disconnected stories. He was quite surprised when Dr. Treece pointed out the common threads that ran through everything.

After he had written his notes of what had happened during the interview, Dr. Treece made a few remarks about things he hadn't mentioned to Rex, since he felt that Rex wasn't ready for them yet.

"Rex didn't comment on the fact that both his present stepfather and the man who made love to his mother were bald-headed as he himself is now, nor did he comment in telling the cantaloupe story about how he described himself at first as 'bald as a cantaloupe.'"

About a week later Rex had another dream.

"I dreamed that my wife and you were in a room with me. It was a very happy occasion. There was an instrument there that nobody knew how to play. There was an organ, that was it. I never did get to play it, though I wanted to."

Dr. Treece thought that this dream, especially the part where Rex said: "I never did get to play it," must mean there was something wrong with Rex's sex life. Rex said:

"Most of the time in sex I just can't come to the end of it. Even after trying for a long time, I have to give up; nothing comes of it. I don't have any trouble getting started; it's just that I can never finish.

"Gala Eris was just another girl as far as I was concerned. I was going with somebody else, until one night I had a wonderful dream about Gala and her oldest sister Lavinia, but it was the same in the dream, nothing came of it. Gala was lying there in a filmy dress and I just stood and looked at her. I wanted to touch her, but I didn't.* She looked wonderful and I felt wonderful. After that dream, she was so nice there, that the next time I met her on the street I looked her over more carefully. That was the beginning of our courtship. I never had any dates with my previous girl friend after that." †

* So strongly did Rex repress his Id instincts before the treatment that even in his dreams he was afraid to express them.

† It turned out later that Gala had not been "just another girl." The first time he had seen her, Rex had been greatly excited by her but through his usual fear of his own emotions, he had immediately repressed his excitement. Consciously, thereafter, she had been "just another girl," but meanwhile his strong feeling for her was hard at work in his unconscious, forming the wonderful image which emerged full-blown in his dream. His conscious regard for his other girl friend could not prevail against his unconscious feelings to-

Near the end of the hour, Dr. Treece interrupted Rex.

"You see that today you are always about to do something and when it comes to the point you don't do it. In real life you get worked up to going to church and to having an orgasm and then you don't do either. It is the same in your dreams. You get ready to play the organ, but you never do play it; in the one about your future wife, you get all excited and then nothing happens, just as in real life."

Rex was quite interested in this and said there was another angle to it.

"The same thing happens when I try to make up my mind about something. I never get to the point of making it up.* For instance, take the time when a rich family once wanted to adopt me, and I couldn't make my mind up to go through with it. It would of been a wonderful chance for me to get whatever I wanted. The Farbantis that was, and they had lots of money. I don't know why they wanted me. It's the same with jobs. Sometimes I've been offered a better job than the one I have, but I dilly-dally about deciding and finally the chance goes by. I guess that's held me back a lot.

"My hair has improved a little in the last two days. It doesn't fall out so easily. You know I believe a lot in dreams. A few days ago for the first time I dreamed that I shot somebody: two men."

"You mean," said Dr. Treece, "that you were at last able to permit yourself to dream that you hated somebody and did something about it instead of just feeling hurt?" †

"I guess that's it," said Rex.

The following week, Rex said something which particularly im-

---

wards Gala, and he married the latter. It is probable that if he had married the former, the marriage would not have been a happy one, since Gala's image would have continued to function in his unconscious, adulterating and confusing his feelings towards his wife. For a similar account of the not unique occurrence of a marriage following "a wonderful dream," see the interesting autobiography entitled "The Book of My Life," by Jerome Cardan, the celebrated physician and astrologer of the sixteenth century. (E. P. Dutton & Company: New York, 1930.)

* Rex described his condition very aptly here. Nearly all his difficulties fell under the heading of being "unable to get to the point."

† This was real progress. Rex at last permitted his feelings to express themselves, even if only in a dream. It is interesting to note that his hair began to grow again just at the time this first happened.

pressed the doctor. He told how he and his cousins were playing house when they were little, and Mary Volk was the mother and he was the father. They took their clothes off to "Do like ma and pa do," and they were caught and Rex got a terrible beating.

"The thing that puzzles me," said Rex, "is how I knew about how to show her such a thing. I don't know where I could of learned about it at such a young age. I was only about six, and I am absolutely sure that I never saw anybody doing it, but I felt like I knew just how it was done."

"What about the time you saw your mother and the man when you were three?" asked the doctor.

"What man?" asked Rex, puzzled.

"The bald-headed man that was making love with your mother in the field," said the doctor, who was not surprised that Rex had forgotten this incident since he had talked about it.

Rex jumped and sat up on the couch.

"That's right," he said excitedly. "So she did. How did you know about that? Did I tell you about that?" *

Here we shall leave Rex and Dr. Treece, at the end of the third week of the treatment. Rex's hair, which had begun to come back slowly before this, now began to grow more rapidly as he expressed his feelings more and more freely instead of keeping them (and his hair) coiled up inside of himself like the spring of an alarm clock which can't go off. In about six weeks, Rex had quite a head of hair, which was almost white at first, but gradually took on its former dark color.

While regaining his hair was a great thing in a way for Rex, it was just the first step in the treatment. As his hair grew back and the treatment proceeded, he began to have pounding of the heart, and became sadder than ever. Dr. Treece expected that just as in the case of Rex's cousin, Horace Volk, when the first symptom was cured it would be replaced by another one. He gradually "rounded up" all of Rex's ungratified libido and mortido tensions into one set of symptoms, which consisted mainly in a terrible pounding of the heart and flushing of the face whenever he came into the doc-

---

* Telling the story about his mother was one time that Rex did "get to the point." He was so frightened at having done this that he promptly forgot he had done it.

tor's office. They spent almost a year in curing this new "artificial" symptom, or *transference neurosis*,* and at the end of that time, when Rex had to stop the treatment, he was quite a new man. He was more talkative and sociable, could make decisions quickly, his sex life was normal, and he was able to handle his new job of bossing a section of the cannery without getting upset every time he had to tell someone to do something. His wife was happier, and their children, who had been depressed and sickly from living in the former atmosphere of the home, began to bloom.

We have not touched on the deeper stages of the treatment, when Rex began to realize that even at the age of three he was stirred up sexually by what he saw his mother do, and felt so guilty about this that he was unable to complete the sexual act properly when he grew up "for fear that a bald-headed man might cut his penis off if he did so," as he dreamed one night. Nor have we touched on the meaning of his baldness, as a self-punishment, as a means of getting some attention, and as a way of saying to his mother: "Look, you like to give your affection to bald-headed men and now I am bald-headed too!" †

The treatment we have described above does *not* apply to all bald-headed men. It can only help (and perhaps only in rare instances) some of those cases where hair comes out suddenly all over the body in large handfuls. It must be remembered that as the hair neurosis disappeared it was replaced by an anxiety neurosis. The mechanism which caused the hair to grow back, therefore, was not a cure, but only a replacement of one symptom by another, the second one being the transference neurosis brought about as part of the treatment. Only when the second neurosis was treated was the patient properly benefited.

* This meant that the doctor's image had now become a powerful driving force in Rex's conscious and unconscious. Rex had transferred many of his abnormal feelings from early childhood images to this new image. The new image was much easier for the doctor to deal with than were the childhood images which caused the original symptoms.

† In connection with a certain type of criticism of psychoanalysis it should be noted that Rex's memory of the sexual incident concerning his mother was *not* unconscious, and that some of his reactions to this incident were also conscious. What *was* unconscious were some of his reactions to the incident, and these the most important for determining his marital happiness and future approach to life (and hence the happiness of his wife and children also).

## 9

## How to choose a doctor

There are so many different professions dealing with the human mind that the average citizen has difficulty telling these "psychies" apart. The men in these professions, on the other hand, are usually proud individuals who do not like to be confused with each other. It is especially necessary to be able to distinguish the various branches if one is thinking of going to somebody for advice or treatment.

A *psychiatrist* originally meant a physician who specialized in diseases of the mind. Nowadays, a psychiatrist means a doctor who not only treats neuroses, psychoses, and emotional disturbances, but also tries to prevent them. He tries to help people improve their judgment and he gives them advice based on his experience with other human beings concerning their feelings about themselves, the world around them, and the people among whom they live. A psychiatrist is invariably an M.D. If he is not an M.D. he cannot be a psychiatrist any more than he can be a brain surgeon.

After he has finished medical school, the student psychiatrist goes through a regular internship, during which he may deliver babies, remove tonsils and appendices, and perform autopsies; or he may prefer an internship where he can concentrate on internal diseases, such as diabetes, heart disease, stomach ulcers, and tuberculosis.

When his internship is over, he goes to a special training hospital for further study, just as do his colleagues who want to become surgeons, heart specialists, and so on. After this training period is finished, he may go into private practice. If he desires national recognition as a specialist, however, he must continue his specialized studies for at least five years after his internship is over. He is then qualified to take a stiff examination, oral, written, and practical, from a group of older, established specialists. When he has passed the examination, he becomes an American Board Diplomate. (This is different from a National Board Diplomate, which refers to something else entirely.)

Thus the psychiatrist, after his interneship, will study for five years more in order to become eligible to take the examinations of the American Board of Psychiatry and Neurology. If he passes the examinations to the satisfaction of his older colleagues, he is recognized as a competent psychiatrist by the medical profession. There are a few qualified psychiatrists who do not elect to take the examinations, but the only way a layman can be sure that a psychiatrist knows his business, unless he is recommended by another trusted physician, is to ascertain that he is a Diplomate of the American Board of Psychiatry and Neurology. There is no law against any doctor calling himself a psychiatrist, but the best way to convince the medical profession is either to be preparing for, or to have taken, the board examinations.

A *neurologist* must also be an M.D. While a psychiatrist specializes in helping people improve their judgment and emotional stability, a neurologist specializes in diseases of the brain, spinal cord, and nerve cords. Many psychiatrists are also competent neurologists and vice versa. There is some connection between the two fields, as is suggested by the name of the examining board, and a doctor may be certified by this board as qualified in either or both of these specialties. Sometimes a man who practices both is called a Neuropsychiatrist.

Some psychiatrists, however, feel that there is more connection between the mind and the endocrine glands than there is between the mind and the brain, at least as far as practical medical treatment is concerned, so that they would rather concentrate on endocrinology than on neurology as a sideline.

A *psychoanalyst*, as we have said already, is a psychiatrist who specializes in the form of treatment known as psychoanalysis. In order to become a psychoanalyst, the psychiatrist must take additional special training after he has had some years of psychiatric training. He goes to a recognized Psychoanalytic Institute and studies under a group of experienced analysts. Every analyst must be analyzed himself before he is recognized by the profession. Thus, he may have a total of six or eight years of training after his interneship before he is considered ready to practice psychoanalysis.

There is a small group of psychoanalysts, many of them very

skillful, who are exceptions to this rule. These are called "lay analysts." They do not have medical degrees. They were carefully chosen for their intelligence, sincerity, integrity, education, emotional stability, and understanding of human nature before they were admitted to the Psychoanalytic Institutes for training. Most of the lay analysts belong to another period, since American Psychoanalytic Institutes no longer train people to be analysts unless they have medical degrees. Of course, many social workers, nurses, psychologists, teachers, lawyers, ministers, and others who have to handle human problems study at these Institutes in order to gain an increased understanding of human nature, and they are heartily encouraged to do so, but such "laymen" are not recognized by the profession as qualified actually to psychoanalyze other people.

In 1929, the British Medical Association made an investigation concerning the use of the term "psychoanalyst," and announced their official conclusion as follows:

"There is in the medical and general public the tendency to use the term 'psychoanalysis' in a very loose and wide sense. This term can legitimately be applied only to the method evolved by Freud and to the theories derived from the use of this method. A psychoanalyst is therefore a person who uses Freud's technique, and anyone who does not use this technique should not, whatever other method he may employ, be called a psychoanalyst. In accordance with this definition and for the purpose of avoiding confusion, the term 'psychoanalyst' is properly reserved for members of the International Psycho-Analytical Association. . . ."

It may be mentioned that none of the "splinter" schools (that is, the schools of Jung, Adler, Rank, Stekel, etc.), except the Horney group, either have the facilities for, or require, such prolonged, rigorous, and self-sacrificing training as is required of those who wish to become orthodox Freudian psychoanalysts.

While psychiatrists and psychoanalysts are interested in the personality as a whole, as it affects the individual's life course, *psychologists* are mainly interested in certain aspects of the personality as they work in various special situations.* A psychiatrist is like a

---

* This way of stating the operational distinction between psychiatrists and psychologists is open to criticism, but it is the best I can do after much discussion with various psychologists.

man who is interested in the meaning of a poem, while a psychologist is more like a person who studies the poet's grammar. A *psychometrist* is a psychologist who specializes in measuring the powers of the mind. Most psychometrists are concerned with measuring intelligence and the ability to grasp and understand problems. The *physiological psychologists* are interested in the connection between the mind and the various organs serving it, such as the brain, the ear, and the eye. There are many other kinds of special psychologists.

After a psychologist is graduated from college, he selects a special field of study for his M.A. or Ph.D. degree. Psychologists, with certain rare exceptions, do *not* have M.D. degrees. Most of the psychologists with M.D. degrees are in the field of physiological psychology, since this is closely connected with neurology and requires considerable medical or pre-medical knowledge. A few psychologists in the past were admitted to Psychoanalytic Institutes and became qualified psychoanalysts, but this is no longer possible in this country, at least as far as the American Psychoanalytic Association is concerned. Some non-medical psychologists practice *clinical psychology* and psychotherapy. Most recognized psychologists are members of the American Psychological Association.

Anyone who wishes psychotherapy or psychiatric advice should be sure to go to a qualified person. In some parts of the country, anyone who wishes may hang out a neon sign reading "Psychiatrist" or "Psychoanalyst," since these words are not copyrighted. This is dangerous to those who seek help, since their condition may be aggravated by such quacks, and they may be swindled out of so much money that they are unable to afford the sound treatment from a properly trained person which is what they really require. There are several ways to check the standing of anyone who claims to be or is called a psychiatrist or psychoanalyst.

The Directory of the American Medical Association, which is available in most public libraries, contains the name of each licensed physician in the United States and Canada, together with his medical school and his specialty, if any, and also notes whether he is a diplomate of his specialty board.

The List of Fellows and Members of the American Psychiatric Association contains the names of all physicians who belong to this association, which includes nearly all the doctors in the country with psychiatric training, and states whether or not they are diplomates of the American Board of Psychiatry and Neurology. The association also publishes a larger Biographical Directory, which contains a life history of every member, so that the reader may judge for himself how competent each one is.

The Directory of Medical Specialists contains the names of all diplomates of all the American specialty boards, including surgeons, obstetricians, psychiatrists, etc. Every psychiatrist who has passed the examinations of the American Board of Psychiatry and Neurology is listed there, and also the various professional societies to which he belongs. A listing in this directory is a guarantee of training and competence. Those who are not listed there may or may not be competent. Many older psychiatrists have not taken the Board examinations, so that their names do not appear in this directory.

Nearly all qualified psychoanalysts in this country are members of the American Psychoanalytic Association; most of the exceptions are in New York City, where new organizations of former members have been formed. Those who belong to these other organizations may have had full psychoanalytic training in the past, but they are no longer recognized as orthodox psychoanalysts, which is why they have broken away and formed their own groups. In most large cities there is also a group of younger apprentice analysts who are not members of the national Association but are connected with the local Psychoanalytic Institute, which is recognized by the Association. Membership in the American Psychoanalytic Association is a guarantee of competence in this field. Those who are not members are reliable if they are connected with the local Institute. If anyone calling himself or herself a "psychoanalyst" does not belong to either the local Institute or the national Association, he or she has either broken away from the orthodox analysts, or else has not had approved psychoanalytic training.

The number of qualified psychoanalysts is limited (probably less than 300 in the whole country), and nearly all of them are collected in the larger centers. Anyone who desires psychoanalysis, therefore, will probably have to move into or near a large city, where he will perhaps find the Psychoanalytic Institute or Society listed in the telephone book. During the next few years, it is likely that many more qualified analysts will come to the smaller cities, but at present they are concentrated in Boston, Chicago, Detroit, Los Angeles, New York, Philadelphia, San Francisco, Topeka, and Washington-Baltimore.

If none of the directories mentioned above is to be found in the local library, the County Medical Society, the State Medical Society, or the American Medical Association (535 North Dearborn Street, Chicago 10, Illinois) may be consulted.

The yellow pages of the telephone book are *not* a reliable place to locate a psychiatrist or psychoanalyst. Many well-qualified men in the field deliberately keep their names out of the sections headed "Psychiatrist" and "Psychoanalyst" in some cities, so as not to be confused with the unqualified people, many of them outright quacks, who claim to belong to these branches and so list themselves in the telephone directory. Anyone who has a neon sign outside his office with either of these words on it is undoubtedly *not* qualified. No neon sign salesman has been known to earn a commission by attending the convention of the American Psychiatric Association and its Psychoanalytic Section. Genuine specialists in any branch of medicine or surgery are highly ethical and do not believe in advertising.

With these hints, anyone who feels in need of skilled help in handling personality or emotional problems should be able to locate a competent, well-trained specialist. If one is fortunate enough to have a family physician who is sincerely interested in finding proper psychiatric help and guidance for those of his patients who need it, his assistance, of course, is important. In many towns there are also recognized psychiatric and mental hygiene clinics, and Veterans Hospitals, to which the individual can go for psychiatric help and advice. Any such clinic will be glad to give the names of some private psychiatrists to anyone who feels the need of more intensive treatment than a clinic is able to give. The local "Physicians Exchange" or "Nurses Registry," which can usually be found listed as such in the telephone directory, will also be glad to refer inquirers to a psychiatrist if there is one in the community. The difference between psychoanalytic treatment and psychiatric treatment should be borne in mind, so that the individual may be sure that he is being sent to the kind of doctor that he wants or that is recommended for him.

In large cities, where many qualified men can be easily found, it matters little which individual doctor is chosen, training and qualifications being equal. It is particularly unwise for those who seek psychoanalysis to go shopping around from one doctor to another. If anyone wants to be psychoanalyzed, or if psychoanalysis is recommended to him, he should make a clear-cut decision and act upon it promptly. Once he (or she) is in the hands of a qualified analyst of either sex, it is usually better to let his or her attitude toward or criticism of the analyst become a problem of the analysis, rather than an excuse for delay or for revoking the decision.

## Footnotes for Philosophers, Chapter Nine

### 1. What is analysis?

If some people wish to define science in such a way as to exclude psychoanalysis from the roster of scientific disciplines, they have this privilege. It would seem, however, that their Procrustean attempts to make "psychology" as they understand it fit a man-made definition of science, somewhat hinders their efforts to find out about human nature. They sometimes give the impression of feeling that if nature does not agree with the book, nature is wrong. Psychoanalysts are willing to change the books, including the dictionaries, if the latter do not agree with nature.

One of the best books on the subject matter covered in this chapter is *Facts and Theories of Psychoanalysis*, by Ives Hendrick, op. cit.

See also: *Psychoanalysis Today*, edited by A. Sandor Lorand. International University Press: New York, 1944.

### 2 & 3. The process of analysis

Those who are particularly interested in the subjects covered in this and the following sections, including the questions of what is and what is not psychoanalysis, and who is and who is not a genuine psychoanalyst, are urged to read:

*Practical Aspects of Psychoanalysis:* A Handbook for Prospective Patients and Their Advisors, by Lawrence S. Kubie. W. W. Norton & Company, New York, 1936.

4. *Who should be psychoanalyzed?*

Certainly, judges and statesmen. We think of ourselves as intelligent beings, and yet let the fate of ourselves and the rest of the world depend partly upon the whims of the Ids of our elected officials. We can see on every hand how men's emotions distort their images of reality, but there are some men who *must* have clear images of reality if justice, peace, and humanity are to prevail. As things are now, a judge's adventures with his parents in infancy, and even what he had for dinner last night, are matters of considerable import to a criminal whose offence merits a sentence of ten to twenty years. Will he get ten or twenty? This should not depend upon the state of the judge's Id tensions, but upon what is best for society and the individual criminal. This applies even more strongly to those in a position of political power. The fate of a nation may hinge upon the energy distributions in its leaders' minds, instead of upon what is best in the long run. It is not the atom bomb which is important, but the decision of certain specific individuals as to what we are going to do with it. It is deplorable that men who have the fate of mankind in their hands do not even consider being psychoanalyzed before undertaking their duties so that they would at least know when they were being taken advantage of by their repressed tensions.

5. *Freud*

See: *Freud, Master and Friend*, by Hanns Sachs. Harvard University Press: Cambridge, 1944.

Also: *Freud's Contribution to Psychiatry*, by A. A. Brill. W. W. Norton & Company: New York, 1944.

6. *The dissidents*

See: *Understanding Human Nature*, by Alfred Adler. Garden City Publishing Company: New York, 1927.

A condensed account of Jung's theories can be found in:

*The Psychology of Jung*, by Jolan Jacobi. Yale University Press: New Haven, 1943.

In the September, 1945, issue of *The American Journal of Psychiatry*, the official organ of the American Psychiatric Association, there is an article by S. S. Feldman entitled "Dr. C. G. Jung and National Socialism." In this article it is stated that Jung was actively co-operating with the Nazis as far back as 1934. This view is documented with an account of his activities, and extracts from his writings, during the period of Nazi ascendancy. An attempt to refute this accusation and defend Jung was published in *The Psychiatric Quarterly* for April, 1946, under the title "Carl Gustav Jung—Defender of Freud and the Jews," by Ernest Harms. The question is not whether Jung's readers approve of his personal life, but whether his personal prejudices unduly influenced the objectivity of his psychological observations.

The most concise and readable account of Horney's views may be found in:

*Are You Considering Psychoanalysis?* edited by Karen Horney. W. W. Norton & Company: New York, 1946.

This book contains several statements which it is difficult to resist the temptation to correct. For example, it is stated that according to Freudian concepts, the desire to grow is "an evidence of something sick." This is not so. Among orthodox Freudians, the patient's desire to grow is regarded as a valuable indicator of his ability to get well. For good reasons, Dr. Horney's ideas have a special appeal in certain political circles, while the conclusions of the orthodox Freudians are quite unacceptable in the same circles. But political appeal, however important it may be, is at least not a valid criterion of scientific truth or therapeutic effectiveness. As far as popular appeal is concerned, the orthodox Freudian theories, since they are based upon the family unit, should have the greatest appeal for those who believe in the family as the basic unit of society, while Horney's theories should and do attract more those who think in terms of larger social units.

For an account of the work of the Chicago group with short-term "psychoanalysis," see:

*Psychoanalytic Therapy*, by Franz Alexander et al. The Ronald Press Company: New York, 1946.

In comparing the results of modified forms of analytic treatment with the results of orthodox psychoanalysis, and in determining whether such methods really deserve the name of "psychoanalysis," the following questions might be asked:

1. What are the energy processes and emotional experiences which take place during psychoanalysis?
2. What are the desirable results of psychoanalysis?
3. How many of the processes and experiences can be eliminated without vitiating the desirable results?
4. How can the remaining processes and experiences be shortened without vitiating the desirable results?

If we bear these questions in mind, it is understandable why many open-minded orthodox analysts feel that no modified or shortened form of analysis so far devised can obtain the same desirable results as regular Freudian analysis, or is entitled in good conscience to be called "psychoanalysis." No doubt all forms of psychotherapy in wise and experienced hands accomplish some good; but before any psychotherapy be called "psychoanalysis," it might be postulated that its method and the patient's experiences should resemble those of psychoanalysis, and that it should accomplish very nearly the same things that psychoanalysis does.

The reader may be curious as to how it happens that some doctors are "Freudians," some "Jungians," some "Horneyites," and so on. The author can speak with certainty only for himself. The following is an account of why I favor the Freudian viewpoint.

Most people will agree that it is the function of a physician to give each individual patient that form of treatment which will be of the greatest benefit to him in the long run. For example, it is often safer and better in the long run for a patient with a hernia to have an operation rather than to wear a truss, even though the truss may give him temporary relief and the operation will cripple him for a few days. It is easy enough for hernia sufferers to sit around and discuss what they have read concerning the relative merits of trusses and operations, but the surgeon is the one who has to make the actual decision and the future of the patient lies in his hands. He can only conscientiously acquit himself of this responsibility by making his decision in accordance with his own past experience and the experience of those surgeons whom he respects.

In the same way, it is easy enough for laymen to discuss what they have read concerning Freud, Jung, Horney, etc. But the doctor who has the responsibility of actually treating neurotics has to make a clear-cut decision as to what form of treatment he is going to give each individual patient in order to give him the most benefit in the long run. The psychiatrist makes his decision in the same way as the surgeon, basing it on his own past experience and on the experience of those colleagues whom he most respects. The responsibility of the practicing psychiatrist is quite different from the responsibility of those who are engaged in academic discussion.

My preference for the Freudian viewpoint is based on purely empiric considerations. During a period of study lasting ten years, I maintained an attitude as objective and as free from theoretical prejudice as I was able. My aim was to find out the best approach to the treatment of psychiatric patients, and not to validate or disprove anyone else's theories. I tried to form my own theories, based on my own observations and on observations of the methods of my teachers, each of whom had his own viewpoint. I then re-read the works of Freud, Jung, Adler, Kahn, Meyer, and so on. This literature was re-evaluated in the light of personal experience. In general, as far as psychodynamics were concerned, the ideas of Freud best fitted in with the results of clinical observation. The general views of Jung, Adler, and Horney did not fit in with personal clinical experience, although each of them said some things which seemed valid. As far as the treatment of neuroses was concerned, the orthodox Freudian approach seemed to promise better results than any of the others, and appeared to give the patient more for his money. One does not necessarily decide to "become a Freudian," or to "belong" to the Freudian school. It is only necessary to decide that one's own observations agree more closely with those of Freud and his orthodox disciples than with anyone else's.

7. *Group therapy*

As indicated, most of the material in this section is based on personal experience. J. L. Moreno developed psychodrama in this country. Two of the outstanding pioneers in group work in America are Trigant Burrow and Paul Schilder. There is a book which gives considerable detail about various aspects of group therapy, including lectures, analytical methods, and musical, dance, and motion picture methods. The methods and experiences of these writers are different from my own.

*Group Therapy: A Symposium.* Beacon House: New York, 1945.

8. *Rex Bigfoot*

This section reports a fictitious composite of material somewhat similar to that obtained during the opening stages of the successful treatment of some cases of alopecia totalis.

9. *Choosing a doctor*

See: *Where Do People Take Their Troubles?* by Lee R. Steiner. Houghton, Mifflin & Company: Boston, 1945.

Those who are interested in obtaining psychoanalytic treatment should read *Practical Aspects of Psychoanalysis*, by Lawrence S. Kubie, op. cit.

The discussion concerning the proper definition of "psychoanalysis," according to the findings of the British Medical Association, may be found in this book, and is quoted from the British Medical Journal for June 29, 1929.

# Appendices

Appendices

# BEYOND SCIENCE

---

In 1922, Freud stirred up great interest among his disciples by publishing an article called "Dreams and Telepathy." Mental telepathy is now considered a legitimate subject for investigation by psychoanalysts. Freud was also interested in certain aspects of fortune-telling.

It is not an original idea, therefore, to include a section on these and allied subjects, which are sometimes covered by the term *parapsychology*, in a book on psychiatry and psychoanalysis. Fortune-telling, intuition, and what is now widely known as *extra-sensory perception*, are all manifestations of the human mind in action. These matters are of such general interest, and force themselves so regularly upon the attention of those who practice psychiatry and especially psychoanalysis, that a book on the human mind as the psychiatrist sees it would seem incomplete without some discussion of them.

There is no known way to acquire or train parapsychological faculties. Each observer is a law unto himself, and can only work under conditions which are suitable for his individual self and which he himself is usually unable to define exactly. The present attitude of psychiatrists toward parapsychological experiences is based on the following considerations:

1. Nearly all psychiatrists, and probably all psychoanalysts, rely extensively on intuition in their daily work, and find that it rarely fails them (or the patient).
2. Many psychoanalysts have published observations indicating their belief in the existence of telepathic phenomena.
3. If the subject is mentioned, almost everyone except certain rigid personalities can and does relate personal parapsychological experiences. Many of these experiences can be ex-

plained in other ways, but because there are other possible explanations does not necessarily mean that the "other" explanation is nearer the truth than the parapsychological one.

I

## What about fortune-tellers?

In this section we shall deal with graphology and palmistry, and mention some other methods of "fortune telling" in passing.

A person's handwriting can be judged in two ways: first, by scientific methods, that is, by studying the characteristics of a large number of scripts and relating them to the characteristics of the writers, so that standards of comparison are set up and can be used for classifying people. This is known as *scientific graphology*. There are many books on this subject, some of them written by reputable psychologists. This method of study is preferred by strict scientists. Some people, however, feel that they can better form an opinion about what an individual writer is likely to do in various practical situations by using *intuitive graphology*.

In practicing intuitive graphology, the graphologist puts himself into a state of deliberate concentration, and retraces in his thoughts or with his finger the exact movements made by the writer in forming one or more letters. If he is fortunate enough to possess the proper intuition, he will then sense things about the writer's emotional state which are not revealed by the known facts or the material in the script, and some of which may be repressed and therefore not even known to the writer himself. From this apparently meager information, an experienced psychiatrist or psychologist may form a good idea of the writer's personality structure and his probable emotional tensions of the moment which will guide his actions in the near future.

One of the biggest problems in graphology is to discover which personality characteristics should be expected to show up in handwriting. In other words, it is as difficult to know which question to ask as it is to find the answer. But the fine movements of handwriting are an expression of the individual's whole personality, and it is reasonable to suppose that some meaning can be found in them if we only know exactly what kind of meaning to look for.

Palmists, phrenologists, and other fortune-tellers who study physical structure probably notice unconsciously the position and movements of the facial and other muscles in making their judgments of people. Consciously, however, they believe that their judgments are based on permanent bodily characteristics, such as the bumps on the skull or the lines on the palm of the hand. Since the bumps on the skull have nothing to do with the personality, we need not consider phrenology any further.

As for reading palms by lines, no one should be so foolish as to think that an anatomical line on a person's hand tells anything about his past or future. Successful palm prophets consciously or unconsciously base their statements on other factors, perhaps including mental telepathy and clairvoyance, if such things exist. An obvious source of information is the shape of the hand. Undoubtedly many palmists classify people accordingly with some success, and they may have an inkling or actual knowledge of the differences between endomorphs, mesomorphs, and ectomorphs. They may realize, for example, that ectomorphs, being usually cerebrotonic, have a certain way of living which influences their life adventures, while endomorphs, being usually viscerotonic, tend to have a different kind of life experience. It is natural to suppose that the young ectomorph is likely to be "preoccupied with love troubles," and that the mature endomorph is more likely to "hear some good news at a banquet." By using such guides, the palmist can increase the percentage of correct hits.

A person's palm may also reveal his occupation and the palmist may use this knowledge in a subtle way with or without realizing it. The much-callused hand of a laborer immediately suggests money troubles, while the smooth hand of a wealthy Bohemian suggests sexual complications. In the first case the palmist might say: "The money will come soon, don't worry." If by chance it does in even one case, her name will be made among the laborer's friends, no matter how many other times she has missed. In the second event she might prophesy: "A blonde artiste will soon come into your life and give you much happiness; later she will cause trouble!" If the rich Bohemian gets around the following week to taking out a dancing girl from the Chimera Club, something he had been planning to do for a long time anyway, and if he later has to make a financial settlement with her, the palmist's future is assured.

With female clients, the case is even simpler. If a toil-worn housewife wearing a crucifix comes in with "diaper hands," the palmist need not hesitate to say: "You will have another baby within the year." If the client is a hard-faced, highly manicured dancing girl in a mink coat, the palmist will not often go wrong by predicting: "A rich man will soon give you a lot of money." If we reverse these prophecies, we can see how obvious and simple they are. It would be unsound to tell the laborer's worn-out wife that a rich man was going to set her up on Park Avenue, and equally poor judgment to tell a tough chorus girl who was obviously out for all she could get that she was going to have another baby within the year.

While a rich heiress who happens to be named Celeste is apt to have a different career from a proletarian girl who happens to be named Mabel, this need not confuse us as to the value of numerology applied to names. It is valueless. Money plays a far larger part than names in determining the careers of their owners. Similarly, many people are affected by the phases of the moon and the barometric pressure, but it should be a matter of indifference to any sensible person, unless he is interested in the science of astronomy, as to whether it is Mars or Mercury who is having a conjunction with Venus at any particular moment. We must attribute lucky hits on the part of numerologists and astrologers either to chance, to vague language, or to the types of observations mentioned previously. The same applies to the readers of tea leaves, birds' entrails, etc.

We have only hinted at the use of intuition, which is probably an important factor in all these cases. The question of mental telepathy and clairvoyance also has to be considered seriously when fortune-tellers hit regularly in questions involving numbers, such as dates, money, ages, and family size.

As for people who read minds and tell fortunes over the radio, listeners would be amazed if they knew some of the fascinating forms of trickery by which professional magicians can "read minds." In any mind-reading act, the moment the victim is asked to write anything down, no matter how innocent the writing paper looks, he may assume immediately that he is going to be made the victim of legerdemain. Even without writing, there are astonishingly effective methods for "reading minds" by trickery. Apparatus and systems for the most mystifying "mind-reading" acts can be easily purchased at any magic supply house.

## 2

## What is intuition?

The matters related in the following sections will have to be accepted for what they are worth as true accounts of personal experiences. Similar occurrences have been demonstrated to fellow psychiatrists and before groups of doctors, and of course the patients and others involved can verify what happened, but there is no way of demonstrating the veracity of these events to the individual reader.

Intuition is the acquiring of knowledge through sensory contact with the object, without the intuiter being able to explain to himself or to others exactly how he came to his conclusions. In other words, intuition means that we can know something without knowing how we know it.

Intuition is a fragile and personal thing, and its study has been easily discouraged by those who cling strictly to scientific principles and refuse to admit that a faculty exists unless it can be exercised and its effects reproduced at will. Unfortunately, at present intuition can be exercised only at such times and under such circumstances as the intuiter himself feels are correct. He is either "on the beam" or he isn't, and until someone can discover how to control intuition so that it can be brought into play at will, and investigated under proper laboratory conditions, we shall have to accept people's word for what happened, just as we did during the "anecdotal" stage of animal psychology, in the days of the good and learned Reverend J. G. Wood.

Now let us study some examples of intuition from the writer's experience.

When on night duty in various hospitals, I have been wont to gather social pleasure and bits of knowledge by passing the time with the patients in the wards whenever opportunity offered. One evening I walked into the office of a ward in a large hospital and found one of the patients sitting on the desk. Knowing that he should not have been there, he got up to leave, but since I felt that I was in an intuitive mood, I requested him to stay. We had never seen each other before and did not know each other's names. The incident took place in a part of the hospital far from the psychiatric section where I worked during the day, on a ward which was completely strange to me.

Before the man had a chance to say anything, I asked him to be seated again, and inquired:

"Does Philadelphia mean anything to you?"

"Yes," he replied. "I was brought up there."

"Well," I said, "but you left home when you were fifteen."

"That is correct," he replied, beginning to wonder what was going on.

"If you will permit me to say so," I continued, "I believe your mother disappointed you."

"Oh, no, doctor. I love my mother very much."

"Nevertheless, I think she disappointed you. Where is she now?"

"She's at home. She's not well."

"How long has she been ill?"

"Most of her life. I've been taking care of her since I was a young fellow."

"What's her trouble?"

"She's always been nervous. A semi-invalid."

"Then in that sense she disappointed you, don't you think? She had to take emotional support from you rather than give it to you, from your earliest years."

"Yes, doctor, that's correct, all right."

At this point another man entered the office, and was invited to sit down. He sat on the floor with his back against the wall and said nothing, but he listened with great interest.

"You give me the impression that your father was ineffective from the time you were about nine," I continued with the first man.

"He was a drunkard. I believe about the time I was nine or ten, he began to drink more heavily."

This conversation took more time than its description does, since it was punctuated by frequent groping silences on my part. The second man now requested that I tell him something about himself.

"Well," I replied, "I think your father was very strict with you. You had to help him on the farm. You never went fishing or hunting with him. You had to go on your own, with a bunch of rather tough fellows."

"That's right."

"He began to scare you badly when you were about seven."

"Well, my mother died when I was six, if that had anything to do with it."

"Were you pretty close to her?"

"I was."

"So her death left you more or less at the mercy of your tough father?"

"I guess it did."

"You make your wife angry."

"I guess I did. We're divorced."

"She was about sixteen and a half when you married her."

"That's right."

"And you were about nineteen and a half when you married her."

"That's right."

"Is it right within six months?"

He stopped to figure for a moment and then replied:

"They're both right within two months."

There was another long silence, but by this time I could feel the intuitive feeling slipping away so I said:

"Well, fellows, that's as far as I can go."

"Doctor," said the second man. "Could you guess my age?"

"I don't think I'm in the groove for guessing ages tonight."

"Well, try, Doc!"

"I don't think I'll get this, but I'll try. You were twenty-four in September."

"I was thirty in October."

These two cases are selected out of quite a large number, mainly because these men later consented to appear at the regular weekly meeting of the staff doctors of the hospital, where they bore witness to the authenticity of the observations. (At this meeting I was attempting to demonstrate how the early emotional adventures of the individual leave their marks not only on his later personality but also on his muscular set, particularly in the face, and these two men seemed ideal for such a clinic.)

Most of these observations were the results of "intuition," specifically, what doctors call "clinical intuition." Just as the old family doctor could diagnose typhoid fever "by the smell" because of his vast experience with this disease, so nowadays the observant psychiatrist learns to judge many things about his patients "by intuition." Since he is continually seeing patients and inquiring about their ages, marital status, home life, parents' characters, and so on, it is to be expected that after some years he should acquire the ability to make pretty shrewd guesses on sight.

Such shrewdness is not confined to psychiatrists, nor to the medical profession. Any professional becomes pretty "intuitive" about his own business. Professional age-guessers and weight-guessers at fairs and carnivals make their living through such intuition, which they cultivate by practice and experience. The average person can judge ages and weights fairly accurately, yet perhaps no one could put into words exactly how he makes such judgments. Not even an artist, who is accustomed to copying intuitively the very visual clues from which such information is derived, could explain how he tells the difference between a man of twenty-three and one of twenty-six.

It is important to realize, then, that we can know something without being able to put into words exactly how we know it; but we can know it surely, nevertheless. This was clearly shown in the first case above, where I knew that the man's mother had "disappointed" him. So sure was I of this knowledge that when he denied it I insisted upon my judgment, and it finally turned out to be correct. On the other hand, the gross error I made in guessing the second man's age, after I had guessed all the "more difficult" things accurately, but after my intuition had worn itself out, shows that without intuition to aid him, even an experienced observer can be easily led astray.

These impressions are not ruled by the laws of chance. It is not a question of being right part of the time through coincidence. When one has "that feeling," one rarely makes a mistake. When one doesn't have the feeling, one's guesses do follow the laws of chance. Guessing the age when fifteen men left home and being right in two or three cases would be one thing; guessing different things about fifteen men and being right almost 100% of the time is another. That is why it is so difficult to study these things properly. They cannot be done by request. The feeling of being "on the beam" comes only at certain times, and then it is gone.

## 3

## How does intuition work?

To understand intuition, we have only to rid ourselves of the belief that in order to know something we have to be able to put into words what we know and how we know it. This belief is the result of an overdevelopment of the Reality Principle and of the modern scientific outlook which has taken us in some ways too far in the direction of *testing* reality, and away from nature and the world of natural happenings. Our Egos, in subduing our Ids, have imprisoned much that could be useful and beneficial. Those with enough Id control might be able to allow intuitive faculties to develop without endangering the rest of their repressions and their necessary contact with reality. As Freud says, "All this is highly speculative and full of unsolved problems, but there is no need to be alarmed by it." Intuition is simply induction without words. When we are able to put into words what we intuit and how we came to our conclusions, we have verbalized induction, which is commonly called Science.

An admirable opportunity for studying the intuitive process at work was offered in interviewing 25,000 men for the United States Government at the rate of two hundred to five hundred per day. Under such pressure, the individual "psychiatric examinations" were a matter of seconds rather than of minutes. With such a strict time limit, one's judgments had to be based more on intuition than on examination. In order to study the problem, two stock questions were first devised. An attempt was then made to predict by intuition what each man's answer to these questions would be. The intuitions were recorded, and then the questions were asked. In a surprisingly large percentage of cases (over 90%), the intuitions were found to be correct. The two questions were: "Are you nervous?" and "Have you ever been to a psychiatrist?" After much study, the grounds for making the predictions in each case could be put into words, so that eventually, instead of using intuition to predict the answers, they could be predicted by applying certain rules which could be written down.

After confirming these rules in several thousand cases, another study was undertaken. An attempt was made to guess each man's occupation before he spoke, simply by watching him come into the room and sit down. The men were all clothed alike in a maroon bath-robe and cloth slippers. Again it was found that the guesses, or intuitions, were surprisingly accurate. On one occasion, the occupations of twenty-six successive men were guessed correctly by this method, ranging through farmer, book-keeper, mechanic, professional gambler, salesman, warehouseman, and truck-driver. Once more the grounds for making the prediction in each case were studied until some of them could be put into words, so that eventually, for at least two occupational groups, instead of using intuition to predict the answers, they could be predicted in a large percentage of cases by applying certain rules which could be written down.

After the rules upon which the predictions were based were discovered, an interesting observation came to light. The conscious intention in the second experiment was to diagnose occupations. It was found, however, that it was not occupations which were being diagnosed at all, but ways of handling new situations! It was found in the two occupational groups that were most clearly understood, that it just happened that those men who handled the examination situation in one way (passive waiting) were nearly all farmers, while those who handled it in another way (alert curiosity) were nearly all mechanics. Thus it turned out that intuition did not diagnose occupations, but emotional attitudes, even though the conscious intention was to diagnose the former.

This was an important discovery. It meant that since intuitions are not known through words, the Ego doesn't really know what it is that is known. All the Ego can do for the intuiter and those around him is to try to put a very subtle feeling into words as best it can, and it often merely comes close to the truth rather than actually hitting it. Secondly (really another aspect of the above), intuition cannot be asked any specific question but can only be guided in one or another general direction; it presents us with an impression and then we have to look for the answer in the material which it puts at our disposal.

It was further found that with each new rule that was written down, the accuracy of guessing by conscious observation went up, but was always less than the intuitive accuracy. It thus seemed evident that the feeling of "things arranging themselves without conscious control" which had been observed during intuition had to do with a large number of factors which were being noticed and arranged without being put into words, by something below the conscious level. Since all of these factors could not be put into words, the intuitive accuracy was always greater than the accuracy obtained by applying consciously those rules which could be written down.

Thus a psychological definition of intuition can be stated. Intuition is subconscious knowledge without words, based on subconscious observations without words, and under the right circumstances it is more reliable and accurate than conscious knowledge based on conscious observation.

As we have seen in the last section and in this section, intuition deals with at least two different aspects of the personality. The first is the early childhood emotional relationships between the individual and those around him, such as his parents and relatives, and the adult representatives of those relationships: emotional attitudes toward various people who are important to the individual. These are based on ungratified Id tensions. The second is the individual's way of experiencing and handling new situations. This, though based on Id tensions, actually relates to the attitude of the Ego, and its reaction to reality. We can say roughly that we may have intuitions about Id tensions, and about Ego attitudes.

Careful study during the experiments led to the tentative belief that intuitions about Id tensions are mostly formed by watching the mouth of the subject, while intuitions about Ego attitudes mainly come from observing the eyes. Thus we may tentatively venture to say that in a certain sense the muscles about the eyes serve chiefly to express Ego attitudes, while the muscles about the mouth serve chiefly to express Id tensions. In the classical anal erotic, such as we have pictured in Mr. Krone, this idea is strikingly illustrated. In the cold eyes of such a person we read his consciously suspicious approach to the world and its new situations, while in his tight-cornered mouth we read his constipation, his stubbornness, his stinginess, his orderliness, and his cruelty, the classical symptoms derived directly (as his suspiciousness is indirectly) from his unconscious anal erotism.

It is worth noting that much intuitive knowledge may depend upon the sense of smell. The odor of a person's breath and sweat can change with his emotional attitude. Some people are more aware of smells than others, and the distance over which smells can influence emotions is incredible; certain moths can detect sexual odors a mile away. The fact that we are not aware of a smell does not mean that it is not affecting our emotional attitude. Smells can change dreams without being perceived as smells.

## 4

## What is extra-sensory perception?

Many people are familiar with the extra-sensory perception or "ESP" cards, which are now sold for use as a parlor game. This is a pack of twenty-five cards with five different designs on their faces, so that the pack consists of five circles, five squares, five stars, five crosses, and five "wavy lines." The game is to try to guess which design is on a card without looking. It seems evident that by the laws of chance, since there are five possible guesses, one guess in five should be correct.

The reason this game is of scientific interest is that in the Duke University laboratory of Dr. J. B. Rhine, who designed these cards, many people were able to guess correctly, in thousands of trials, an average of more than one time out of five. Dr. Rhine felt that these good guessers must become aware of what the next card should be by some method other than the use of their senses; he therefore chose the name of "extra-sensory perception" for this ability to guess correctly more often than was expected by the laws of chance.

Dr. Rhine designed the cards for the purpose of studying mental telepathy and clairvoyance. If an assistant looks at a card and thinks about it hard, as though he were trying to telegraph what it is to the guesser, that is called mental telepathy. The guesser may be sitting behind a screen in the same room or he may be in another room many miles away; but, in any case great care is taken to prevent him from seeing the card.

If the guesser tries to guess which card is coming up next, a card which no one has seen and no one can be thinking about, this is called clairvoyance. In both cases, by the laws of chance as we know them today, over many thousands of trials, an average of one guess in five should be correct.

In the course of years, with millions of trials by different subjects, Dr. Rhine found out many interesting things. The most important was that certain people nearly always got a high percentage of correct guesses, while others hardly ever did. It seemed as though some people were regularly more telepathic or clairvoyant than others. Secondly, if the high guessers got tired, or if they were given sedative drugs to dull their minds, their percentage of correct guesses went down until it averaged just about the expected one out of five; while if they were given coffee or some other stimulant, their results improved.

The results seemed to show that certain people have clairvoyant or mental telepathic abilities, and this naturally caused a sensation in scientific circles. His work was immediately criticized from many quarters. First, his mathematics was questioned. It was said that in the way he did the experiments, chance alone could account for the high results. Since the Institute of Mathematical Statistics formally declared in 1937 that his mathematics was correct and approved of the way he applied the laws of chance, this kind of criticism is rarely heard any more. It can still be said, however, that our ideas of the laws of chance have only been worked out on paper. It may even be that Dr. Rhine's results are the true laws of chance and that all the calculations of mathematicians are wrong, since they were never proven by trying them out as many times as Dr. Rhine has done.

Secondly, the quality of his cards was criticized. With a little practice they can be read from the back by sight and from the front by touching them without seeing them, and this disposes of some of his experiments. There are some experiments with good results, however, where there was no chance for the subject to see or touch the cards at all, especially those carried on over the telephone or with the subject in another room, sometimes many miles away.

Thirdly, the conscious and unconscious sincerity of the experimenters was questioned. It was felt that they might have been fooling themselves, deliberately or unconsciously. Many of the experiments can be questioned on these grounds, but not all by any means.

Fourthly, the experiments do not work for others as regularly as they do at Duke University. The British Society for Psychic Research, which tried to be open-minded about Dr. Rhine's ideas, but criticized his methods, was unable to find any subjects who showed convincing evidence of telepathy or clairvoyance when tested by this method.

Taking all his experiences and all the criticisms into account, it is difficult to avoid the conclusion that either this is a method for demonstrating extra-sensory perception, or else the laws of chance are different from what we think they are. Many interested people believe, however, that mathematics is not the best way to study this problem; that telepathy and clairvoyance exist, but should be studied by other methods. The most interesting problem, of course, if one accepts the belief that people can perceive extra-sensorially, is *how* they do it, and it seems unlikely that mathematics could ever answer this question.

Dr. Rhine is now working on another problem which will be of interest to a good many people: namely, can the thrower influence the dice? So far, his answer seems to be yes. People who just roll without caring don't seem to roll their point as often as people who roll with "plenty of schmaltz on the bones." By using a mechanical roller, Dr. Rhine eliminates any chance of "educating" the dice. This problem is not so difficult to study in everyday life as the problems of clairvoyance and telepathy. In every group of dice players there is always someone who makes his point regularly, and someone else who hardly ever makes it, and this can go on for years. In poker, some people fill an inside straight with startling frequency and others never can (including the writer).

## 5

## How does extra-sensory perception work?

We can only communicate clearly with ourselves and with others by using words, but we can know things without using words. Ordinary knowledge is based on sense impressions which we can describe in words. We know that the girl is wearing a red coat because we see that the coat is red. Intuition is based on more subtle sense impressions which we cannot describe in words. We know that the girl has a red coat in her trunk because we "can tell" that she is "the kind of a girl who likes red coats." What seems to be clairvoyance or mental telepathy is based on something else. We suddenly suspect, for no known reason, that the girl's older sister has two red coats.

Clairvoyant-like and mental-telepathy-like happenings are most strikingly brought to our attention when they deal with numbers. When we become aware in the case of a complete stranger of the correct number of teeth which she has, or the correct street in New York where she is going on a visit, we are practically forced to conclude that such knowledge is arrived at by some method other than the use of the senses.

It is almost safe to assume that we have three ways of getting knowledge of our surroundings; that these are not sharply separated, but blend subtly into each other; and that each probably makes a contribution in sizing up any situation. First is ordinary knowledge, gained through the Ego by means of the Reality Principle; second is intuitive knowledge, gained "subconsciously" (perhaps through what analysts call the Preconscious) without consciously realized perceptions; third is extra-sensory-like perception, gained by unknown means of communication.

We do not know how extra-sensory perception works, if it exists. Psychoanalysts have written a good deal about mental telepathy. This generally takes the form of "extra-sensory perceptions" which have to be interpreted by psychoanalytic methods before the thing which was perceived becomes apparent. This is evidence that extra-sensory perception may be a function of the Id.

## Footnotes for Philosophers, Appendix A

1. *Fortune-telling*

The method of intuitive graphology may remind the interested reader of the Stanislawski method of dramatic training and of the James-Lange theory of the emotions. The validity of such intuitive methods of judgment can be adequately controlled by using as material the Bender Gestalt test instead of handwriting, subsequently verifying the conclusions by clinical studies. Careful work on graphology has been done by Saudek.

*Experiments with Handwriting*, by Robert Saudek. William Morrow & Company: New York, 1929.

With two to ten minutes of coaching, depending upon which method of trickery is used, any person of average intelligence can become a "mind-reader," and call off playing cards, street addresses, and the numbers on dollar bills which he has never seen, either from the same room, or over the long-distance telephone.

2. & 3. *Intuition*

For a review of the literature on this subject see:

*Intuition*, by K. W. Wild. Cambridge University Press: London, 1938.

An interesting discussion of the properties of smell can be found in:

*Aromatics and the Soul*, by Dan McKenzie. Paul B. Hoeber: New York, 1923.

4. *ESP*

For details of Dr. Rhine's work, see:

*New Frontiers of the Mind,* by J. B. Rhine. Farrar & Rinehart: New York, 1937.

For criticism of Dr. Rhine's work, further interesting material, British experiences covering the whole field of psychic phenomena, and bibliography, see:

*Fifty Years of Psychical Research:* A Critical Survey, by Harry Price, Honorary Secretary of the University of London Council for Psychical Investigation. Longmans, Green & Company: London & New York, 1939.

The precautions which Mr. Price took in conducting his investigations of psychic phenomena are impressive; the things which happened in spite of his precautions are even more impressive. Some of the incidents are verified by committees of distinguished and presumably hard-boiled gentlemen.

5. *The nature of ESP*

One of the basic papers on the psychoanalytic approach to the problem of telepathy is found in Freud's *New Introductory Lectures on Psychoanalysis,* Chapter 2, "Dreams and the Occult." Other articles in English can be found in various psychoanalytic journals, especially the easily available *Psychoanalytic Quarterly,* but these are difficult to evaluate, since many of the perceptions were not appreciated directly, but had to be dug out of the material by technical psychoanalytic interpretations, which in some ways obscures their validity.

# MAN AS A POLITICAL ANIMAL

IN THE OLD DAYS, scientists left politics to the Wilsons and Haps-burgs, but nowadays it is the duty of every citizen to interest him-self in world events, lest they overwhelm him and all his fellow citizens. The psychiatrists and the physicists, who are deeply con-cerned with studying the realities of man and nature, can no longer remain aloof, but must tell the world what they know of its prob-able future, even at the risk of becoming involved in outside affairs and of being criticized. It is no longer wise for scientists to refrain from expressing strong opinions and bringing strong influence to bear in a vigorous attempt to change the trend of history.

The following short sections are an attempt to show people how psychiatrists can help them think more clearly about political events. A few selected subjects only have been touched upon, but even today, psychiatry has enough to say about the psychology of masses of people in political situations to constitute a separate de-partment of "political psychiatry," and to fill a textbook in the near future with useful and pertinent observations and principles. Psychiatrists, even more than physicists, should and must concern themselves with political affairs.

I

## How do people think about politics?

The rule of images applies most tragically in the all-important field of politics: namely, that men do not act in accordance with reality, but in accordance with their images of it. We know how images can be distorted by emotions even when reality is there to guide them in the direction of truth. In politics, which is really speculation about the future and about men's characters, there is little reality to go by. There are few beacons to direct the Reality Principle, and these are camouflaged by the unscrupulous so that many people are left at the mercy of such leaders.

The average citizen's political images are almost completely determined by his emotions. Politicians realize this well, and the one who makes the shrewdest use of this knowledge is often the most successful. It is a simple matter for him to manipulate people's selfishness so as to make them forget that the first qualification of a good congressman is that he be a good legislator, that is, that he draw up and support laws which will bring the most benefit to the greatest number. Instead, if he is evil, he presents them with a simple image of his own making of what a good congressman should be like, an image based on their prejudices and their selfish desires of the moment, and then he tries to show them that he is that man. Instead of basing this image on a judgment of the future which he hopes they don't have, he bases it on the simple wishes which he knows they do have, such as the wish to believe that their names are worth remembering and their babies worth kissing, and other wistful thoughts which have little to do with their futures in a shifting world of competition.

So we have the spectacle of a man being elected to Congress not because he is wise, but because he is jollier than his opponent, or because he can play the banjo better or make better pancakes; or, even more frequently, because he is a better talker, that is, a better influencer of other people's images, regardless of his honesty. Of course good oratory is an asset in Congress, but if it is applied to distorting images instead of to making them truer, it is highly undesirable for the good of the people.

The average voter has little chance of forming an accurate image of what a candidate is like. He only knows what the candidate and the newspapers tell him, and they both have their axes to grind and will present images fashioned accordingly for public consumption. The tragedy is that the public adopts these images, and acts and feels accordingly without regard to the realities.

A good example of how political images affect political feelings was offered by the occupation and liberation of France. The

French had their image of what the Germans would be like when they came in and prepared their feelings in accordance with this image, which was an evil one. The result was that it was not too difficult for the Germans to please many of the French people. Since the French expected them to be entirely bad, anything good they did seemed praiseworthy because it was better than the image the French had of them. On the other hand, the French had a rosy image of how the Americans would behave and what they would do for France. Since the French expected them to be entirely good, anything bad they did seemed blameworthy, so it was not difficult for the Americans to offend them. In other words, the French praised and blamed not in accordance with reality, but in accordance with the differences between reality and their image of it. This principle applies to our own politics, as well as to marital relations and religion. In marriage, a good husband may be less often praised for his goodness than blamed for some little trespass, while a bad one may be less often blamed for his badness than praised for some little show of affection. In religion, the repentant sinner causes more rejoicing than the man who lives a good life throughout.

To show how easy it is to form the public's images for them without regard to reality, one has only to think of how public opinion concerning certain countries in Europe has swayed back and forth during the past few years. The newspapers have recently been at pains to promote a "bad" image of certain European nations. The average citizen feels that he has a pretty good idea concerning the realities of these nations and their people. What he has, actually, is an image of them which is made up by newspaper publishers and which he has accepted. Most Americans with opinions about these things have not only never been to these countries, but have never even talked to any of their citizens. These are subjects which affect the future of every human being in the world, and about which accurate images are urgently needed. Realistic information about these countries is usually available at public libraries, yet most Americans base their images on emotional incidents carefully selected by the newspapers for publicity from among the thousands of incidents which happen every day. Each man is at liberty to approve or disapprove of other nations as he sees fit, but on such important subjects he should be sure his information is not one-sided.

## 2

## How do evil men gain followers?

A competent leader knows that morale is more important than butter, and a feeling of security and satisfaction more inviting than a fine banquet. An evil leader, such as Hitler was, knows that there are three types of people to whom he must appeal before he can succeed, three types of people with three different goals, all of them selfish and largely useless to society, but which can be turned to advantage by unscrupulous men who know how to use other people's selfishness, a field in which Hitler was a genius.

1. The Egotists, the cold and power-hungry, of whom he was the leader. The others went with him because they saw, and he made it plain, that following him was the most likely way to get what they wanted.

2. The Ego-searchers, those who were weak and searched for security in leaning upon a stronger personality. Any strong and unswerving leader can win some following among these two groups. To the first he promises power, to the second he offers support and a feeling of security, if only by making their decisions for them and saving them this tedious and distressing task for which they are so ill-equipped.

3. He was now ready to attempt the Egocentrics, those who sought not power and not decisiveness, but approval: the human sheep. This meant that they would not join his organization willingly until by doing so they would win approval from their neighbors. Thus the larger his organization became, the more attractive it appeared to the egocentrics, and so it fattened like a snowball: the bigger it was, the faster it grew.

The egotists are the executives, and the ego-searchers form the machine, of any political party, but this is only the nucleus. No political party is a success until it starts to attract the egocentrics, for only then can it grow by geometric bounds.

Hitler was an evil leader, and appealed first to those who like himself had questionable or selfish interests at heart. There are also good leaders who are interested in the common welfare, and appeal to those of like mind, and these must have similar groups of followers. The leader is the one who determines the policies of his disciples, and he can only get most of them by appealing to their unconscious minds. The policies of his group are determined by whether he takes the easy way of the Id (always with a "valid" excuse): rape, kill, grab; or the harder way of the Superego, which needs no excusing: love, help, give. So we have two types of leaders, the good and the evil, each at bottom lonely, and each with his nucleus of ambitious followers and his club of admiring ego-searchers, gradually winning over the bulk of egocentrics, the conventional churchgoers and party members. The masses of humanity, the ego-searchers and egocentrics, will follow their leaders and not the rightest, but the strongest, will win for the moment. It is our task, therefore, to make the leaders "of the Superego" stronger than the leaders "of the Id."

## 3

## How does an evil leader hold his followers?

A "good" leader holds his followers by demonstrating the truth of his teachings through the Reality Principle, and by continually appealing to their Superegos and their Physis, their desire to do right. He convinces them that only by keeping the common good in mind can they attain maturity and happiness for themselves. An "evil" leader holds them differently. He first changes their Superegos to suit his own ends, so that they will think it a duty and a "should and ought" to do as he wants them to. This is the harder part of his task, and the more important one for his own stubborn interest. He then keeps them interested by supplying them with opportunities for crude Id satisfaction. With their old Superegos they would not have allowed themselves to indulge in the infantile and selfish gratifications which he now offers, or, if they did, they would have felt guilty and uncomfortable. With their new Super-egos, however, they can permit themselves such indulgences with less guilt, providing they have been successfully taught that they no longer owe any duty to their old consciences but only to their new leader. If the leader has the privilege of bringing up his followers from birth, this shaping of the Superego can be started from the very bottom so that it is practically unchangeable in later years. He gives them breeding camps for their libidos and extermination centers for their mortidos, and in exchange they give their devotion to him instead of to humanitarian ideals.

Life is complicated, and the evil leader holds his followers by making it appear simple. Hitler stated the principle of his kind of leadership as follows:

"The great masses' receptive ability is only very limited, and their understanding is small, but their forgetfulness is great."

The evil leader knows that there are many ignorant people who are unhappy because they feel their own stupidity and must remain silent and obscure while the learned speak. But they have votes, and their votes are as good as anyone else's and their shillelaghs as strong. So he lulls the already drowsy intelligent ones to sleep while he woos the ignorant. He woos them by giving them answers, so that they become convinced that they too are intelligent, and they fear the enlightened no more. He raises them in their own estimation and brings them a happiness they never knew before: the happiness of the sure and informed. The answers he gives them are simple: so simple that even the dullest can use them to answer all questions, new and old, they who never dared answer a new question before, but waited first for the enlightened to speak. He gives them an image of the world and he gives them a sureness about this image, and sureness is what they want above all. Once they accept this image, they act in accordance with it, even in the face of all reality to the contrary. So the poor, ignorant, beaten-down peasant becomes a Superman.

The evil leader does all he can to use his power to twist reality so as to make it appear like the images he gives his people to go by. It is not for his followers to seek the dark causes of war and poverty, or the complicated reasons for their own unfortunate position. He gives them a simple answer for all to say aloud confidently. Who causes war? The Aztecs! Who causes poverty? The Aztecs! Who causes them to lose their pitiful jobs? The Aztecs! Who devised the devilish laws of nature? The Aztecs! With such a simple catechism, it is no wonder he wants to kill off all the intelligent people as fast as he can before they can ask any questions about such a silly way of looking at things.

He puts on demonstrations to show his followers that he is absolutely right in case there is any doubt left in their minds. Which is the dirtiest race in the world? They know the answer and they all shout it in unison: "The Aztecs! They all have dirty feet!" A party is sent out to find proof of this. They find an Aztec on the street, and drag him to headquarters. His shoes are removed and his feet are examined. They are clean.

"Well, of course," says the leader, "this fellow isn't a typical Aztec. You know, some Aztecs are all right. In fact, some of my best friends are rich Aztecs. But the usual run of Aztecs, they are the ones who are foul."

The gang sallies out and brings back another Aztec—again with clean feet. It is the same story. He is not the typical, dangerous, dirty Aztec. So they bring in another—and another—and another— always the same story. They bring in ninety-nine Aztecs, all with clean feet. Finally they find a broken-down Aztec, an old drunkard who has fallen in the gutter and got his feet dirty. They bring him back to headquarters. His shoes are removed, the leader peers at his feet, spies the dirt, and a cry of triumph arises as they shove him onto the platform before the assembled throng.

"See!" shouts the leader. "It is just as I told you. All Aztecs have dirty feet!"

From that time on, all the members of the party are convinced of one truth: all Aztecs, as far as they are concerned, have dirty feet. If any of them haven't, it is because they are not only dirty, but hypocrites into the bargain, and have been slyly washing their feet for years. The party members know the truth underneath this false appearance of cleanliness: the dirty Aztecs, like true hypocrites, have for generations been teaching their children to take baths. Ah, the slippery swine!

## Footnotes for Philosophers, Appendix B

1. *The voter's image*

   In this connection, the works of Korzybski, op. cit., and the more easily available book of Hayakawa, op. cit., may be thoughtfully consulted.

2. *The psychology of the follower*

   The ideas about the life goal of the individual and its relationship to the common good are modified for political psychology from Kahn's "teleological" concepts. See *Psychopathic Personalities*, by Eugen Kahn, op. cit.

3. *The evil leader*

   Hitler's *Mein Kampf* is the textbook on the technique of the evil leader in the modern world. See also Nietzsche, Machiavelli, Carlyle, etc.

# WORD LIST

---

THE DEFINITIONS BELOW give the meanings of the words as they are used in this book. In most cases these are the same as the meanings generally understood by psychiatrists and psychoanalysts, but a few words have been given broader meanings than the generally accepted ones, and in other cases the words are defined from an unusual point of view though much the same happenings are referred to as in the conventional definitions. The list is intended as an aid to the reader, and not as a psychiatric dictionary. Words which are used only in a single section of the book, therefore, are for the most part not included, as their explanation can be located by referring to the index. Most of the words here are those which have been used again later after they have first been explained.

There is an excellent book for those who seriously wish to acquire a psychiatric vocabulary; this is the *Psychiatric Dictionary, with Encyclopedic Treatment of Modern Terms*, by Leland E. Hinsie & Jacob Shatzky. (Oxford University Press: New York, 1940.)

## A

ACTIVE  Taking the initiative. Normal men are usually more active than normal women.

ADRENAL GLAND  A small piece of tissue adhering to the kidney on each side. One section of the gland manufactures a chemical which helps prepare the body for extraordinary feats in time of emergency, as in the face of danger or frustration. Another section of the gland manufactures a chemical which affects the secondary sexual characteristics, such as the growth of the body hair and the depth of the voice. It is the former with which we are mainly concerned here.

AGGRESSION  An attempt to inflict damage upon an object.

AGGRESSIVENESS  The intensity with which the individual expresses his constructive and destructive impulses in his behavior.

AIM  The specific act which reduces emotional tension, such as kissing, striking, watching, repairing, creating.

AMBIVALENCE The existence side by side in the same individual of two apparently "opposite" feelings toward the same object, such as simultaneous love and hate of the husband or wife. Both feelings may be either conscious or unconscious, or one of the pair may be conscious and the other unconscious.

ANAL Referring to the rectum, anus, and feces. Anal pleasure, or "anal erotism," may be seen in children and psychotics quite undisguised, and in neurotics and "anal characters" in disguised form, as in the pleasures of being stingy or messy.

ANXIETY The feeling which arises when a conscious or unconscious tension is stirred up and seeks a method of relief.

AUTONOMIC NERVOUS SYSTEM The part of the nervous system which "automatically" controls the organs and functions which cannot be controlled by the will. It supplies nerves to the heart, lungs, stomach, blood vessels, skin, etc. It consists of two parts: the sympathetic nervous system, which is the one chiefly stimulated by the adrenal glands and which prepares the individual for emergency action; and the parasympathetic, which prepares him chiefly for the pleasures of life, such as defecation and sexual intercourse.

## B

BARBITURATES A class of drugs used as sleeping powders. The most widely known are phenobarbital, sodium amytal, nembutal, and seconal.

## C

CASTRATION COMPLEX The system of ideas and feelings, conscious and unconscious, frank and disguised, and their effects as shown in behavior which results from the infantile idea that females once had a penis and lost it, and that males may lose theirs if they do not behave properly. The castration complex shows itself chiefly as "penis envy" in women, and as "castration fear" in men.

CEREBROTONIC An individual who is mostly interested in thinking rather than in action or sociability. The lanky, serious-minded college professor is often a good example. Ectomorphs are usually cerebrotonic.

CHARACTER The ways each individual develops to handle his energy. Some can store energy and some cannot. Some express it through muscular action, others shackle it due to suspiciousness or other psychological defenses. Each individual has his own way of dealing with his energy problems.

CLAIRVOYANCE The ability to predict what is going to happen without any observation of the situation.

CLITORIS A little penis-like organ which is found in women just above the urinary opening.

COMPLEX A system of ideas and feelings, conscious and unconscious, which influences behavior as well as many "intelligently thought out" decisions. Example: castration complex.

COMPULSION An inner urge which cannot be controlled by the will even when its uselessness or harmfulness is realized. It usually involves doing the same thing over and over, such as washing the hands four times, again and again, throughout the day. Adolescent masturbation usually has a compulsive quality.

CONSTITUTION The qualities and make-up, both physical and mental, that the individual is born with. Large bones and good intelligence are constitutional.

### D

DEATH INSTINCT A tension which has as its aim separation, injury, destruction, or killing. The energy of the death instinct is called mortido, which may be directed inwardly or outwardly.

DEPRESSION Sadness. A "depression" is an illness characterized by sadness and loss of energy, appetites, and interest in life. When severe it may be called "melancholia." Its manifestations are mainly due to inwardly directed mortido.

DISPLACEMENT The use of an aim or object other than the one really required or wished for, in order to relieve a tension partly or temporarily. Sarcasm may be an aim displacement for killing, and loving a parrot may be an object displacement for loving a man.

### E

ECTOMORPH An individual who develops lengthwise rather than in thickness or breadth, with emphasis on the tissues which come from the outside layer of the egg, namely the brain and skin. The lanky, long-faced college professor is an example. Ectomorphs tend to be cerebrotonic.

EGO That part of the mind which is in contact with the outside world on one hand and with the Id and Superego on the other. It attempts to keep thoughts, judgments, interpretations, and behavior practical and efficient in accordance with the Reality Principle. Here we have used the word somewhat inexactly as almost synonymous with the conscious part of the mind.

EGO IDEAL The ideal image which the individual has of what he would like to be like, and which he tries to live up to. It is the Ego Ideal which leads men to imitate their fathers, Clarence Darrow, William Osler, Jesse James, or Jesus.

ENDOCRINE GLANDS Small pieces of tissue found in various parts of the body, including among others the adrenal, thyroid, and sex glands, which manufacture special chemicals that percolate into the blood and affect the way the body and mind work.

ENDOMORPH An individual who develops in thickness rather than in length or breadth, with emphasis on the tissues which come from the inside layer of the egg, especially the digestive organs. The stocky, paunchy, thick-necked politician is a good example. Endomorphs tend to be viscerotonic.

EXTROVERT. One whose Id instincts are directed outward.

## F

FREE ASSOCIATION Reporting every thought and feeling which comes to mind during the psychoanalytic sessions, when the mind is kept free of all censoring, control, or sorting of thoughts.

FRUSTRATION Inability to relieve a tension because of difficulties in outside reality or a conflict within the mind. A convict is frustrated by reality and a prohibitionist is frustrated by his own conflicts.

FUNCTION The way things work. A functional illness or change means a change in the way the body works without enough detectable structural change to account for the amount of disorder. Many stomach disorders, such as excessive belching, and heart disorders, such as pounding, are of this variety.

## G

GENITAL The adult stage of personality developments wherein the individual gets his greatest satisfaction from making other people happy because *he* likes *them* (and not in order to make *them* like *him*, or to square his conscience, or because of what they give him). In the genital stage, pleasure is shared, and the individual uses the sexual organs, rather than the mouth or the lower digestive tract, to obtain the most direct and intense satisfactions.

GRATIFICATION Any thought or act which relieves tension and anxiety and brings the human energy system closer to energy balance.

## H

HEREDITY The process by which qualities come from the parents so that their possibilities are present in the egg from the moment it is fertilized.

HORMONES The chemicals manufactured by the endocrine glands, which affect the functions of the body and the mind.

HYPOCHONDRIASIS A form of self-love which manifests itself as paying undue attention to bodily sensations and attracting the attention of others by continually referring to one's inward organs.

HYSTERIA An illness wherein an emotional tension is partly relieved by a physical symptom which has some connection with the expression of the emotion. A man with an unconscious impulse to strike his father may suddenly find his right arm paralyzed for no reason that he knows of or that physical examination can reveal. The people who are especially likely to get such illnesses are overemotional, dramatic, changeable, and unreliable in their behavior, and are called "hysterical characters." Such people are particularly subject to the sudden outbursts of emotional expression which are popularly called "hysterics."

## I

ID The reservoir of psychic energy, of which the individual is not aware, derived from the raw life and death instincts. The Id works according to the pleasure principle. Its energy is libido and mortido, whose aims and objects can be made conscious through psychoanalysis.

IMAGE The idea which the individual has of himself and the things around him, and according to which he acts, thinks, and feels. An image consists of a representation, or picture, and an emotional charge, or feeling, about the picture. A man in love is a man under the strong influence of a highly charged image which even if it is far different from the reality as other people see it, nevertheless guides his ideas, feelings, and behavior.

INFERIORITY COMPLEX A system of thoughts and feelings which results in the individual continually comparing himself unfavorably to other people, even when the facts do not warrant such discouraging comparisons.

INTROVERT One whose Id instincts are directed inward.

INTUITION Knowledge based on observations which cannot be put into words.

## L

LIBIDO (libee'doe) The energy tensions which are relieved by construction, creation, and bringing closer together. The energy of the life instinct. Its greatest satisfaction is obtained in the adult by a sexual orgasm, and its "purpose" seems to be the preservation of the race.

## M

MASOCHISM An effort to satisfy inwardly directed mortido at the same time as libido is being satisfied. Masochistic women often choose drunkards for husbands because they know from experience or by intuition that a drunkard will be cruel to them both mentally and physically.

MESOMORPH An individual whose chief development is in breadth rather than in length or thickness, with emphasis on the tissues which come from the middle layer of the egg, such as the muscles and connective tissue. Li'l Abner and athletic lifeguards are good examples. Mesomorphs tend to be somatotonic.

MORTIDO (mortee'doe) The energy tensions which are relieved by destruction, injuring, elimination, and separation. The energy of the death instinct. Its greatest satisfaction is obtained in the adult by murder or suicide, and its "purpose" seems to be the preservation of the individual.

## N

NARCISSISM Inwardly directed libido.

NEURASTHENIA An old term for a form of self-love manifested by unwillingness to expend effort, multiple physical complaints, undue worrying, and lack of pleasure in normal relationships. Nowadays such conditions are usually classified as either anxiety neuroses or neurotic depressions.

NEUROLOGIST A physician who specializes in diseases of the nerve cords, spinal cord, and brain.

NEUROSIS An illness characterized by excessive use of energy for unproductive purposes so that personality development is hindered or stopped. A man who spends most of his time worrying about his health, counting his money, plotting revenge, or washing his hands, can hope for little emotional growth.

NEUROTIC ACTIVITY The use of energy for unproductive purposes, which may be part of a neurosis and hinder development, or may partly relieve bothersome tensions and thus help to leave the individual free to concentrate on other things. Smoking is a good example of the latter.

## O

OBJECT That person or thing which may be used to relieve tension. The object of libido may be a rare postage stamp or a woman, and the object of mortido may be a crooning radio or a Fascist. Many people have mainly themselves as libido and mortido objects.

OBSESSION An idea, feeling, or impulse which keeps intruding into consciousness and which cannot be suppressed by will even though the individual realizes that it is unreasonable or harmful. Jealousy of a faithful wife or husband may become an obsession.

OEDIPUS COMPLEX The feeling of a child that he would like to gratify his libido by being closer to one parent and his mortido by eliminating the other. These feelings often persist into adult life in disguised form.

ORAL Those tendencies of behavior and feeling which firs. arise dur-

ing the nursing period and often persist into adult life in frank or disguised form. The infant who cries when he is without the bottle may grow up into an adult who is not happy without a bottle.

## P

PHOBIA Exaggerated fear of a specific object or situation

PHYSIS The growth force of nature, which makes organisms evolve into higher forms, embryos develop into adults, sick people get better, and healthy people strive to attain their ideals and grow more mature. Possibly it is only one aspect of inwardly directed libido, but it may be a more basic force than libido itself.

PLEASURE PRINCIPLE The tendency of tensions to seek immediate and complete relief without regard to the consequences. The Id is guided by the pleasure principle, and therefore has to be curbed by the Ego in accordance with the Reality Principle.

PSYCHE (sykee) The human mind, conscious and unconscious, including its ideals and aspirations.

PSYCHIATRIST A physician who specializes in helping, advising, and treating those who suffer rom emotional difficulties, faulty judgment, or more obvious difficulties in interpreting their feelings and surroundings correctly. A qualified psychiatrist is *always* an M.D.

PSYCHOANALYSIS. A system of studying, changing, and thinking about human behavior developed by Sigmund Freud. It deals mainly with the psychology of the Id and the way the Ego handles the Id tensions. As a method of treatment, it usually requires almost daily sessions of one hour for a year or more, since the Id is difficult to domesticate.

PSYCHOANALYST A physician with psychiatric training who specializes in treating his patients by means of the long, detailed treatment developed by Sigmund Freud and known as psychoanalysis. There is also a handful of qualified psychoanalysts who are not physicians. All recognized psychoanalysts are connected with official psychoanalytic institutes affiliated with the International Psycho-Analytical Association.

PSYCHOLOGIST One who studies the mind. As usually used, the term refers to one who studies behavior and conscious mental content in special situations. Most psychologists do not have medical degrees. Recognized psychologists are usually members of the American Psychological Association.

PSYCHOLOGY The study of the mind, usually referring to behavior and conscious mental content in special situations. Psychiatry is concerned with the prevention and treatment of emotional and mental disorders. Psychoanalysis studies chiefly the psychology of the unconscious mind, while the word "psychology" as generally used refers to the psychology of the conscious mind. Properly speaking, however, psychology includes the study of both the conscious and unconscious minds.

PSYCHONEUROSIS Used here as exactly synonymous with neurosis.

PSYCHOPATH An individual who does not restrain himself from doing things which are harmful to others. It is also used to refer to any individual whose personality structure is not well balanced.

PSYCHOSIS A mental illness resulting in the unconscious becoming conscious and taking over control of the individual. Since he then attempts to act in accordance with the pleasure principle instead of the Reality Principle, he can no longer get along in society. Psychosis is the medical word roughly corresponding to the legal term "insanity," which implies that the individual is a danger to himself or others or is likely to cause a public scandal, and that he is of unsound mind and judgment for undertaking to make decisions about financial and other matters involving the law.

PSYCHOSOMATIC This word is used by some in an attempt to emphasize the idea that emotions can contribute to diseases of the body, and that diseases of the body can affect the emotions.

PSYCHOTHERAPY Treatment of illness through professional relationship with the physician as a person rather than by means of medication or surgery.

R

REALITY The way things actually are. That is, the possibilities for interrelationship at any given moment of all the energy systems in the universe. A clear understanding of reality would enable the individual to predict the results of various ways of behaving in any situation.

REALITY PRINCIPLE The guiding principle which leads the individual to attempt to judge beforehand the consequences of various courses of action, instead of acting immediately in accordance with the Id tensions of the moment. The Ego has to curb the Id in accordance with the Reality Principle.

RELATIONSHIP The connection between two or more people, ideas, feelings, or things.

REPRESENTATION The shape or form of a mental image, conscious or unconscious, without regard to the kind or amount of feeling it is charged with.

REPRESSION Pushing something into the unconscious, or keeping something from becoming conscious. Repression keeps the individual from being in a continual state of confusion by preventing him from becoming aware of many things, though what is forgotten or unknown still remains an active force in the unconscious part of the mind.

## S

SADISM An attempt to satisfy outwardly directed mortido at the same time as libido is being satisfied. Drunken women make good mates for sadistic men because they often encourage men to be cruel to them physically and mentally.

SCHIZOPHRENIA (skitsofree'neeya) A mental illness characterized by a loss of normal emotional responses and normal contact with reality, so that the patient lives in a private world where little affects him except his own fantasies and dreams.

SOMATOTONIC An individual who is interested in expressing himself mainly through muscular action. Li'l Abner, Superman, and athletic lifeguards are good examples. Mesomorphs are usually somatotonic.

STRUCTURE The way things are made and what they are made of.

SUBLIMATION Aim displacement or object displacement (or both) of libido or mortido with partial relief of tension through socially acceptable, creative, or useful activity. A hammering sculptor attacks and destroys as he constructs and creates, thus relieving both mortido and libido with a result which is valuable to society.

SUPEREGO The images charged with inwardly directed mortido which guide and restrain the free expression of the Id impulses, and even overrule the judgments of the Ego. Any conscious or unconscious thought, feeling, or action which is out of accord with the Superego gives rise to a tension which, if it becomes conscious, is called "guilt." The Superego consists mainly of the conscious conscience, the unconscious Superego, and the Ego Ideal.

## T

TELEPATHY Receiving knowledge from another individual without communication through any medium known to us at present.

TENSION A state of energy imbalance. All processes in nature are based on the principle of restoring energy balance and reducing tension.

TRANSFERENCE The emotional relationship which develops between any two or more people, especially between an adviser and his client or a doctor and his patient, when it is based on emotional attitudes left over from childhood which are transferred to the current situation.

## U

UNCONSCIOUS Mental processes which the individual is not aware of. "The Unconscious" is a part of the mind where repressed images and their charges are stored and whence they continue to influence the individual's behavior.

## V

VISCEROTONIC An individual who is chiefly interested in absorbing energy. He likes to absorb food, air, and affection. The stocky, sociable politician is a good example. Endomorphs are usually viscerotonic.

## W

WISH An urge which tends to guide the individual toward definite aims and objects which will relieve his tensions. Only living organisms can wish, and wishes are what distinguish living matter from dead matter.

# NAME INDEX

*(Subject Index starts on page 313)*

---

# SUBJECT INDEX

Abnormal development, 121
Abortions, 154
Absolute ideas, 145
Abstract intelligence, 31
Abstraction, 56
Acting out, 150
Active personality, 50, 82, 126
Addiction
  alcohol. *See* Alcoholism
  curing, 190
  drugs, 179, 186, 188
Adjustment, 21, 96
Adolescence, 99
Adrenal gland, 7, 40
Adults, 72
  sexuality, 92
Affect, flattened, 178
Age-guessers, 282
Aggressiveness, 40, 58
Aim displacement, 48, 109
Air encephalogram, 225
Alcoholics Anonymous, 191
Alcoholism, 111, 138, 172, 179, 185,
  189, 228
  and marriage, 191, 192
  curing, 190
  delirium tremens, 59, 172, 192
Alopecia, 251
Ambition, 35
Ambivalence, 53, 249
American Board of Psychiatry and
  Neurology, 262, 265
American Psychoanalytic Associa-
  tion, 238, 264, 265
American Psychoanalytic Institutes,
  263
Amytal, sodium, 147, 218, 222
Anal personalities, 82, 85, 91, 109, 114,
  286
Analysis
  psychoanalysis. *See* Psychoanalysis
  self, 242

Analytic psychology, 242
Anesthesia
  hypnotic, 218
  local, 239
Anger, 125, 133
Anxiety neurosis, 35, 36, 136, 143, 151,
  237
Aphasia, 13
Apoplexy, 12
Approval, desire for, 35
Arguments, 21
Arranging, 54
Arthritis, 133
Artists, 22, 48, 282
*As if* concept, 24, 55
Asthma, 132, 143
Astrology, 278
Astronomy, 278
Autonomic nervous system, 211

Backache, 123, 132
Balance of energy, 35
Baldness, 5
Barbiturates, 189
Battle neurosis, 220
Beautiful women, 99
Bedwetting, 98
Behavior
  and alcohol, 179
  and drugs, 179
  compulsive, 60, 136, 143, 144, 146,
    237
  conscienceless, 195
  neurotic. *See* Neuroses
  normal, 138
Belching, 123
Birth marks, 133
Biting, 78, 83
Blood pressure, 14, 59, 124
Blushing, 10, 133
Bodily energy, 7
Body-image, 148

— 313 —